life-drawing walking b   ar
erleading bingo dodg   li
arties lawn bowls lear   la
sitting on a bench cold-water swimming dinner p
veterans' football ecstatic dancing edible garde
una cruising conversation volunteering farm anim
dwatching camping singing in a choir finnish saur
akeboarding talking to strangers pilgrimage birdv
flying life-drawing walking book club pottery wal
ding cheerleading bingo dodgeball improv fishing
arties lawn bowls learning Welsh bridge roller bla
sitting on a bench cold-water swimming dinner p
veterans' football ecstatic dancing edible garde
una cruising conversation volunteering farm anim
dwatching camping singing in a choir finnish saur
akeboarding talking to strangers pilgrimage birdv
flying life-drawing walking book club pottery wal
ding cheerleading bingo dodgeball improv fishing
arties lawn bowls learning Welsh bridge roller bla
sitting on a bench cold-water swimming dinner p
veterans' football ecstatic dancing edible garde
una cruising conversation volunteering farm anim
dwatching camping singing in a choir finnish saur
akeboarding talking to strangers pilgrimage birdv
flying life-drawing walking book club pottery wal
ding cheerleading bingo dodgeball improv fishing
arties lawn bowls learning Welsh bridge roller bla
sitting on a bench cold-water swimming dinner p
veterans' football ecstatic dancing edible garde
una cruising conversation volunteering farm anim
dwatching camping singing in a choir finnish saur

HERE COMES THE FUN

Also by Ben Aitken

Dear Bill Bryson: Footnotes from a Small Island
A Chip Shop in Poznan: My Unlikely Year in Poland
The Gran Tour: Travels with my Elders
The Marmalade Diaries: The True Story of an Odd Couple

HERE COMES THE
FUN

A YEAR OF MAKING MERRY

have **BEN** _fun!_
AITKEN

Ben

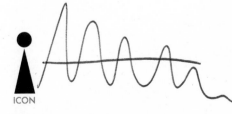

ICON

Published in the UK and USA in 2023 by
Icon Books Ltd, Omnibus Business Centre,
39–41 North Road, London N7 9DP
email: info@iconbooks.com
www.iconbooks.com

ISBN: 978-183773-005-6
ebook ISBN: 978-183773-007-0

Typeset in Baskerville MT by SJmagic DESIGN SERVICES, India.

Printed in the UK.

For Winnie Carter (1936–2023), who knew something about fun.

Contents

1

Fun is a funny thing alright

Wherein the author discovers his biological age, freaks out, goes cold water swimming, freaks out, joins a veterans' football team and attends the birthday party of an 8-year-old.

8 November, 2021

I've decided to spice up my fun life. Why? Because I recently did a sort of health and personality test online and scored 2.7 out of 10. The test found me to be somewhat guilt-laden, rather self-conscious, and likely to die from a heart-related issue. My 'word cloud' (if you can imagine such a thing) was dominated by two of the most sought-after adjectives in the dictionary: preoccupied and lacklustre. Apparently, my idea of a peak human experience is playing charades in a pub garden with a friend I haven't seen for six years.

I'm not going to claim that my score on the test was a wake-up call, because it wasn't. For one, the test was crude and simplistic, and for two, I was already fully awake to the fact that I wasn't winning at life. I'm also not going to claim that prior to the test my personality was so rank and insipid that my own mother had filed for a divorce, because it wasn't. I don't want to turn this chronicle into a version of *An Idiot Abroad*, with me as Karl Pilkington and the realm of fun as the promised land to which I am congenitally ill-suited. That would be too easy a contrivance. Too obvious an exaggeration.

The truth is that I'm pretty average. Neither fun-starved nor fun-fat. Neither depressingly dull nor exceptionally jolly. Neither constantly pulling my hair out, nor meditating thrice daily. My motivation for embracing fun is neither especially existential nor deserving of tabloid news coverage. At no point in the immediate future am I likely to be the subject of an article with the headline 'World's Least Fun Person Found Loitering in Argos'.

If I'm none of those things, then what am I? Well, I'm just someone who fancied that they weren't getting enough. Someone who realised (for the umpteenth time) that life isn't a rehearsal. Someone who had a mild epiphany that the meaning of life isn't craft lager and subscription TV. Someone who fancied a bit more laugh, and a bit less groan.

I'm also someone who, to get a handle on his subject and gain a useful sense of direction, conducted a comprehensive and statistically significant survey of 42 people and discovered that the big hit in their lives is swimming in freezing-cold water. (Closely followed by knitting.) As a result, there's talk of me kicking off my fun era with a swim in the local pond. I'm against the idea on principle – the principle being my aversion to cold water. I don't care what lies in store for me on the other side (uber endorphins, a superhuman sensation), if unbearable coldness lies between us. Start how you mean to carry on, they say. So I'll start with knitting – if you don't mind.[1]

9 November

I walk to the pond gingerly, not least because some of the potential side effects of cold water swimming don't sound fun at all. Hypothermia. Hyperventilation. Cardiac arrest. Pulmonary

---

[1] At this stage, I need to tell you something. Because it's kind of important, and it's the kind of thing I'd be interested in knowing if I were reading this sort of book – that is, a stunt memoir wherein the author puts normal life on hold as if it were as easy as flicking a switch, in order to dedicate themselves to saying yes or living biblically or being scared every day or searching for people with the same name. Writing is my full-time job. I have no dependents. My income is much less than the national minimum wage, and I don't have any assets or wealth to speak of. I'm delighted to say that I didn't have to pay for the two-week cruise of the Baltic that I went on in the summer of 2022 (more of which anon). I'm less delighted to say that I did have to pay for more or less everything else, including the ecstatic dancing, which, at fifteen quid a pop, didn't represent value for money. If you think the above attempt at transparency was unnecessary, don't worry, it won't happen again.

collapse. Arterial explosion. Ocular combustion. I could go on making things up, but you get the point – it's not for the faint-hearted. Which means it's not for me.

It may not be for me, but it certainly *is* for plenty of others, which is why I'm here – to investigate what floats other boats. Cold water swimming is having what you might call, perhaps inappropriately, a moment in the sun.

Leading up to today, I did a bit of homework – which is to say I watched a documentary. The documentary featured people like Peter, who, when asked to justify his lust for frigid torment, said something along the lines of: 'It's ace because a swim in the pond when it's super cold just makes me forget everything for up to twelve hours.' Call me precious, but I don't want to forget everything for up to twelve hours. I don't think that would be helpful. Another dipper featured in the documentary, meanwhile, said that the delightful thing about swimming in the pond was its knack of making the ghosts disappear. Call me impoverished, but I don't have any ghosts. At least I don't think I do.

Although the documentary did little to warm me up to cold water swimming, it did equip me with various ways of making the experience less likely to be fatal. A flask of tea should be sipped slowly for eleven years upon exiting the icy depths. At least sixteen layers should be put on within seconds of leaving the pond. Speed should be demonstrated immediately after leaving the water, to ensure the period of time between trauma and recovery is as short as possible. And exaggeration should be employed wherever possible.

When I reach the pond, there's a guy in a kiosk taking payment, which is a bit like charging someone to stub their toe.

'It's my first time,' I say.

'Welcome,' he says.

'Bit nervous actually.'

'You picked a special day – the water temperature is five degrees.'

'Is that warm for this time of year?'

'Er, no. It's cold for this time of year.'

'Which makes it special?'

'Exactly.'

'Any tips?'

'Know where the exits are.'

I've never undressed so slowly. I had hoped to engage in a bit of changing-room banter with some of the regulars, so they might expand a little on the relationship between distress and entertainment, but there's nobody around, which is ominous.

I've borrowed some aqua shoes – chiefly to avoid being barefoot on the icy, stone jetty that juts into the pond – but they're several sizes too small, meaning that when I hurriedly tiptoe towards the water in my trunks, I must resemble the least aesthetically pleasing ballerina known to humankind.

When I reach the ladder, I actually manage to muster some nerve and display some sangfroid by climbing straight into the water without dicking about, i.e. without hopping from foot to foot, arms clasped around me, hoping something tragic or miraculous might occur that would result in me not having to proceed any further.

In the end it's not too bad. Granted, upon entering the water I can't breathe and inwardly swear about 42 times, but compared to the cold showers I've been taking in preparation for this moment, getting into the pond is somehow less disgustingly abrupt and shocking. I think it's because in the pond you're completely submerged, meaning the attack is spread out, rather than focused on your head or back or midriff. There's a life lesson in that. I think.

I'm not saying it's nice; by no stretch of the imagination is it nice; but what I am saying is that I'm able to spend 47 seconds in the pond approximating someone doing a version of the doggy paddle, without screaming wildly for assistance.

On second 48, I decide that that's enough fun for one day. I return to the jetty a happy if slightly petrified person, then run back to the changing space as fast as I can without courting disaster. I dress exceptionally quickly, which brings to mind those lines of Shakespeare regarding schoolchildren going to school sluggishly and leaving it with haste. I enjoy sipping my tea wearing every jumper I own. I might even be smiling. Relief is fun. Survival is a hoot. I reckon I could do this again.

21 November

I've joined a gym. I know I should have waited until the new year like the rest of the world, but what can I say, I'm precocious. Anyway, the gym has this machine – perhaps yours has one too – that is designed to essentially scare the crap out of you. It's called Boditrax. You basically take your socks off, step onto a set of scales fitted with a bunch of sensors, grab a pair of analytical handles, and then hope for the best. Twenty seconds later, the machine gives you about 45 readings, including visceral fat levels, Body Mass Index, bone density, muscle content and so on. When my results appear, they don't make for easy reading. Apparently, I'm on the fringes of clinical obesity, am the proud owner of almost no core muscle, and have a biological age of 54, which is nearly twenty years my senior. I step off the scales feeling deflated about my rate of inflation.

Not that I expected much better, mind you. For the last twenty years – since I left school, really – my lifestyle has been sub-optimal. I routinely self-medicate with Guinness and cider. The only time I lift weights is when I'm unloading the dishwasher. And I get most of my aerobic exercise walking to Chicken Cottage. It has clearly taken its toll.

I leave the gym newly resolved: never to step on that bloody machine again.

4 December

One of the few things you can say with confidence about fun is that it's subjective. In fact, it's massively subjective. If you tell me that fun is six donuts in succession, at a particular café in Minneapolis, when a storm is raging outside, I'm not going to get above my station and tell you you're wrong. While we might be able to agree on a set of potential characteristics for fun (energis-ing, absorbing, not likely to result in trauma), we'd struggle to find even one activity or pastime that is consistently and invariably those things (or a combination thereof). We can say what things *characterise* fun, but not what things *are* fun.

When I did some research – that is, posted a tweet that gar-nered eleven replies – I learned that for Adrian from Wrexham fun is taking the bus with nothing on but a raincoat, and that for Caroline from Minnesota it's tripping over. I repeat, *tripping over*. She absolutely loves it. Can't get enough. It gets her chuckling. While Caroline concedes that it can't easily be scheduled, and will sometimes leave her modestly injured, she also wonders if it's these very characteristics that make the pastime so appealing to her.

When I spoke to some of the older people in my life about what they did for fun as kids, it kind of blew my mind. When my partner's mum, Kim, was about eight or nine, she used to spend most of her leisure time pretending to be the Chelsea captain Ray Wilkins. According to Kim, she loved nothing more than pretending to be a famous footballer out on the town after three points on a Saturday. She used to dress up in the football kit and spend hours improvising dialogue befitting this scenario. Interesting.

While Kim was being Ray, my dad and his mates were either playing a game called Split the Kipper – which involved a sheath knife, another person's legs, and a high degree of jeopardy – or a version of darts wherein the board would be substituted for whichever of his mates pulled the short straw and the oche situated no less than 30 metres from the target. It can surely be no coincidence that A&E admissions plummeted after the launch of the Nintendo Gameboy in 1989. So what if kids developed braindead personas if they got to stay in one piece?

At least my mum's idea of fun wasn't dangerous. 'Knock, Knock, Ginger' involves knocking on someone's front door and then running away before the door is answered. My mum reckons she could have played this game for days on end if she'd been given half a chance. She reckons the feeling she got from confusing local homeowners was somehow good for the soul. Since she told me this, I've not been able to look at her the same way. Make no mistake, fun is a funny thing alright.

For the purposes of this book, I don't think there's much to be gained (or much fun to be had) in labouring to come up with a definition of fun. Instead of trying to pin fun down, I'd rather concentrate on dipping a toe in the stuff itself. (If this looks like a dereliction of duty, or like I'm prioritising play over work, then I'm guilty as charged.) If the stuff I dip a toe into happens to overlap with such things as amusement and merriment and enjoyment and diversion – so be it; we'll roll with the punches.

For those of you who are desperate for a rule of thumb, however, who simply couldn't carry on reading without one, let's say that if it gives you a lift and stops you thinking about work, then there's a good chance it's fun; while if it doesn't do either (like changing a nappy or sitting in traffic, or changing a nappy while sitting in traffic), then there's a good chance it's not. Now, where's a kerb I can trip on?

21 December

I've joined a veterans' football team. My partner Megan isn't supportive at all. She doesn't, for a start, like the idea of me being eligible. (You've got to be 35+) She asked me not to go. Looked on in despair when I bought the boots and shin pads. 'My grandad plays walking football,' she said. 'Shall I see if they need anyone?'

I've not played football for 23 years, in which time my muscles and physique and general sporting ability have grown accustomed to televised drama and burritos. I enter the changing room and am hit by the smell of Deep Heat, which prompts a wave of bad nostalgia.

'Where do you play?' says a man wearing the glow of retirement (and very little else).

'Nowhere.'

'Nah, come on. Striker? Full-back?'

'No, honestly mate. Nowhere.'

I don't fit in the shirt, which is surely a portent. Problem is there's only a small one spare, and I've got too much spare to be small, if you know what I mean. My warmup is off-the-scale self-conscious. I do some things I remember seeing others do years ago: high knees, star jumps, that sort of thing. The gaffer comes over and says that some of my teammates are genuine veterans. 'One of these blokes fought in Vietnam. Another in the Falklands. If you don't put your head in the way of things they'll be on to you.'

After this attempt at encouragement, the gaffer then makes the mistake of confusing age with ability and puts me in the centre of midfield – the most dynamic position. After 47 seconds (which, coincidentally, was how much fun I had in the pond that time), I feel my right calf muscle creak. It's not a snap, or a pull, but it's something. A howl, maybe. A protest.

Then, ten minutes later, and not yet having touched the ball deliberately, it's the groin. Another creak, another howl. When, just before halftime, I kick the ball awkwardly with my weaker left foot and half the nail on my big toe comes off, or very nearly comes off, I'm ready to throw in the towel and put football down as a failed experiment.

And yet despite the knocks and strains, and my gross incompetence, and the fact that I resemble a walrus in a crop top, I'm loving it. The steady adrenaline. The slight risk. The pleasant anarchy. The feeling of returning to childhood. The low-stakes camaraderie. The *game*.

Also pleasing is the halftime team talk, wherein our 69-year-old winger displays a knowledge of complicated footballing matters that was neither demonstrated nor hinted at during the first half. Andrew's opinion (that we need to pass in triangles), sets off a flood of others, including the need to keep it simple (from James), the need to throw caution to the wind (from Mike), and the need to exploit their old boy at the back, who's seen more general elections than Ricardo's had hot dinners (from Ricardo).

Each opinion is earnest and passionate, and paid absolutely no attention whatsoever.

My opinion – that I ought to be taken off – is also ignored. And so, for another 50 minutes that feels like a full calendar month, I waddle around like an awkward bollard. Until, that is, an unlikely ball is sent over the top and I'm clean through on goal, at which point, instead of dropping a shoulder or just putting my laces through it, I display all the composure of a rabbit in the headlights and just kick the ball tamely into the goalkeeper's tummy. We lose 5–1.

I walk home with less a spring in my step (too injured for that), and more a spring in my mood.

25 December

In bed with the new variant of Covid. Generally speaking, novelty gets a good press. But the sobering truth is that not all novel things are equal. New shoes – great. New variant – less so. On a positive note, I do well for presents: an Allen key and a Waitrose voucher. God bless grandparents. They sure know how to keep your spirits up.

9 January

My year of making merry hasn't exactly got off to a flier. First a near-death experience, second I join a veterans' football team, and now an eighth birthday party. The birthday boy is William, my friend's eldest. When said friend mentioned the party and I was like, 'You know what? I might pop along to that – could be fun,' his only response was to ask me very seriously if everything was okay.

When I arrive, the church hall is lit by revolving disco lights. A load of parents are lined up stiffly around the edge, while their kids are on the dance floor expressing themselves to 'Get Lucky' by Daft Punk. The DJ – DJ Anthony – is quite a funny bloke. His patter is operating on two levels – one to amuse and engage the kids, and one to stop the adults from imploding with boredom. During a lull in proceedings, the man next to me asks which one's mine. In retrospect, my response – 'None of them, actually. I just popped in for some fun' – could have done more to put his mind at ease.

My mate Mark's just been dragged up to the front by DJ Anthony and asked to show the kids some dance moves, which they have to copy, with the best copier getting a handful of sweets from DJ Anthony's jar. Mark's never been shy (which is a shame if you ask me), and doesn't need to be asked twice. DJ Anthony drops Taylor Swift, and Mark's off, out of the blocks with a parody of the Macarena. I've not seen him so animated since he won an award for best effort in geography. Next, Mark segues into a set of moves that suggest a ridiculous and sped-up version of tai chi. If he's improvising, then the man's a genius. If he's not, then he's got some questions to answer.

Personally, I'm thrilled when the 'lawnmower' comes out. It's a move Mark would routinely perform on nightclub dancefloors in Portsmouth, back in his early twenties when he wasn't a married accountant with two children. The 'lawnmower' basically involves pushing an invisible lawnmower around the dance floor in a jaunty fashion with an ecstatic look on your face. The sight of Mark bouncing around with his lawnmower with twenty-odd children doing likewise before him is at once heart-warming, oddly inspiring, and, yes, somehow fun. I'm not saying I could watch the spectacle forever, but I could happily manage another ten minutes.

When Mark is invited to step down so the kids can freestyle, not all of them are as unabashed and carefree as I thought they might be. It's easy to think that kids don't give a hoot about anything, that they're essentially boisterous puppies with an insatiable thirst for play, but of the group before me only about half fit this description. About a quarter can't look beyond all the pizza lying around (and probably have similar biological ages to me); a couple are clearly outlaws in the making because they're only interested in trying to pilfer DJ Anthony's sweet jar; and the rest look like – well, like I would on a dance floor, which is to say awkward and unsure and a trifle embarrassed.

But on the whole, there's no denying that the kids are far more candid and exuberant than an equivalent group of adults would be. Which is for better and worse, of course. These kids might well be quick to boogie like there's no tomorrow, but they are also quick to have a punch-up on the floor over a bit of cake whose ownership was claimed by the one and doubted by the other. So I'm not going to make your average eight-year-old my role model just yet, if it's all the same to you. My inner child can stay inner for now.

There's a slightly unsavoury episode at the end of the party, I'm afraid to say. When DJ Anthony calls it a day and the music dies down, I go over to the birthday boy to give him his present. No word of a lie, the ungrateful little sod gives it straight back to me. Really, the sooner these kids learn how to repress a few things the better.[2]

---

2 It wasn't William.

2

Silliness can go too far

Wherein the author starts doing the crossword, considers the serious matter of being silly, plays cricket in a pub, stops doing the crossword and considers why fun is a virtue.

17 January

Initially, the idea was that this fun project would be sort of dual aspect. There would be the practical side – containing accounts of trampolining and fishing and so on – and there would be the theoretical side – containing all the interesting ideas other people have had on the matter of fun and merriment. I wanted to know how the concept of fun had evolved historically, and how it differed from culture to culture. (Did the ancient Egyptians ice skate, for example?) I wanted to know if fun could be pigeon-holed as the momentary release of certain chemicals (including serotonin, dopamine, adrenaline and endorphins) in response to certain experiences that are largely pointless and somewhat silly, like volleyball and karaoke. Basically, I wanted to get the low down on fun, and so I spent a couple of weeks at the library, where I read four books entirely and about 100 books in part. I learned that the ancient Egyptians didn't ice skate. I learned that hippos do backflips. I learned that neoteny is the retention in adults of childlike traits, including an appetite for play. I learned that there's a positive correlation between having fun and having a larger cerebellum (which raises the question of whether fun produces more brain, or more brain produces fun). I learned that for Catherine Price, author of *The Power of Fun*, fun can be found at the confluence of play, connection and flow. I learned that it's a good thing that notions of fun are inherently unstable, because in medieval Venice it was considered fun to shave off your hair and then headbutt a cat. I learned, through the work of Michael Foley, and in particular his book *Isn't This Fun?*, that evidence of ritualistic fun involving dressing-up, dancing and getting pissed has been found in prehistoric art on every continent. I learned that far from being frivolous in the grand scheme of things, fun has served an evolutionary purpose, by encouraging us to innovate, socialise and get jiggy. I learned all this and then pressed stop. I pressed stop because if I didn't I would have found myself down a rabbit hole with no choice but to continue burrowing southward until I emerged in New Zealand with a fully theoretical and completely impractical book on my hands. In summary: I did the homework and then left the work at home and went out looking for some action.

19 January

I meet a retired maths teacher at a greasy spoon in South London for a cryptic crossword induction. Jim is the goalkeeper of my football team, and reckons (unrealistically) that such puzzles are his chief means of diversion. We both arrived at the café with a copy of *The Times* under our wing, and after ordering two plates of saturated fat, we turn in sync to the crossword at the back. The idea is that Jim's basically going to think aloud as he works through the crossword, and so doing introduce me to some of the tricks of the trade (anagram indicators, anagram fodder, coded directions) and inspire a lifelong love for the pastime. That's the idea. Basically.

'We'll start with an easy one,' says Jim.

'Okay, hit me.'

'2 down.'

'With you so far.'

'Determined late series of games at Wimbledon? (4,3).'

I stare at the clue for 30 seconds, then at my plum tomatoes and fried bread, then back at the clue, hoping that by shifting my focus in this way the clue will somehow unscramble itself.

'Let's break it down,' says Jim.

'Let's.'

'Determined is the concise clue, so the answer we're after is a synonym for determined.'

'If you say so.'

'I'd hazard that "Series of games at Wimbledon" is "set", and that "late" is probably "dead", as in my late gerbil or wife.'

'Gerbil or wife?'

'Which gives us "dead set", as in to be dead set against such-and-such, which of course is another way of saying determined. Shall we move on?'

'How did you learn to do this?'

'By doing this. So, now we've got the "d" from dead set, let's have a look at 20 down. Righteous man's best friend turned 50 on fourth of July. Five letters, the third of them being the "d".'

'Brown sauce?'

'No, it doesn't fit. I reckon it's godly.'

'Of course you do.'

'Man's best friend – dog – which when turned around gives us god. Do you follow?'

'Entirely.'

'And 50 is L in Roman numerals, of course.'

'Are you gonna eat that, Jim?'

'While fourth of July – meaning the fourth letter of July, I fancy – is "y".'

'Do you not you like black pudding or something?'

'Which gives us godly. (Not especially, no.) And godly happens to be a synonym for righteous – or sort of, anyway. Help yourself.'

'Nice one.'

'Moving on. 25 across. Four letters beginning with "y".'

'Hit me.'

'Elusive figure still leading India …'

'Do you reckon I should have taken that chance on Saturday, Jim?'

'Yeti.'

'Rather fluffed my lines, didn't I?'

'Comic blunder turned opening into pancake …'

'I wouldn't go that far, Jim.'

'Look, Ben. Shall we concentrate for a second? We haven't got all day.'

'Speak for yourself, mate.'

20 January

Being daft can be fun. Not always, not reliably, but it certainly has the potential. By way of example, I was in a shop this afternoon – of the bric-a-brac variety – and said to the lady minding the wares, 'Do you know the problem with Russian dolls? They're full of themselves.' The lady appreciated the observation; indeed, it tickled her. I can't say the observation was original – I got it off my dad, who doubtless got it off his – but what does that matter? If one effect of recycling pointless silliness is a chuckling vendor, I'm all for plagiarism.

Similarly, I asked a waiter the other day how their weekend was. They said they went back to Wolverhampton, where they had four birthday parties over the course of a few days. To which I said, 'You're ageing quickly, aren't you?' On that occasion, the recipient of my daftness just shook their head, dramatically unimpressed.

Silliness of this kind won't always be welcomed, or provoke a titter, but that shouldn't count against it. My dad, whenever ordering a soft drink in a pub, likes to say, 'And I'd like some

ice in that please. Fresh ice, mind. None of that frozen stuff.'
This little gag of his tends to go entirely unacknowledged, which
doesn't bother him, for it nevertheless serves a purpose – to act
as a tiny reminder that life is essentially light, is basically daft, is
inherently unserious, notwithstanding all its travails and gravitas
and setbacks.

I don't know. Maybe I'm barking up the wrong tree here.
Maybe such drollery and daftness are too inconsequential and
ordinary to warrant a mention here. Or maybe it's exactly those
properties – inconsequentiality and ordinariness – that qualifies
silliness for serious consideration. What am I getting at? Be silly,
I guess. Be daft. When you can, if you want. There's no reason
to, of course, and therefore every reason indeed.[3]

22 January

I have a game of cricket in a pub. Yep. That's right. It seems
like watering holes have gone full circle and are now, once
again, as much about playing games as they are pouring drinks.
Old-fashioned public houses would offer darts, billiards, skittles
and so on. Then bars and gastropubs came along, and it was
about nice décor and sophisticated ambience and oxtail bao
buns and rhubarb gin. When this happened, the onus in terms
of entertainment and amusement was shifted squarely onto
the punter and the pinot noir, and if that combination didn't
work for you as a means of diversion then you were pretty much
stuffed. Which I often was. There's only so much fun I'm going

---

[3] Silliness can go too far, however. A salutary lesson was offered by
Salvador Dalí, who, in search of kicks, once delivered a lecture in a
deep-sea diver's suit, and almost suffocated.

to get out of three pints of Stella and my mate Chris telling me what a financial derivative is (again).

Anyway. Some pubs are reintroducing games. Are reincorporating play. Not in a tokenistic way – a dartboard in the corner, say – but in a major one. It's not yet a trend or a movement as such, but there are now pubs and bars in the UK offering, as their unique selling point, golf, cricket, darts, table tennis and even kabaddi, an ancient Indian sport that involves being chased while breathing out constantly.

Sixes. That's the name of the pub. It's got everything you'd expect from a pub, plus half a dozen cricket 'nets' – or simulators. I'd spotted the pub online, and found the concept appealing, though I think it's fair to say the company behind Sixes is probably stretching the truth a notch when it claims on its website that 'nothing says freedom more than playing cricket in a pub'.

I meet some friends. We get some beers. We enter our details. And then I enter the net to face a pixelated spin bowler. It's not much fun to begin with – I fail to make contact with the first six deliveries. But after I reacquaint myself with the small amount of hand-eye co-ordination I possess, and manage to clobber a couple – I start to get a bit of a kick out of it, which is to say my brain serves up a pint of endorphins and a shot of adrenaline, the potency of each amplified by the presence of an audience.

When it's someone else's turn to step up to the plate, I enjoy offering feedback on their efforts, and improvising a bit of pitch-side commentary – 'The ageing Liverpudlian has caught that one nicely; his parents would be proud were they not otherwise engaged in Corfu', and so on. If not quite an out-of-body experience, role-playing in this way certainly allows a certain escapism, a bit of selflessness, a touch of the old getting lost in the moment. (It would be odd if it materialises – over the course of my funathon – that peak emotional experiences essentially involve people not being who they are.)

The addition of a cricket experience to the traditional British boozer doesn't please everyone. Megan, more accustomed to wielding a paintbrush than a cricket bat, takes no pleasure in being hit on the kneecap not once but twice. She describes her batting debut as stressful and unnecessary, though she does have the grace to admit that there might be a relationship between enjoyment and competence, i.e. without a sliver of the latter, one will struggle to gain a measure of the former.

The cricket also has a fracturing effect on the social experience as a whole. Just as you're getting into a conversation with a mate about their Christmas or week at work, one of you is called into bat, or something happens in the net that takes your attention away from each other and pulls it towards a moment of calamity. It's a bit like tenpin bowling, which always promises to be a heightened social experience but tends to end up being a slightly underwhelming and disjointed one.

On top of the social damage, by the time I've batted for the fifth time, the law of diminishing returns has well and truly set in and the cricket itself is starting to suffer. I guess that's the thing with novel experiences – they don't stay novel for long. Here's a thought: activities that are truly our cup of tea remain satisfying and fun and engaging long after they ceased to be novel. Activities that aren't truly our cup of tea, like playing cricket in a pub, tend to stop being so after roughly 45 minutes. Nonetheless, it's good to give these things a shot, because if you don't, you wouldn't ever discover the things that bring you lasting joy.

After our net session is up, we retire to a table and do what you normally do in a pub – sit and talk about work. This is pleasant enough, but not helping things is the noise pollution of cricket balls being thwacked every few seconds. We could be in a warzone. We are all subconsciously on edge – a psychological state not thought to be conducive with fun. Hey-ho.

The pub offers membership, I'm intrigued to learn. For 50 quid a month you can play as much cricket as you want, Monday to Friday, 10am–4pm. The idea, I suppose, is for people that work at home to stop working at home and start working at the pub instead, where they'll be at liberty to smack a few balls while on the phone to their line manager. I'm not going to become a member. I dipped a toe into pub cricket, and that will be the extent of my immersion.

23 January

If we accept that things that are funny are fleeting shards of fun, then we might accept that eavesdropping can be a supplier of such shards. Case in point: I was walking back from the shop this morning when I heard one person telling another person that 'the thing about facts is – you have to take them with a pinch of salt'.

26 January

Having established what fun is (i.e. just about anything really), it might be worth establishing why exactly you should go after the stuff. For one, fun is much easier to target than happiness. It's less nebulous and abstract. (Which isn't to say it's not nebulous and abstract, only that it's less so.) For two, fun comes with a gener- ous package of benefits: it is a reliable mood swinger; it is good at building bridges and fostering relationships; and it has been proven to reduce stress (and therefore the risk of a plethora of negative health outcomes). For three, fun is hardly a bitter pill to swallow. In fact, it's a piece of cake to swallow. It's not as if I'm saying: here's a bunch of unequivocally positive outcomes, but what you have to do to get them is ruin your life. Instead, what I'm saying is: to stand a chance of winning all the afore-mentioned prizes – the well-being, the reduced stress, the social boost, the uptick in optimism – all you have to do is have more fun. As Catherine Price says in *The Power of Fun*, adding more fun to your life is like going on a diet that requires you to eat *more* of the foods that you love.

Having said all of the above, let's not lose sight of the fact that fun is its own reward. Frankly, it shouldn't matter what happens as a result – fun should still be pursued. Even if fun didn't have the positive effects that it does, it's got enough intrinsic appeal to make plenty of other sensations blush. The appeal of fun isn't that it reduces the risk of coronary heart disease down the road. The appeal of fun is that it reduces the risk of you being bored and sluggish right now. The appeal of fun isn't that it reduces the chances of you having a stroke in later life. The appeal of fun is that it energises, and engages, and exhilarates; that it injects a sense of lightness and levity into your Tuesday afternoon.

But even those things (energy, exhilaration, levity) are still too far down the road for my liking. Even those things are outcomes, are consequences. Such things may well be important elements of fun's resumé, but the act of promoting them still feels a bit like putting the cart before the horse. Is the truth not that we have fun because we want to play pickleball? (Don't ask me what pickleball is; I've just heard of it.) Is the truth not that we have fun because we want to take part in a cuddle puddle? (Asking for a friend.) Is the truth not that we have fun because we want to sit around a table and reflect with old friends? Because we want to sing? Because we want to dance? Because we want to perform? Because we want to create? You don't invite someone to have fun, you invite them to a roller disco. You don't put fun in the diary, you put shopping with your nan in the diary. Fun is an outcome, not an event. And the less we think about it, the better. (I am aware that by promoting less thought about fun I am undermining the already unstable foundations of this book.)

In short, fun has lots of benefits, short and long term. But try not to think about them too much. Instead, just do something and see what happens. Like the way a watched kettle never boils, if you keep too much of an eye on fun it's liable to hide.

30 January

Second crossword session with Jim. Or should I say: Puzzling meeting plus homophone of gym (8, 7, 4, 3). First things first, Jim reminds me of the various tricks I was introduced to last week, and then, armed with these, I read through the clues.

The exercise is fruitless: I can't even spot the tricks, to say nothing of solving them. I'm utterly blank. Clueless even, which is ironic given what I'm gaping at gormlessly. I can't spot the indicators, the hazard lights, the coded instructions to reverse, to turn upside down, to get on my feet and do star jumps. None of it.

Jim's got a few by now, needless to say, but is keeping schtum; he wants me to persist unassisted a while longer. I do so, and it isn't fun, not for a second. Engaging? Sure. Testing? Certainly. But in terms of fun, I've had more brushing my teeth.

What it comes down to is that racking your brain without confidence and for no compelling reason isn't inherently rewarding – no shot of dopamine or wave of endorphins is readily forthcoming. There's definitely – I'm coming to see – a relationship between competence and fun that I'd be wise to pay attention to: namely that you will struggle to be amused and delighted by things you are utterly – and apparently unswervingly – crap at. We saw it with Meg playing cricket, and we're seeing it now.

I throw in the towel (4, 2) after half an hour, and the pair of us resort to chitchat. I ask Jim what it was like being a maths teacher for umpteen years (good); what it was like growing up in Crewe (bad); and, finally, what it was like manning a picket line in the 80s (occasionally ugly). Jim's stories – abbreviated here for the sake of concision – are more stimulating than the crossword by a factor of several thousand. When I share this opinion, Jim can't believe what he's hearing. For him the cryptic crossword is sacred, which means that what I've just said amounts to profanity.

'I'm easily pleased, Jim.'

'And you're easily challenged 'n' all. You need to show a bit more resilience.'

He persuades me to give it one more shot. Says there's fun to be had, just not the low-hanging variety. We arrange to meet next week, same time, same place.[4]

---

[4] I'm pleased to say that four days later Jim got Covid, and so couldn't meet for round three. We are yet to reschedule.

3

To be without some of the things you want is an indispensable part of happiness

Wherein the author goes downhill, goes to a yoga class, abandons his phone and sings the praises of conversation.

5 February

Football. We're away to Walton-on-Thames, which I'm told is a historically spicy fixture for the Comics.[5] I get a lift to the match with the gaffer. I do my best to butter him up en route, but it's no good – he sticks me on the bench. Says that since making my debut I haven't exactly been on fire.

A funny thing happens prior to kick-off. In short, one of our players gets locked in the toilet. He arrived at the ground discreetly and somewhat late, entered the cricket pavilion (where we'd been invited to get changed), and headed straight for the loo. Just a minute later, and with kick-off imminent, the captain of the opposition locked up the pavilion, as per his routine.

It was only because one of our players (winger Darren) had to search for something in his kit bag a few minutes into the match (talent, perhaps) that he was in a position to spot his phone vibrating. It was Oggy, explaining his situation, which in short was that he'd turned up unnoticed and been locked in the bog. Were it not for Darren's chance rummage, our Lithuanian talisman would have remained in captivity for the duration of the match. Perhaps Walton-on-Thames do this every home game? Pinpoint a potential playmaker and then trap them in a cubicle. Needless to say, the sight of Oggy emerging from the boggy is a pleasant one indeed.

Also pleasant is not being a substitute for long: someone gets injured within five minutes and I'm promptly summoned by the

---

[5] The team is technically – or tenuously – an offshoot of the London School of Economics, where several of the starting eleven claim to have been educated.

gaffer, albeit without enthusiasm. And he was right to be hesitant. My first contribution is to fall over attempting a backheel.

There's a lovely moment just after the restart when a member of the opposition is sent off for dissent. The referee had adjudged the player in question to have been offside, an adjudgment the player in question evidently disagreed with, if his response – a set of menacing propositions regarding what he would like to do to the ref given half a chance – was anything to go by.

The infuriated striker is finally forced off the pitch and sent to the cricket pavilion to cool off. (There's an awkward moment when he arrives at the pavilion, finds it locked, and has to march back for the keys.) He must cool off pretty quickly, because the hothead is back at the side of the pitch within a few minutes, bearing a cup of tea, a cigarillo and an infant aged roughly eighteen months. It must be the case that the infant was passed to the hothead while my attention was elsewhere, rather than discovered in the cricket pavilion by chance, which is how it appeared to me.

I'm pleased to say that, even with a babe in his arms, the dismissed striker spends the rest of the match hurling abuse at both the referee and his assistant – who by this point is yours truly. (I got injured ten minutes into the second half, and was asked to run the line.) The most memorable utterance bellowed in my direction goes something like this: 'Get a pair of f**king glasses you potbellied tart.' I shout back that I'm actually wearing contact lenses so that can't be the issue, which seems to confound the gentleman sufficiently to take some of the heat out of the moment. For the next minute or so, limping up and down the side of the pitch, trying to stay in line with the last defender, I can't stop thinking about what I've just been called and laughing, which suggests that on paper being gratuitously insulted can be a source of merriment.

When I get home, I show Megan some footage of the match that the assistant manager took and shared with the squad. She makes two remarks: 'It's like you're playing in slow motion,' is one, and 'Can't they get you a bigger shirt?' is the other. Charming.

7 February

In an indication of how one thing can lead to another, the manager of my football team – a keen cyclist – has invited me to join him in the saddle. And he's prepared to lend me one so I might do so. It is fair to say that Andrew's by no means short in the saddle department. He buys a new set of wheels every year, can't bear to part with the old set, and so has dozens of bikes in the shed/living room/guest bedroom, to the delight of his wife, who, although appreciative of the wheel as a design concept, isn't so fond that she desires such an array of examples.

Having familiarized myself with one of Andrew's old rides – a carbon-framed number worth more than I am – we proceed via Wimbledon Common to Richmond Park. The latter was established by King Charles I and is a jewel in London's crown. When I mention to Andrew, upon entering the park and drinking in its inestimable charms, that the saddle of my bike is taking the shine off the afternoon's delight by causing a deal of pain (it feels like I'm straddling a railing), he says something questionable about the road to pleasure being paved with discomfort.

Notwithstanding the saddle, it's fair to say I'm in a good mood. The motion, the exertion, the novelty, the hint of danger, the visual scenario, the sporadic education (e.g. when Andrew points to Pembroke Lodge and tells me it was once the home of the philosopher Bertrand Russell, who's on record as saying that to be without some of the things you want is an indispensable part of happiness) – it's all conspiring to elevate my spirit and heighten my mood and make me positively hormonal.

The best part of the ride is a stretch of downhill after a long, slow climb (which suggests that both Andrew and Bertrand might have been on to something). During the descent, I clock a group of deer to my right and a group of towering flats to my left, and somehow the combination of the deer and the flats and the downhill sensation awakens me to the gorgeous, pointless, fleeting thickness of life. By the time I reach the bottom, I'm feeling on top of the world. If I could bottle the feeling and put a drop of it in my tea each morning, I most definitely would.

Speaking of tea, after a couple of laps of the park we stop for one at an unassuming café near Roehampton Gate. The tea is better than normal – improved, like my mood, by the occasion and its ingredients, including Andrew's anecdote concerning a bike holiday during which a lad called Isaac spent a night behind Italian bars after being done for speeding. Reflecting on the anecdote, and Andrew's decision to share it, it occurs to me that different scenarios will necessarily provoke different memories; that there is a conversational bonus inherent in doing new things.

All things considered, my cycling debut proves a truly excellent experience. Until, that is, Andrew has his bike stolen, while he was briefly in the loo and I was briefly daydreaming. I attempt to temper Andrew's fury by reminding him of what the philosopher said about being without certain things that we want. It doesn't work. I guess philosophy can't be right all the time.[6]

8 February

Conversation can be fun. It can also be plenty of other things – dull, infuriating, revealing and so on. But it can surely be fun – as sure as eggs is eggs. I mention this now because I just had one – a long one – with an old friend who I hadn't seen for yonks. Without design or agenda, our chat covered a range of topics, including but not limited to nut allergies and Elvis.

For me, having a good conversation is like opening a book, or putting on the television, or drawing back the curtains and discovering a pleasant and droll and emotive set of surprises.

But that's not quite right, because the person opening up or turning on or drawing back is also the co-author or -architect or -engineer of all those surprises. And what's more (more special, more mad) is that the authoring and engineering and archi-tecting is happening in real time, as we speak, off the cuff. A conversation is a marvel, really. And when the interlocutor is a dear old friend, you have a large and irresistible stake in all that

---

[6] That ride in Richmond Park was the first of ten or so 'training rides' I did in the run-up to the London to Brighton charity bike ride in May 2022 (which I didn't do in the end owing to injury). At the time, the ride described above was not a training ride, it was just a ride. As a result, it was by far the most fun of the ten. Sometimes goals serve to *improve* the quality of an activity, but often they don't. For me, a bike ride is optimal when there's nothing riding on it, when you can just smell the flowers and go as slow as you like, pausing for tea when-soever you wish.

they say, all that they tell. Their utterances and confidences and quips have extra salience and value because *they* have extra salience and value. And when you throw in a bottle of something, and a congenial ambience, and a gap of months since the pair of you last bumped heads, you've got one hell of a hobby on your hands.

Imagine a climbing wall. Imagine all the holds – the bits to reach for, to cling to, to rely on. There's more of those holds when talking with a friend. There's more of those holds because there's more shared experience, more shared files. The abundance of holds makes the going good, the climbing fair, the talk fluid and diffuse and self-generating. And when there's a lull, or a peak, or a pause for breath, then there's always the here and now to turn to, the shared environment, the symposium itself (a pub in Oldham), which is itself a buffet of further footholds, of conversational sparks. In this light, it's easier to understand why conversations had on the phone have such a different quality to those had in person.[7]

All of the above isn't to say that conversations with strangers or people you're less familiar with can't be as good as conversations with friends, because they can; but they can also be handicapped by that lack of familiarity, and by some of its consequences – self-consciousness being one, distrust being another.

And yet sometimes talking to strangers can be more fruitful and free-flowing and frank than talking to friends. Less shared

---

[7] It has been suggested that 85 per cent of communication during in-person chats is non-verbal. Ergo, a conversation minus the majority of its comms is bound to occasionally falter. So don't be hard on yourself if, like me, you're awful on the blower.

files can mean more ground to cover; less pre-existing connection can mean a reduced fear of judgment. In the face of a stranger, we are at liberty to truly open up, because we don't stand to lose anything by doing so. Unless that stranger is a priest, of course, in which case the consequences can be hellish.

Aside from the very fact of them, I also find the *process* of conversations enjoyable at some level. I like the way a chinwag works. I like the way it leads from one thing to another, almost unscripted, almost dreamlike. I like the way it issues micro-doses of surprise and intrigue and novelty and suspense, as it improvises its course. I like the way it nourishes, and edifies, and reduces to tears, as it goes invisibly onward to nowhere in particular.

It won't come as news that a good talk requires a good listen; that a good chat requires each converser to care as much for taking as giving. Conversation requires the provision of care and interest, and it requires trust – that all parties might speak freely without fear of mockery or censure.

Though a conversation needn't be peaceful. Back in the good old days, disagreement used to be encouraged and enjoyed. It used to be one of the points of talking: to share viewpoints, compare takes, and then go away with food for thought. In the sport of fencing, a conversation is the play of blades in a bout; and didn't Nietzsche say that our best friends are also our best enemies because they are prepared to rebut and discredit some of the waffle we come out with? Don't be under the illusion that good conversation depends on the swapping of compliments, or the sharing of niceties. As crucial as respect in conversation is candour.

Ironically, conversation isn't easy to talk about. It isn't much discussed. Perhaps it's because conversation is so ordinary and ubiquitous that it manages to go under the radar, somewhat unseen, somewhat unsung – in terms of fun, I mean. When it comes to gabbing, we are like the fish who haven't a clue what water is, but depend on it nonetheless.[8]

As previously stated, conversations won't always be hilarious or light-hearted. They might not even *tend* to be these things. And yet when I close my eyes and imagine myself laughing, I'm laughing in response to something someone's said. I'm laughing opposite someone. I'm laughing in conversation.

One way of illustrating conversation's value is to imagine a world without it. I can do this with many things – tenpin bowling, skydiving, peanut butter – and the prospect doesn't alarm me. But a world without conversation, whether spoken or signed, whether written or performed – bereft! Another way of illustrating its value is to look at the etymology. The word 'conversation' can be traced back to fourteenth-century France, where it meant *a place where one lives*. Which says it all really.

At the end of my conversation with a dear old friend in a pub in Oldham, they insisted on giving me a hug. I attempted to sabotage the moment by rationalising his affection.

'That'll be the oxytocin, mate,' I said.

'Nah,' he said, still hugging me.

'I promise you, mate. That's what chat does. It issues the cuddle hormone.'

'Can't you just hug in silence?'

'Or rather it triggers the hypothalamus to issue the cuddle hormone.'

'And is that why you won't shut up about it? Because you want more cuddle.'

---

[8] Said fish make an appearance in David Foster Wallace's essay *This is Water*.

'I'm saying nothing.'

'That's better.'

He let me go. And we swam away.[9]

14 February

At the beginning of the year, I made it an ambition to sample every single one of the classes offered by my gym. In short, I wanted to add some spice to my exercise life. By sampling all the classes, I knew I'd be taken out of my comfort zone, and introduced to a host of novel ways of getting a sweat on. It's inarguable that exercise is good for you. (Unless, that is, you powerwalk off a cliff.) Indeed, it's because of exercise that *Homo sapiens* has a brain three times bigger than it should be. Our distant ancestors were really into something called 'persistence hunting', which is a type of long-distance running in pursuit of one's meals for the week. Because of persistence hunting, the human brain was producing a vast amount of proteins called neurotrophins, which caused it to put on weight. Fast forward several thousand years, and exercise remains a friend of the brain. Because exercise is good at both reducing stress and boosting one's mood (by triggering the release of endorphins and serotonin, chiefly), it is also good at *enabling* fun, at being a reliable accessory to it. Simply put, after exercising one is more likely to feel open and available to various sources of merriment. So when I resolved to give all the gym classes a go, I knew that even if the classes themselves weren't tremendous fun, they would still be doing me a favour by getting me into a headspace where fun was more

---

[9] For further reading on the value of chatting, *Let's Talk: How to Have Better Conversations* by Nihal Arthanayake is a lovely book.

obtainable. If, as well as serving as gateways to more fun down the road, the gym classes proved to be fun in themselves, then so much the better.

Yoga isn't fun. Or, put more precisely and politely: yoga isn't fun for me on this occasion. Instead, it's, erm, awkward and painful and embarrassing. One thing I learn within a few minutes of the class starting is that it's all very well going in with an open mind, but if your hamstring's closed and has been for years, yoga is unlikely to be a combo of epiphany and exhilaration.

It's not anyone's fault. Maria – the teacher – does her best. But her biggest mistake is to treat me like an equal. Of course, she can't offer me a bespoke package – I get that. She can't just focus on me and tailor her lesson according to my limitations – I get that too. She has to behave democratically – I get that as well. But by pandering to the people as a whole, she just about ruins the trapezius of this person in particular. To her credit, Maria does attempt now and again to personalise her feedback by whispering things to me as she goes around the studio ('other way, Ben'); but to be frank there's only so much she can do. I mean, I was a car crash before the session had even started, when I couldn't even help myself to a mat and a foam roller without causing a scene. The closest I get to a state of flow is when Maria tells us *not to let our minds mislead us* – a somewhat cryptic request that I devote my full attention to for roughly a minute.

Things get worse before they get better. We're asked to stretch our legs out – this I can do. Then we're asked to open them as wide as possible – this I can do less. The greatest angle I can muster – and bear in mind that Maria is asking for something in the 150–180 degrees range – is about four degrees. You can barely tell my legs are open at all. When Maria asks us to bring our foreheads down slowly until they are touching the floor, I decide she's taking the piss. When I lift my head to confirm my suspicion, everyone's head is touching the floor.

I get through the session, and notwithstanding all of the above, it does me some good. I like the almost aphoristic quality of a lot of Maria's guidance. There's one thing she says – about pain – that speaks to me on several levels. She says that when a stretch begins to hurt, that is the beginning of its goodness. Worth remembering, that; it's a take on suffering that can be applied to a lot of situations in life. Though of course what Maria is really saying in this situation is: 'Don't you dare capitulate at the first twinge of discomfort, young man, because in case you weren't aware somebody missed out on this session because of you'.

I will go again. Once a week – that's the aim. I know enough about cost-benefit scenarios not to expect well-being and jollity on a plate within seconds of entering the room – or yoga studio, in this case. No, I'll be back. For some more yin yoga. For some more unnatural lunging and illogical overextension. For some more unnerving exhortations to send my breath to the floor from the chin via the pancreas. Only next time I'll avoid brassicas in the morning.

16 February

An eavesdropping. 'I can't see anything, Mummy. All the phones are in the way.'

19 February

Spending hours on your phone every day probably isn't fun, but you do it anyway. You do it anyway because smartphone usage is closely bound up with the administration of dopamine, which makes smartphones feel deserving of your time. Simply put, dopamine makes you want to do something again. That's its job, and it's been in the post for some time. Dopamine serves an evolutionary purpose: it encourages us to have sex and socialise and try new things. The reason the act of checking a smartphone triggers the release of dopamine is because, in theory, when we check a smartphone, *anything* could happen. Anything doesn't happen, of course, but it could, and that's what matters: by picking up our phones we are stepping into the unknown, and our brains reward us for doing so. When we don't find what we were hoping for, we put our phones down – until we check them again. We check them again because – once more – anything could happen. This cycle will continue until we've checked our phones dozens of times in a single hour, and been rewarded with a biochemical pat on the back on each occasion. For most humans, it's an unprofitable cycle. For a select few, it's worth a fortune.

A few weeks ago, I went to reach for my smartphone while I was on my smartphone. That was a low point. It was also a light-bulb moment. Now I don't have a smartphone. Now I have a phone that is as stupid as a phone can be. It can barely cope with phone calls. It was built when Bill Clinton was in power. But it doesn't make me think it's in my pocket when it's in my hand, so it's got that going for it. My new phone isn't as good as my old phone, but it makes me better. So it goes.[10]

---

[10] Since I got my new stupid phone, I probably ask to quickly look at Megan's smartphone about 149 times a day.

4

Oh to possess once again that nine-year-old style!

Wherein the author flies a 1938 biplane, goes skiing, is bowled over by soufflé and learns about the different types of fun.

21 February

I'm not a huge fan of skiing, truth be told. I've only been a few times, most of them in Poland, where it doesn't break the bank so much, and there's less chance of you coming a cropper, if only because there's less mountain to come a cropper on.

I fly to Geneva, where I'm met by my uncle and two cousins, aged, in no particular order, nine, 62 and twelve. Mike is quick to get something off his chest: that he has to stay at home this evening to prepare an important presentation about protons, meaning I'll have to drive the children to the chalet, where their Austrian mother will reward the safe delivery of her children with (if she hasn't changed a bit) a bit of cheese and a gherkin.

I can't say I'm delighted by the prospect of the journey. I hardly drive, you see, and drive even less on mountainous roads in French cars with precious cargo on board. In the event, the drive proves pleasingly uneventful. The most memorable element of the journey is when I ask the girls what they consider to be fun and Erin says 'revenge' and Anya says 'vichyssoise', which I believe is a cold soup of pureed leek and potato.

Upon arriving at the chalet, Anya and I play a version of hide-and-seek. In the first instance, this involves me compiling a crossword for her, with each correct answer yielding five seconds' worth of hiding time. Naturally (given that this is a child who gives the answer vichyssoise to the question 'what is fun?'), Anya gets all the questions right and uses her 60 seconds to find a hiding place so effective as to be undiscoverable, meaning nobody sees her for the next hour and a half – an outcome not lost on (or unappreciated by) the rest of her family.

22 February

The view from my bedroom window is quite something. I stand and stare for several minutes, which means I can tick mindfulness off today's to-do list. Would this alpine view be subject to the law of diminishing returns? I fear so. There's such a thing as hedonic adaptation and it rains on the parade of felicity. Basically, our brains get used to a good thing and return to their baseline levels of happiness before the ink is even dry on our status updates. If the neuroscience is reliable, we can safely hazard that within a week this alpine view will fail to trigger what it triggers today. At which point it will be necessary – to maintain my good mood – to move to a bedroom facing a bigger mountain.

It's not exactly fun renting my ski gear. For a start, the cost of doing so is a bit of a fun-repellent. (Sadly, fun is not impervious to questions of value.) Second, when attempting to get the boots on, I always think I'm about to break my ankle. And third, the helmet never fits because the back of my head is unusually protrusive. It's like my skull's got a conservatory, where it keeps pointless comparisons and similes.

We hit the slopes. That's what we do – we hit them. We don't awkwardly and painfully make our way towards them for the next half an hour – oh no, we hit them. And once we've hit them, I resemble, in principle if not in all actuality, an alpaca in heels. All the while my legs and brain are struggling to get on the same page, even the humble snowplough is beyond me. Which isn't ideal: the snowplough is an amateur skier's crutch; life without a working one is parlous. Not a few times over the next twenty minutes do I say to myself – legs akimbo and approaching a dead end – 'And this is fun how?'

When my period of gross incompetence eventually runs out of steam, and I start to get the hang of it, it is going fast in a straight line that I like the most. I like it because it feels both exciting and relatively safe – relative, that is, to leaving the main drag and 'riding the bumps', which is what my cousins prefer to do. The fun of going fast in a straight line is added to by the visuals – or the environment, as it used to be called. Unless you are a regular, coming once or twice a year, the alps on a clear day in winter – or indeed any mountain range on a clear day in any season – will shock and startle the senses beautifully, elevating whatever one is doing to a higher experiential plane.

Did I mention my cousins' tyrannical streak? I didn't? Well here it is in action: the pair are presently demanding that I forgo my independence and follow them forthwith. When I'm too cowardly to turn them down, and make a sporting attempt to keep up and follow their lead, I spend the next several minutes sharing some uncharitable thoughts with the wintry atmosphere.

The bumps are no fun for me, you see. Their survival is fun, but the bumps themselves, the bumps per se, are not. I am too out of control. Too bodily at odds. Too endangered for the experience to have a feel-good factor. It's not only because I'm a poor skier. It's also because of my height, which is letting me down badly. My cousins, on the other hand, remain partially grown. Their lower centres of gravity mean they are less affected by the ups and downs, and, simply put, there is less of them for things to go wrong to.

Though it's not all plain sailing for them either. Anya, in particular, never looks far from disaster. To speak truthfully, it is Erin, the eldest, who loves the bumps. Anya follows because she must; and the reason she must is because she cannot allow her sister to triumph in any way – not here, not now, not there, not ever. By following, Anya pays homage to a sisterly compulsion as old as time. And by following, she falls over – always comically, always calamitously, and always to the delight of her bigger sister, which *incenses* Anya, which causes the wrath of a dozen tortured souls to rise up inside her and spill forth in a venomous Germanic shriek, '*Nein*, Erin! *Das ist nicht lustig! Hör auf oder ich töte dich!*' I don't speak German. But let's assume that Anya isn't telling her sister how much she loves her.

When it's my turn to fall over, I don't mind the experience so much. To be honest, I kind of even like it. There's fun to be had in falling over. Tumbles are, by their nature, spontaneous. This is a feather in their cap. They are so abrupt and unexpected and anomalous as to be somehow delightful. They are such a break from the norm that their randomness can't help but thrill the brain. And when it becomes clear that nothing is broken or out of joint, and relief has been added to the cocktail of serotonin and adrenaline, basically the brain has a little party. On its own. For about a minute. After which point it's time to get up and find one's cousins.

The chairlifts are also fun. They provide a chance to chat in a unique context, with the mountains all around and hundreds of people in bright costumes swooshing along below. We talk about school and their friends and the German language; about their favourite food and their favourite words (annihilate for Erin, *schleim* for Anya). And when we're done talking, I instigate a game called Bogeys. One person says 'bogeys' very quietly, almost whispering the word. Then the next person says it a tiny bit louder. And then you keep going until someone is shouting 'bogeys!' as loud as they can. At first the girls are a bit cool for this game, a bit suspicious of its value, and will only say 'bogeys' sullenly, half-heartedly. But before long they're fully on board and in hysterics. In fact, once she's figured out that the game is in essence an act of rebellion, a form of civic disobedience, it's a tall order getting Erin to stop shouting 'bogeys'.

Next to the bumps and the tumbles and the chairlifts and the chatter, making our way back to the chalet is considerably less fun. One of the girls suggests a shortcut, across the back gardens, and has set off before I've had a chance to question the proposal. It's off-piste, alright. It's trespassing even. And it's treacherous to boot – not least when a river appears before me.

'It's not wide,' says Erin. 'Just don't think about it and don't slow down. And when you get to the river, sort of lift up the front of your skis.'

I attempt to do as I'm told, but instead of not thinking about it, I definitely think about it, and instead of not slowing down, I definitely slow down, and instead of lifting up the front of my skis, I definitely don't lift them up, with the result that instead of crossing the river I sort of end up wedged between its banks. While Erin laughs, and Anya takes a picture, I dream of being back in the relative comfort of the yoga studio.

But, here's the thing. You can't cherry pick when it comes to fun. You have to accept the whole package, including the bit where you end up in a river. Fun things acquire their value in relation to, and in opposition to, things they are not – like awkwardness and discomfort. Without the things it's not, fun would hardly make any sense. Which is something to bear in mind the next time you're stuck in a river, or the couple in the flat above decide to use their tumble drier at 3 a.m., or you get a massive ulcer on your tongue. Bad things are good for us – when all things are considered.

Another thing about fun – while we're giving it some thought – is that it will often come out of nowhere. You'll go skiing and get a fair amount of fun from going downhill on planks (which is to be expected), but not half as much as you get from the sight of a man (well-to-do, English, mid-forties) turning around in anticipation of an approaching chairlift, only to find said chairlift fully occupied with a German family, leaving the man no option but to try, in an understandably panicked fashion, to climb aboard the lap of the German father, who, again understandably, opts to rebuff the man's advances and send him crashing to the ground, at which point the chairlift attendant clocks what's going on and brings the conveyance to a halt. If you offered me a scene like that every day, I'd snap your hand off.

Later that evening, after another round of gherkins and cheese, I ask my uncle what the most fun thing he's ever done is. Without giving it too much thought, he points out the window, towards Mont Blanc, and says:

'Climbing that thing.'

'Yeah?'

'Oh come on. You push yourself to the limit. You almost kill yourself. And you do it because when you get up there you feel like you've never felt before. It's the terror. The exertion. The relief when it's over. I'm actually noticing overlaps with parenthood. It's Type 2 fun.'

'Type 2 fun?'

'You don't know about the types of fun?'

'No.'

'Aren't you supposed to be writing a—'

'Yes, but do continue.'

'Type 1 is fun while it's happening. Type 2 is largely horrible while it's happening, but unbelievable afterwards.'

'I see.'

'And there's also Type 3 fun.'

'Which is?'

cookery class, skiing, aerobatics

'Neither fun during nor afterwards because the experience leaves you injured or traumatised.'

'Not one for the whole family then.'

'Well. I guess it depends how much you love your family.'

When it comes to Type 1 fun, it would appear that Anya is an addict. She is relentless in her pursuit of the stuff. When we finally got back to the chalet after my ordeal in the river, she instantly set about making a snowman (her appellation, not mine; if you want to imagine a non-binary snowperson, be my guest). Then she fashioned a bobsleigh and bobsleighed down every slope within 100 metres of the chalet. After that, she wanted to play hide and seek, and after that she wanted to play it again. Compared to the rest of us, Anya was winning at life. Oh to possess once again that nine-year-old style! Oh to shake off the existential kilos of maturity! Oh to remove the wool of adulthood that has been pulled over my eyes! Oh to—!

Ah. Hold up. She's just cracked her head open trying to hide on a bookshelf.

27 February

For a recent birthday, I was gifted a voucher for a cookery school in South London. The Avenue Cookery School is based in Wandsworth, which is where Hugh Grant (playing the prime minister) goes door knocking in search of Martine McCutcheon in *Love Actually*. The school is a relatively junior establishment, opening its ovens just a couple of years ago. As a result, the communal kitchen is looking a million bucks. One half expects Greg Wallace to emerge from a pantry clutching a spotted dick and custard.

When I arrive, I'm seated at a cooking station with four other solos – Paul, Brenda, Ahmed and Tilly. We compare excuses for coming. Ahmed was also gifted a voucher by his mother; Brenda's trying to get over the loss of a family member so is generally avoiding being at home; Tilly's actively trying to have more fun this year (idiot); and Paul clearly signed up for the wine. Booze is included in the ticket price, you see, and the fact isn't lost on my tablemates. Indeed, it's a good job some soda bread turns up when it does, else a few of us might have been done before the starter.

Our instructor for the evening is Richard, who looks like a young Gary Rhodes, if Gary Rhodes were Scandinavian and built like a scrum half. Richard tells us a few things off the bat: that he used to be a builder; that he loves the science of cooking as much as the art; and that we'll be doing cheese soufflé followed by coq au vin followed by crème brûlée. A fair trio if ever there was one.

After bringing the rowdiest tables to heel, Richard goes through the menu in more detail, giving short demonstrations of certain techniques as he does so. Briefing complete, now it's our turn to get stuck in, starting with the custard for the crème brûlée. Being a relative innocent in the kitchen, I find even the simplest of tasks – like separating eggs and weighing sugar – totally absorbing. Time may well fly when you're having fun, but I fancy it also has wings when you haven't got a clue. Unless, that is, you're doing a cryptic crossword.[11]

---

[11] The mental health benefits of being a beginner – and by extension, of lifelong learning – are set out nicely in Tom Vanderbilt's *Beginners: The Joy and Transformative Power of Lifelong Learning*, which I urge you to commence, cluelessly, at once.

Speaking of not having a clue, it's quickly apparent that Ahmed isn't the handiest in the kitchen, and that he'd much rather talk about his difficult day at work (as a researcher for an MP) than keep an eye on the custard. But the eggy nectar comes out beautifully nonetheless: mopping up its dregs with a finger is objectively the most pleasurable and meaningful thing I've done all year.

Post pudding prep, we turn our attention to the starter. Richard returns to his demonstration counter to demystify the electric whisker and underline exactly what he means when he says he wants us to *fold* the egg whites into the bechamel. When Richard calls me up to assist with the whisking, he soon wishes he hadn't. When he says 'go', I press the wrong button and the whisk pops out of its socket and falls into the bowl. *Nul points.*

With our soufflés in the oven (for fifteen minutes at 140), it's time to crack on with the coq. As we brown thighs and char lardons, the wine and conversation continue to flow. Ahmed is waxing lyrical about the MP he works for. Tilly is saying the most fun she's had this year was quitting her job as a primary school teacher (which is hardly a ringing endorsement for people under seven). And Brenda is telling us how she's retired these days but used to be in oil, not unlike the shallots we've been tasked with caramelising. At this juncture, Richard pops over to offer tips about freezing egg whites. He's just that kind of guy.

He's also the kind of guy that believes mashed potato should contain a potentially fatal amount of butter. He's dead serious on the matter; won't countenance any recipe that doesn't call for equal parts potato and clarified butter (which is butter that's been reduced until cleansed of anything healthy, like water).

When we've browned our thighs, added our wine, and our stews are bubbling away, it's time to extricate the soufflés, which

we top with gruyere, splash with cream, and finish with a sprin-
kling of pepper. They are sublime. Who would've thought that
baked egg could taste so good? It's like the best omelette you'll
ever have, times seven. It's the texture. That's what does it. If I
could be made of anything, I'd be made of soufflé.

Then I have a spoonful of the mash-butter and decide I'd
rather be made of that instead. Christ, it's good. And yet it's not
even the standout element of the course, for it's the sauce that
makes the main. The sweetness from the caramelised shallots, the
depth from the wine, the intensity from the tomato, the saltiness
from the lardons: if a dish deserves an OBE then it's this one.

During dessert, Richard takes questions from the audience.
Because several people are by now pickled, some of the questions
are a bit below the apron. 'All that whipping and beating must
keep you really lean, Richard?' asks a lady with more front than
Buckingham Palace.

When it's my turn to pose a question, I ask Richard about
the pros and cons of running a cookery school.

'The answer is the same for each,' he says.

'And what's that?'

'You're cooking all the time.'

'So you can have too much of a good thing, can you?'

'You bet your arse you can.'

And on that note, Richard tells us to drink up and sod off.

Outside, my tablemates gather in the winter chill for final
exchanges. Brenda asks what I made of the evening. I tell her
that if I had the means, I'd be down here every weeknight. Or
most weeknights, anyway. Because although the cookery school
is social and comic and educational and so on, I wouldn't want
to put my fondness for it under pressure. You've got to go easy
on delight, I fancy, else it will stop coming out to play.

6 March

I'm starting to get the impression that fun is self-perpetuating; that one instance will lead to another, and so on. Well here's an example. I did one fun thing a few months ago (accept a random invitation to attend the book club of a lady who was smitten with *The Gran Tour*, at which I mostly looked on while the book club members – about a dozen affluent mothers whose children all go to school together – got swiftly and amusingly pickled on pink champagne) and it resulted in an invitation to fly an aeroplane, one of the mothers having a father who's heavily into aerobatics. It transpires that once a year, at an airfield north of London, said father invites a bunch of people to climb into the cockpit and go for a quick spin – literally so. I don't actually remember accepting Alison's generous invitation. Nonetheless, a few days later, a formal proposal arrived in my inbox, and, having got into the habit of doing so recently, I said yes, despite having as much appetite for life-threatening antics at 3,000 feet as I do for Matt Hancock.

My co-pilot will be a bloke called Nigel, who, I'm told, has been flying planes since he was practically in nappies, and who first applied to join the air force aged eleven. After eventually joining up aged eighteen, Nigel jumped ship a few years later to join an aerobatics demonstration team. He hasn't looked back, or down, since. Nigel was British Aerobatic Champion eight times on the trot, and won the Red Bull Air Race World Championship in 2014. Ordinarily I'd be comforted by such credentials, but on this occasion I remain in two minds. Nigel is clearly top-drawer stuff, but his track record is also evidence of an alarming proclivity for danger. Alison attempts to put my mind at ease, by reminding me that Nigel has racked up nearly 2,000 public displays of aerial gymnastics over the course of his mania –

I mean career. She tells me I'm in the hands of a master, then asks why I'm trembling.

I'm trembling because the plane doesn't have a roof. And because masters are often unhinged, no matter their forte. And because one person having survived flying upside down umpteen times doesn't mean I will. I've heard it said – or seen it written – that the brain 'loves maybe', that it gets a kick out of uncertainty. Let me say this: the brain doesn't love maybe when the conditional thing is survival, when the thing up in the air is, well, oneself. It doesn't love maybe when Nigel is striding towards me with intent, and the unknown is whether I'll be around for dinner.[12]

When Nigel asks a simple question – 'Are you up for this?' – I don't offer a simple answer. Indeed, I don't say a thing. I just smile. Why? Because I don't trust my mouth: it's so desperate to say no, that I daren't give it the chance.

Nigel's appearance – or aura, rather – is doing nothing to calm my nerves. He looks a bit … possessed, to be honest, though with what I can't say. It could be the devil, or it could be supreme confidence. That he looks a bit possessed shouldn't come as a surprise: I guess you're bound to look a bit spooky when your idea of sport is courting disaster. For most people, recreation is about reducing the chances of one's imminent demise – by unwinding, decompressing, letting off steam. For a select few, it's increasing them. But calm down, Ben. You're catastrophising. Everything's going to be—

'I'll take that as a yes, will I?' says Nigel.

I nod.

---

[12] For the record, it was Dr David Greenfield, author of *Virtual Addiction* (1999), who said that our brains 'love maybe'.

'So have you flown before?'

I shake my head.

'Do you know how flying works?'

'I know how *your* flying works.'

'Look, Ben. When you're in a car doing 80 miles per hour on the motorway, are you scared?'

'Sometimes, yeah.'

'Christ, really? Look, what we're going to do is exceptionally safe.'

'Have you got any data?'

'Data?'

'Like – how often does something go wrong? When you take someone up there?'

He looks up there. For quite a long time. He's deciding whether he's going to pull the wool over my eyes. 'I'll be honest. If I'm on my own – nothing goes wrong. The only time something might go wrong is if I'm with someone else and they panic. So all you need to do is not panic. Do you think you can manage that?'

'I'm honestly not sure but I'm going to say yes.'

'Good. So shall we get to it?'

'Okay.'

'Before the weather changes. Because apparently there's a storm heading across from the North Sea, and that wouldn't be fun.'

We don't get off to a flier. In short, I get cramp in my glutes trying to mount the aeroplane. Turns out that a 1938 biplane isn't the easiest thing to enter. Once in situ, Nigel illuminates what's around me – all the gauges and switches and sticks and so on. He tells me that everything I've got to hand, he has too. The plane is dual-control, if that's the right way of putting it. I'm somewhat perturbed not to see an eject button.

'I'm somewhat perturbed not to see an eject button, Nigel.'

'If you want to eject, let me know via the intercom and I'll see to it.'

'Roger that.'

'And that thing between your legs.'

'Yeah?'

'Only touch it when I tell you to.'

'Right.'

'That's the joystick.'

'A misnomer if ever there was one.'

'Just do as you're told and we'll be fine.'

And we are fine. Boy, are we fine. Taking off is a bit ropey – the runway is made of grass, which doesn't help – but once we're up, all fear goes out the window – if there was a window. We climb to 2,300 feet, then cruise over the green and pleasant fields of the English countryside. We cruise over small towns, and big towns, and church towers, and hedgerows, and electricity pylons, and roadways, and railways, and several million people (at a guess) going about their business, in a far more reasonable fashion than I'm presently going about mine. Flying has never felt so good, not least because the gap between flying and the sensation of flight, which tends to be quite significant in an Airbus A380, has never been so small. I'm now happy we haven't got a roof. Nigel's trying to say something to me via the intercom. The sound quality is awful. I think he's saying something about—

'We're going to do a spin!'

'Am I strapped in?'

'We're going to do a—'

'I heard you mate. Just pulling your – wooooaaaahhhh …'

We do a spin. And it's horrible. And I take back what I was just saying about not having a roof. Until ten seconds ago, I was under the impression that to have one's heart in one's mouth was a figure of speech, but now I'm not so sure. Something feels out of place, in any case. Something other than my joystick that is, which, through no fault of my own, is currently doing somersaults between my legs. Here's a one-word description of doing a spin in a topless Edwardian aeroplane: novel. And here's another: petrifying. For the several seconds it takes for us to rotate about our lateral axis, I swear to God all the blood in my body comes to a standstill.[13]

'How was that?' says Nigel.

'Horrible.'

'Did you enjoy it?'

'Yes.'

Before I've had chance to unpack my feelings further, we've made a start on a loop, and the word loopy is suddenly striking me as distinctly onomatopoeic (something about the upward start, and the elongated middle …). It takes us about ten seconds to do a complete loop, during which time we travel about a kilometre. Not that I was counting. Instead, I was remembering what Nigel said about not panicking, and wondering, seeing as my brain was now upside down, whether catastrophe was currently at the front of my mind or the back. When the madness is over, and Nigel asks how it was, I'm sorry to say that I address

---

[13] Of course, the opposite is actually happening, i.e. blood is moving in unprecedented directions, and at unhealthy rates, which is how g-force induced loss of consciousness occurs. In case you were curious.

the man in a fashion not commensurate with his standing in the flying field.

'Now you're going to fly,' says Nigel.

'Smashing.'

'Are you holding the joystick?'

'No.'

'Well you better start because I'm not.'

'Sorry, Nigel, I didn't quite catch—'

'Now keep her steady.'

'Are you actually fucking—'

'That's good. And now push gently to the left … That's it. And now straighten her up. And now push gently to the right … And now straighten her up – good. You're a natural.'

If I had a spare hand, I would use it to engage the intercom and tell Nigel that I'm a natural at shitting my pants.

'Let's go for a loop,' he says.

What?

'What you're going to do is drop the nose down by pushing the joystick away from you.'

Am I fuck.

'I said you're going to drop the nose down by pushing the joystick away from you.'

I heard you, thanks.

'And you're going to do that before we reach Scotland if you don't mind.'

Very well. If this is how you want to bail out …

'Good. Though a bit steeper please.'

Oh my actual Jesus—

'And now pull back on the stick.'

Happily.

'Harder.'

Fuck.

'Harder!'

This is hands down the single most counterintuitive thing I've ever done.

'Harder, Ben!'

For the love of Mary and Joseph I think we're upside-down.

'Now hold it there, hold it there ...'

I wasn't planning to let go at this point, Nigel.

'And now ease the stick forwards ... Until we're on the level ...'

I think it's all over.

'And that's it!'

It is now.

'You did it!'

Yeah and no thanks to you.[14]

'I've got control now, Ben. You can relax now.'

I engage the intercom. 'I was relaxed the whole time, Nigel.'

'My arse you were. Want to do it again?'

'No, but thanks for asking.'

'Oh come on! You only live once.'

'And that's precisely why I don't want to do it again, Nigel.'

'Sure?'

'I'll try all things once, but not twice.'

'Fair enough. We'll head back.'

'If you'd be so kind.'

'I would.'

'You are a dear.'

'Don't mention it.'

---

[14] Things said in anger can be deeply irrational and laughably inaccurate.

5

I can't lose the sight of myself

Wherein the author goes to a wake, comes unstuck at the gym, considers the magic of everyday moments and has dinner with the enemy.

10 March

I'm back at the pond. I haven't exactly been going regularly, truth be told. My argument – that my introduction to cold water swimming needs to be incremental if I'm going to stay alive – doesn't really hold up under scrutiny. If I was genuinely trying to gradually assimilate, I'd've been going at least a couple of times a week since my first dip several months ago, increasing the length of the dip by about a minute on each occasion. Instead, what I've done is to go once every few weeks, and barely increase the length of the dip at all. In fact, my dip two weeks ago was shorter than my dip five weeks ago. At that rate, it won't be long before I'm not getting in at all. (Which is probably the optimum outcome, all things considered.)

Today I mean to actually do some swimming. That is, get in, calm down, say a prayer, and then actually swim from one set of steps to another – about fifteen metres. We can put this fresh determination down to Wim Hof. Also known as the Iceman, Wim Hof loves the cold. He once climbed Mount Everest wearing only shorts and sandals, and now he has a television show on the BBC (as a reward, I suppose). In the show, Wim Hof tries to persuade ten celebrities (or approximations thereof) that when it comes to immersing yourself in freezing cold water, it's simply a case of mind over matter – i.e., if you *think* it's not cold then it won't *be* cold, which as far as I'm concerned is unabridged bananas. Try telling someone on fire that all they require – rather than immediate assistance – is to imagine that things were otherwise.

Don't get me wrong. I'm all for a positive mental attitude, and don't doubt for a second that such an attitude, in plenty of situations, can increase one's resilience and improve one's performance and so on. But I also think that some things are just what they are, which is to say not ideal or at all advisable. In short, sometimes you're on fire and just need to be put out.

Mr Hof holds several world records for cold-exposure feats. He's plainly a brilliant, record-breaking exception, and should be duly recognised and celebrated; I'm just not sure he should go around telling everyone to give it a crack, not least because most of us, instead of being brilliant or exceptional, are just kind of normal, especially when it comes to exposure to freezing temperatures. You don't see many other world-record holders (the woman who ate eleven snakes in an hour, for example) going around encouraging others to give it a go. They accept that they're a human anomaly and leave the rest of us in peace.

Having said all that, here I am back at the pond, determined to stay in longer than ever before. Clearly at some level I've bought in to the folly of Hof.

When I reach the kiosk, I put off what's around the corner by having a little chat with the attendant.

'What's the temperature today?'

'About 9 I think.'

'Not bad. Creeping up. How long would you advise I stay in for?'

'What I always say is: When it starts to feel nice, get out.'

'When it starts to feel nice?'

'Yeah. Because that's when your body is shutting down.'

'So you're suggesting I stay in until my body starts shutting down?'

'Yeah, kind of.'

I don't stay in until my body starts shutting down. I have absolutely no interest – I'm starting to realise – in knowing the limits of my endurance, or the extent of my ability. Not regarding cold water, not regarding Scotch bonnet chilli peppers, not regarding anything. Call me pusillanimous. Call me dead inside. I don't care.

I last less than 30 seconds. Despite my exposure to Wim Hof, and despite being slightly seduced by the idea of mind over matter, when I actually get into the pond, all that matters to my mind is when the hell I can get out again. I escape the pond long before it starts feeling good, vowing never to return. I'm done.

21 March

Celebrations tend to be fun. Indeed, they are reliably so, not least because they are emotionally primed to go off. What's more, they have structure and form and context – which makes it easier for those present to engage with the elevated emotional atmosphere and let loose. Weddings are an example. Birthdays are another. And book launches are another still. This evening sees the launch of a book I wrote about being locked down with an 85-year-old widow. About 30 people have come together to celebrate the start of its shelf life. As is often the case with organised celebrations, there is free wine and nibbles – what the Italians would call *cicchetti*, and what Icon Books would call Wotsits.

Something about the wine, and something about its freeness, and something about the fact that the thing being celebrated is finished, is done, is complete – unlike at a christening, say – makes the occasion unusually animated and boisterous. Which is to say that much is said in jest, and much is said in earnest, and much fondness is alleged and exchanged, as the celebration grows out of its allotted time and space and spills out onto the street, where it finds a new home in a pub in Camden that is rumoured to be dodgy. In its new home, the celebration persists, and as it does so all the sundry bothers and burdens of life are momentarily pushed aside.

Celebrations benefit from their ritualistic character. They possess a sense of order and purpose, that makes them easier to enter into, and get lost in. The vibe is not in doubt. The presiding sentiment is pre-ordained – it is cheerful, benevolent, celebratory. Granted, celebrations have the whiff of organised fun about them; but I'm tempted to suggest that celebrations are reliably merry and mirthful in no small part *because* they are organised, rather than in spite of them being so. Organised fun gets a bad press, but I don't mind the stuff – especially when someone else has done the organising. There's less to decide, to deliberate, to doubt; when everything is taken care of, it's easier to be carefree and surrender fully to the occasion. Celebrations also give us a good, solid, indisputable reason to indulge in our favourite elixirs. We needn't be in two minds as we order another Porn Star Martini – not at all – for the justification is authentic rather than dubious, the emotional rationale sound rather than vague, which isn't always the case when we find ourselves half-cut on a Tuesday.

Speeches lend something to the occasion as well, don't they? An element of performance, a touch of theatre, a different emotional register. Speeches are emotionally generative, and tend to be amusing, even if (especially if) they are indisputably bad. No, I'm resolved: celebrations are liable to be fun. Invite me to yours please.

23 March

Eavesdropping. A builder is asked by his mate what he's got for lunch. 'What day is it?' he says. 'Thursday,' says his mate. 'Then it's a bacon lardons sandwich.'

28 March

Another gym class. This time it's something called Total Body Workout, which consists of eight six-minute 'sets', with each set consisting of three 'exercises', which are carried out continuously until it's time to switch to the next amusement. The exercises include squats, burpees, crunchies and so on. Of the suite, it's the squats that truly do my nut in. Prior to today, I don't think I'd squatted once in my life, and now here I am squatting over a hundred times in the space of ten minutes. Muscles can't talk, but if they could mine would be flying off the handle. I've myself to blame, of course. Over the last fifteen years, I've carefully lulled my muscles (all of them, the entire musculature) into a false sense of security. They thought they had it made. They thought life was a doddle. Only to be rudely awoken one afternoon by a series of inexplicable demands. And it's not only the squats that I'm not down with. I'm not up to the burpees either. Doing them, I resemble someone trying to stand up while their hands are superglued to the floor. To add insult to injury, the studio is blessed with a wraparound mirror, which means I can't lose the sight of myself. I don't like my own reflection at the best of times, and I like it significantly less when I'm flushed with exertion, slimy with sweat, and trying to make one press-up last 30 seconds. The writer Bill Bryson once said Bradford exists to make other places look better by comparison. Well, for the time being, I exist to make everyone else in this class look better by comparison. For the final two sets the instructor allows me to just lie on my mat reminiscing about life before I entered the studio. And even that hurts.

29 March

I go to my mate Andy's flat for what he's calling an 'empathy dinner'. Andy's a recently qualified life coach (and therefore potentially dangerous). He endeavours to get people on track, to put a spring in their step, and to generally foster love and understanding. To this end, he organises the above-mentioned dinners, which involve feeding two people with strongly opposed viewpoints Thai curry and then getting them to talk.

I've been invited – as someone who is pro-vaccines – to chew the fat with a French anti-vaxxer called Penelope. To my surprise and disappointment, upon being introduced to Penelope, we don't immediately tear each other's heads off. We don't snarl, we don't grimace, we don't even roll our eyes. Instead, we shake hands and compliment the hummus. (But you just wait until I come across her on Twitter! Grrrr!)

Over a starter of tiny fried fish, Andy gets the ball rolling. He asks us to share our views on the matter in hand, then encourages us to repeat what the other person has said (in an effort, presumably, to make them feel heard and understood). Then – because ideas tend to have roots and seeds and fertilisers and whatnot – Andy gets us to talk about what factors might have contributed to us having the views that we do. For Penelope, the roots of her viewpoint are a deep-seated mistrust of authority, the seeds a father with a deep-seated mistrust of authority, and the fertiliser every family gathering since she was born. So it goes.

By the time the curry arrives it is quite clear that despite our differences, Penelope and I are in many ways on the same page. We both want the same thing – the best possible outcome for as many people as possible – but just have different ideas as to how that thing might be realised. And by the end of the meal, while our attitudes remain opposed, there is no trace of enmity or tension between us. Instead, there is laughter, and lightness, and levity (notwithstanding some disquiet about the rice pudding).

All things considered, the dinner is an emotive, formative and exceptionally novel experience. It is a good conversation raised to a new level by its structure and agenda. Importantly, the first question Penelope and I were asked was: What do you value in the world? We both gave similar answers. People. Friends. Family. Loved ones. Health. Already, then, I was no longer sitting opposite an 'anti-vaxxer', but rather a person, who cherishes others, who values friendship, who loves her family and wants the best for everyone. Much easier to brook disagreement on a certain issue when you understand the extent to which you are fundamentally alike.

Is empathy fun? If we look at the science (or some science, at least), it would appear that, if not fun, empathy and compassion are reliably *enjoyable* sensations. Owing to the administration of oxytocin – a hormone that has enabled our species to bond, to get on, to cooperate – behaving empathically makes us feel good. And because it makes us feel good, it also makes us more likely to behave empathically again. You might legitimately claim that empathy is *all* good. (And better still when it comes with a three-course dinner.)

In summary: a memorable evening. I'm certainly glad I pushed aside my initial dubiousness and said yes. Not only can I now empathise with a particular French woman, I can also go

HERE COMES THE FUN

forward in the knowledge that getting under the bonnet of one's opponents is a nourishing and expanding experience. One significant blot on the evening's copybook was that pudding. Andy burnt the hell out of it, and I don't care what his excuse was.

1 April

To write only about fun is to write about nothing at all. Fun is made sensible by boredom, as joy is made plain by despair. It's my grandad's funeral. The service is horrible – in that it's painfully upsetting. The sight of the coffin, of the congregation, of my grandmother shaking in grief – it all solidifies the loss, the tragedy. The wake is at a pub on top of a hill, overlooking Portsmouth and its harbour. It is good and comforting and moving to speak with my grandad's oldest friends, to hear about his early escapades (and the odd later one). The stories I hear are stirring in a way that no other stories could be. They are new, and important, and personal, and revealing – they confirm why I love my grandad; they add further colour to my memory of him; and they lengthen and thicken the strings of his bow.

Wakes are underlined with such sadness, with such grief, that moments of joy and exuberance – however they are provoked – can feel misplaced or inappropriate. During this wake in particular, I remind myself of Grandad's wish for there to be no sadness in his farewell, which although unviable, is nonetheless a quiet permission to smile and laugh in his honour. The resultant mix of high and low makes the wake a deeply animating experience. It lightens my heart, and as it does so, it gives me ever greater reason to grieve. The honesty, the sharing, the fraternity, the love, all in memory of a beautiful being – it is a remarkable constellation of things. For better or worse, reminiscence is a part of the jigsaw puzzle of life; it contributes to the meaning and value of the whole.[15]

I will never look forward to wakes. Of course not. The idea is absurd. But nor shall I dread them, for they are moments of rare emotional intensity, as brilliant as bleak, as healing as painful. They force reflection. They arrest the ordinary activity of our minds and make us look back – and so doing make us look forward, to life and all its small wonders.

My grandad was such a wonder. He knew how to have fun. A few years ago, he found himself in hospital after a spot of heart trouble. When I went to visit, I learned from a consultant that despite still being in a relatively perilous condition, Grandad was somehow in a better mood than anyone else in Portsmouth. Upon arriving at his side, the first thing Grandad did was to relay something that had happened that morning, when the nurse had paid him a visit. Grandad told the nurse that there was good and bad news. The bad news was that he was going to lose both his legs. The nurse had said, 'Oh, Ted. I am sorry. You poor thing. What's the good news?' And Grandad had said, 'The good news is that I've already found someone to buy my slippers.'

From what I could tell, Grandad's heart and soul were serious things, but they were also as light as life allowed them to be. I aspire to that lightness, that seriousness, and the harmony of the two.

---

[15] MRI studies suggest that the act of recalling something can be as pleasurable as experiencing that same something, which is an enticement to take a trip down memory lane if ever there was one. A nod to Mike Rucker's *The Fun Habit* for providing this insight.

2 April

It's my first shift at the local community library as a volunteer. I'm on duty with Sally, and it will be our responsibility to man the lending desk, where books are issued and received, and enquiries fielded etc.

Before getting down to action, Sally gives me a tour of the library. There's the adult library, which holds a collection of fiction and non-fiction, with about a quarter of all the books on offer being crime novels. It's such a dominant genre, I'm slightly concerned about the intentions of the membership.

Opposite the adult library, across the entrance hall, is a children's library of equal size. Here the tables are lower and the books less skewed towards illegal activity. Having said that, there's currently a young girl sitting on a beanbag reading a book called *Gangster Granny*, which could be seen as a worrying indication of the girl's long-term plans.

There's a small garden at the rear of the building, which contains benches and plants and occasionally someone reading the *Guardian*; while joined to the adult library is an office and a kitchen, where volunteers are welcome to make themselves endless cups of tea, which are crucial if a long day is to be safely and happily negotiated.

After my tour, Sally gives me a rundown of the library's history. The library was for many years owned and run by the local council. Things changed about ten years ago when the council wanted to close the library down, in line with the governing coalition's austerity programme. A local community campaign to rescue the library was launched (which involved leaning on all the neighbours for some cash), and that campaign proved successful. Jude Law – who I understand is a gorgeous actor – played his part, as did Alan Bennett – who I understand isn't. In total,

£400k was raised, which enabled the local community associa-tion to lease the library and its contents off the council. It was the Big Society in action – i.e. government shirking responsibility, and normal people bailing them out.

Having successfully filled me in, Sally says it's time for me to do some work – by handling the enquiry of the member stand-ing before me, who is carrying a stack of books and appears to be about four years old. When I try to scan the girl's member-ship card with the computer mouse, Sally isn't impressed – but I get a smile out of the kid. Sally takes over and issues the girl her books without ado, apologising on my behalf. The kid – who is about four, remember – brushes off Sally's apology with a tiny hand, before dismissing the incident as 'just one of those things'.

'That girl is a regular,' says Sally, after the young bookworm has retired to the children's library. 'It's quite something. She speaks four languages and comes in unaccompanied every Friday, reads two books, takes out three or four more, then goes home.'

I have a little chat with the precocious polyglot on her way out. She says (in English) that she's Swedish, French and Japanese, and is moving to Portugal forever. When I ask why she's moving to Portugal she shrugs her shoulders and says, 'Work.'

All in all, my first shift is rather fun, albeit in a low-key, low-octane kind of way. A keeper.

7 April

A nice thing happened this afternoon. I was walking down the Caledonian Road when I saw a man using a zebra crossing while carrying a ladder that was about the same width as the road. However, it was watching him waiting to use the zebra crossing that was the best bit, because of course he couldn't stand facing the direction he wished to proceed in, as anyone not so encumbered would have done. Had he done that, his ladder would have been both blocking the northbound traffic and causing a fuss in the baker's. Instead, the man had to face towards the oncoming traffic, side on to the road, and try to communicate from that position to the approaching vehicles that it was his wish to cross, rather than just stand where he was all day, carrying a ladder. It was only a long glimpse I got of the man and his ladder, but it was enough for me to understand what was going on and to appreciate – nay, delight in – the specialness of the scenario. There was something beautiful about the oddity of the moment that made it fun to behold; that gave it – by perfect accident – a kind of magic.

8 April

Because liberty sometimes depends on restriction, and a sense of freedom on a measure of restraint, I only sit on the same bench. Its location is urban. I trialled one or two that were in more rural or picturesque spots, like at the top of Primrose Hill for example, looking down on Regent's Park and London's iconic cityscape, but felt that, in the final analysis, they were a bit too nice for my liking.

The bench I went for has got more about it – literally. It offers some theatre, some action, some day-to-day commotion – and all the complex charm and mellow drama that come with those things. It is on Berkley Road, just off Regent's Park Road, which is the little high street that runs through the village of Primrose Hill in North London. You can see a good chunk of the high street from the bench's position. A popular café with a terrace.

A surgery. A charity shop. A convenience store. An off-licence. A pharmacy. A pair of pavements.

I've not brought anything with me. No book, no phone, no picnic. In lieu of diversions, I take some mental notes. I note the scenario's immovables – those things not likely to budge any time soon. The amount of sky and road and pavement and rooftop. The number of lampposts, the number of trees. I don't scrutinise or attempt to put my finger on things (is that an ash? are they Georgian?), and nor do I whip out a pencil and sketch the scene as John Ruskin, who worried that people didn't ever truly see anything, would have me do. Instead, I merely note. It's a Sunday, after all, and I'm not here to cross-examine brickwork.

Is there beauty? Of an underlining or undeniable sort? That would still be here in the absence of the sun and the flowers and the people sitting outside the café? That would still be here on a drab, uneventful Thursday in November? I'd say, yes. And I'd say – to explain or justify that 'yes' – that the beauty comes, as all beauty does, from the shape of things, and the colour of things, and the arrangement of things, and from what those shapes and colours and arrangements evoke, and imply, and promise. God knows why we find things good-looking, but we surely do.

Someone sits down next to me. Even though I vowed just a few minutes ago to say hello to anyone who chanced to land beside me, and ask them how their day has been so far, I say nothing to my new neighbour, for fear they'll rebuff me, or not want to be spoken to, or reckon me unhinged.

I say nothing because I'm confident that's what they want. London has a certain code of conduct, and chatting to strangers isn't in it. Just because we give ourselves a pep talk in the run-up to an event, and tell ourselves to be something we're reliably not (outgoing, gregarious, someone who shoots the breeze with strangers) doesn't mean we'll be able to pull it off. So I say nothing to the person next to me, and he says nothing to me. And then, about five minutes later, he stands and walks away. To live a life unknown. A life elsewhere.

From an evolutionary perspective, our negativity bias, our kneejerk scepticism, used to be a lifesaver. But now I'm not so sure.

12 April

I bomb it down south to get a friend called Arthur to the hospital in time for an appointment scheduled for 12 June. Of course, Arthur *thought* it was 12 April, but in situations such as these, it's not the thought that counts. While open to the idea that doing things for no reason is an avenue to fun, I'm not sure if driving across London to take someone to a hospital appointment two months ahead of time quite fits the bill. And to think I was worried we'd be late! Oh well. All things issue a fruit. And on this occasion, it's Arthur's answer to my question about what he does for fun: 'I don't follow the news, Ben. That's what.' In many ways, Arthur is a good case study when it comes to salutary approaches to life. Once – after falling flat on his face for the third time in a matter of months – he brushed aside his mother's concerns about his new pastime thus: 'Mother. What's a face for if not to fall on?' Legend.

6

Never doubt yourself, people!

Wherein the author gets down on one knee, starts volunteering in a charity shop, gets booked by the ref and sits on a bench.

13 April

We've lost every game of the season so far, though you wouldn't think it based on today's display. It's not the easiest fixture on paper. The opposition are near the top of the table, and I've suspicions about whether their nippy midfielder who looks about twelve is actually over 35.

Nonetheless, the match is evenly poised with just a few minutes to go. It could go either way, or it could stay the same – that much is indisputable. Also indisputable is that no more than 30 seconds after we have a goal ruled out for off-side, the referee awards a penalty against us, adjudging our centre half (Alan, 71, former Master of the Rolls) to have deliberately handled a projectile he knew nothing about.

It's an unsporting decision, given the situation in the match and the fact that up to now the referee has only very occasionally felt it necessary to follow the letter of the law, preferring to keep the game flowing and officiate in a style in keeping with the status of the fixture.

Which is why the Comics are, to a man, utterly incensed about the decision. The gaffer, leading by example, gives the ref an absolute, unprecedented earful, of such vim and vigour and ferocity that it remains a wonder the ref's ear didn't actually explode with the overload of stimulation and French language.

The gaffer, when he was of working age, was by most accounts a mild-mannered and level-headed accountant, not prone to fits of anger or flights of venom. And yet here he is for all intents and purposes giving Vesuvius a run for her money (in the sense that he's going off, if that's not clear).

The ref, to his credit, takes the gaffer's earful on the chin (if an earful can be taken on the chin), offering nothing in response save to point to the spot – a model of officious conviction. That said, the ref can't resist making just the one comment, and that is: 'I am merely applying the rules.'

For me this is a bit rich, a bit much, a bit off the mark, so I say to the ref, barely loud enough to be heard, 'But you *haven't* been applying the rules, have you, ref?' Compared to some of the other things that have been said to him, what I've offered is practically a sweet-nothing.

But it's also the straw that breaks the camel's back. The ref is incensed by what I've said – more incensed than the gaffer was a minute before. He comes at me, a look of fury on his face (where else would it be?), his hand reaching for a back pocket.

'Right. That's it. I've had enough of this. You're getting a red—'

He hesitates. Looks at his back pocket. Realises he hasn't got a red card, only a yellow one, which he decides to show me instead. Fast forward two minutes, and the penalty has been scored, meaning the Comics remain (some would say fittingly) completely pointless.

When I get home, I tell Megan I got booked.

'What for?' she says.

'For dissent,' I say.

She looks away, thinking, then turns to me and says: 'What, did you fall over?'

I laugh. Heartily. As heartily as one can. And am glad, and happy, in this moment, to have been cautioned by the ref, for without that punishment, there would not have been this reward – this reward of laughter.

15 April

Encouraged by my experience at the library, I've enlisted as a volunteer at the charity shop on Regent's Park Road. It's a Shelter

Boutique, and let's just say that you're not picking up much for 50p in here. Generally speaking, I'm not over the moon about shopping. But if I had to go shopping – on pain of death or similar – I would go to some charity shops. The best thing I've ever bought in a charity shop was a three-piece suit in Egham, which I wore to the 'Summer Ball' at my university in 2008. There is a picture of me somewhere (probably in a charity shop) wearing the suit at dawn while being given a 'backie' down Egham Hill. I'm clearly under the influence of several buckets of moonshine, and feeling a million dollars in a suit that cost me fifteen. I fell off that bike about ten seconds after that picture was taken. Evidence, should you require some, of the inherent instability of pleasure.

Another thing I like about charity shops is running an eye over the spines in the book section. There are some titles you just know you're going to see: Bill Bryson's *At Home* for example, or Tony Hawks' *Round Ireland With A Cupboard* or whatever it's called. It must be a bittersweet moment when a writer ends up being a bestseller in a charity shop. It shows they've sold enough copies to achieve a kind of critical mass, a type of ubiquity, while also hinting that their work wasn't worth keeping.

The best charity shop story I'm familiar with concerns a woman in her twenties, living in Leeds but from Reading, who unwittingly buys a satchel in a charity shop that was lost by her mother on a bus in Normandy 50 years earlier. The worst story concerns a man who goes into a charity shop in Adelaide (where they're known as thrift stores, I believe) and buys the umbrella he later impales himself on. It's that sort of unpredictability I enjoy.

I must admit to being somewhat apprehensive about volunteering at the shop. I used to be a retail assistant in a branch of Burton Menswear, and I hated the experience so thoroughly that

I've never set foot in a branch of Burton Menswear since (and I'm not the only one, on the face of it). Indeed, I've hardly set foot in a clothes shop of any denomination since my time as a retail assistant. The wounds are still too fresh.

And yet here I am now, volunteering to be a retail assistant, with a perhaps misplaced confidence that the social side plus the philanthropic element might prove – well, kind of fun. The manager of this branch of Shelter, Natasha, looks like she's wearing half of the stock – glamorous is the word I would use. She gives me a tour of the shop and the basement, where all the behind-the-scenes stuff goes on, like sorting and labelling and steaming and so on.

Natasha's keen to know how much I know about fashion – whether I can rifle through a bag of donated clothes and spot the decent gear etc. She only has to ask one question to ascertain that I haven't got a flipping clue, but she asks a few more for good measure, just to confirm that when it comes to matters of the cloth, I'm as stupid as I appear.

'Have you heard of Joseph?' she asks.

'Does he work here?'

'Where do you normally shop, Ben?'

'Lidl.'

'And what was the last item of clothing you bought?'

'A pair of swimming goggles.'

'And if I said Prada or New Look, what would you say?'

'Prada.'

'Are you sure?'

'No.'

'Okay. Let me think about this.' She thinks. I don't. I just watch her thinking. 'Have you ever used a steamer, Ben?'

After introducing me to the steamer (which gets the creases out of all the clothes that turn up in bags) until I know it better than my own siblings, Natasha wants to check if I'd be any good at valuation. She hands me a scarf and asks what price I'd sell it for. My valuation is within 50 per cent of the figure she had in mind, which she says isn't bad. Then she hands me a pair of shoes and because I wouldn't wear them with a barge pole, I suggest a price which is out by a whopping 8,000 per cent.

'They're Valentino, darling,' explains Natasha.

'Are they? Right. Well there you go. You learn something every day.'[16]

Next, Natasha wants me to fill out a questionnaire that's designed to get to the bottom of my motivation. One question asks for any relevant experience vis-à-vis homelessness, and so I recount how I used to have a food truck called Eggonomics, which was essentially a campervan with signage. I used to go to markets and minor festivals and issue omelettes out of the window, probably illegally. I'd use local cheeses and eggs, and serve each omelette with some percolated coffee and a little paper ramekin of banana chips and grapes and strawberries, and charge £3 for the ensemble, which is why I didn't make any money.

Another reason why I didn't make any money is because I used to do free breakfasts for the local *Big Issue* vendors. If I was in Liverpool or Bristol or Newcastle or Cambridge or wherever, I'd find out where the *Big Issue* vendors picked up their mags in the morning and then pull up outside and dish out gruyere and marmalade omelettes for anyone that was up for it. I write all this down on the questionnaire, somewhat convinced that next

---

[16] Yes, learning is fun, and education is energising etc., but not all learning is equal, not all fresh information is liable to give you a thrill. I swear to God, learning that the shoes were Valentino didn't move me an inch. Indeed, I think the lesson might even have made me less happy.

to my utter cluelessness regarding Valentino and Joseph, it will count for nothing.

Questionnaire complete, Natasha wants to see what I'm like with customers. She asks me to serve the next person who comes in – in whatever manner I see fit. It goes alright until we get to the till, which I struggle to operate despite being thoroughly introduced to the thing by Natasha just a few minutes ago. You'd be forgiven for thinking I was conducting the transaction blindfolded. Natasha doesn't look impressed, and nor does the customer. All things considered, I'd say my appointment was in the balance.[17]

16 April

I like sitting on the bench because it's pointless. I always come unencumbered, and the lack of purpose and intent is jarring, but in a nice way. It always comes as a gentle shock. The stillness. The aimlessness. The just sitting and looking and listening. It's a kind of blank. A type of pause. And is welcome for being so.[18]

Not that my mind doesn't wander. Although appreciative of the here and now, my mind is also deeply and stubbornly attracted to the there and then, to its pet concerns, its dull

---

[17] The jury wasn't out for long. Not long after my struggles with the till, Natasha asked if I could stay on for another few hours, sorting out the shoes downstairs. Which suggests I made a better impression than I thought. Never doubt yourself, people!

[18] The idea of contemplation being somewhat unsettling / perturbing is borne out in one study, led by a psychologist called Timothy Wilson, that found that two-thirds of the sample group would rather give themselves a series of electric shocks than suffer fifteen minutes with nothing to do but sit and think. Yikes.

preoccupations. I'm helpless to stop it wandering away from what's in front and towards what's beyond, what's underlying – things to do, things done wrong, things to come. I notice when it wanders, and when it does I try to stop it in its tracks. I try to return it to what's before me – to this tree for example. Its roots are running amok. The paving slabs around its base are crooked and gaping. It's too late for reparation. Way too late. On this occasion, what's beneath can't be contained, no matter the volume of concrete.

I'm sitting next to a workman (unless he wears high-vis for fun). When I ask about his work, he says he sweeps the streets – tidies them, cleans them, takes away their rubbish. He points to his wheelbarrow, and its brooms, idling outside the pharmacy. I don't really know where to go from here, but I don't want to abort the conversation just yet, so I suggest (moronically) that this road is a special one, and list some of its attributes. He says that the reason it's special is because it gives him the most work to do. The man is satisfied with the remark. He puts the ribbon on it by saying, more to himself than to me, 'More than one way of looking at things, I suppose.'

18 April

I'm back at the library, and I'm no longer trying to scan things with the mouse – a sign of progress if ever there was one. Am volunteering today with Maureen, a pillar of the local community, or if not a pillar then a post at least. She provides a run-down of some of the people that live (or have lived) in the neighbourhood: Sylvia Plath, Joan Bakewell, Jamie Oliver, Imelda Staunton … It's quite an impressive list. Maybe there's a good pub round here that I don't know about.

HERE COMES THE FUN

'I used to live next door to Jude Law,' she says.

'And what was he like?'

'He was alright, I suppose.'

'Just alright?'

'He used to have orange juice delivered by the milkman.'

'And what's wrong with that?'

'You know someone fancies themselves if they're doing things like that.'

It doesn't take me long to work out that a major plus point of working in pairs behind the issue desk of a community library is that you get to chat freely and at length, and without fear of sanction from an overbearing busybody boss-figure. Case in point: an entire half-hour vanishes while Maureen tells me the story of how she managed to lose a bottle of white wine last night. In short: it was in the fridge, and then it wasn't, and God only knows where it is now. That was half an hour taken care of.

Now and again we'll have to stop talking to assist somebody, of course, but even those occasions provide an opportunity to natter. Whenever a kid comes up and puts a book on the desk to be issued, for example, I like to pick it up and make a thing of reading the title and speculating about the contents. If the book is called *Susan the Scary Spider*, or something, I'll wonder aloud whether this is the one about the spider who eats too many sandwiches and turns into a post-box. Occasionally the kid will laugh, but more often than not they'll just shake their head and then look up to the big person next to them for reassurance.

I also enjoy getting a swift review of the books people are returning. 'I wouldn't like to live in Ireland if that's what it does to you,' said one lady about *Beautiful World, Where Are You*, the latest by Sally Rooney. While another member considered David

Cameron's autobiography to be 'disappointingly long', which struck me as a bit impudent.

Granted, most of the time when I ask for feedback I get pretty straight answers – 'Oh, it was fine', 'Yeah, not bad' – but every so often I'll get something pleasant or amusing or incisive or beautifully put, which is why I keep asking. My favourite so far – and, yes, I am jotting the best ones down – was a review of the new Richard Osman. 'Pointless!' said the man, laughing incredulously. 'Absolutely flipping pointless!'[19]

Towards the end of my three-hour shift, an older gentleman enters the library and asks Maureen whether any of his CDs have been purchased. Maureen says she's sorry but they haven't, and returns the lot to him.

'Mightn't we give it a bit more time, Maureen?'

'It's been several years now, Alan.'

When I show an interest in the CD, the man kindly gives me one to take home. After he's left, I study the gift: its front cover shows four men (presumably Victorian) all tucked up in bed together. Below the image runs the title of the album: *The Bed*. The back cover, meanwhile, tells us that far from being a slice of experimental techno, *The Bed* is a collection of reminiscences, anecdotes and reflections, set down for posterity by five old boys who've lived in the area for donkey's years. I'm taken by the premise: just five fellas sitting around talking – about the good old days, about the bad old days, about the prospect of there being no days at all. I'll have to give it a listen.

I like how life can do that. Can be fruitful in that way. Can offer you something out of nowhere. Well, not out of nowhere

---

[19] For anyone reading this in the year 2046 – I'm not going to explain. You'll have to live with the confusion.

perhaps. It helps if you're standing in the right place – behind the lending desk of a library, for instance, looking curious and open. By involving yourself in the community, I'm starting to notice, you tempt Fate to throw you a few favours, you encourage Chance to issue odd and unexpected dividends. It could be a CD called *The Bed* (which might yet prove to be utter drivel), or an insight of Maureen's, or a turn of phrase from Mrs Davies, a longstanding member who didn't think much of Dolly Alderton's *Ghosts*. It could be anything, really. And that's the beauty of it.[20]

20 April

Lawn bowls involves the rolling of big balls across a manicured green towards a smaller one called a jack. It's an ancient game, almost as ancient as the bloke who's about to teach me how to play it. It's reckoned the Romans played a version of it, and it's nigh on certain that Sir Francis Drake was in the process of rolling woods (as bowls are known by those in the swim) when the Spanish Armada rocked up in Plymouth Sound in 1588.

Although the game remains beloved by many, there's no denying that dozens of bowling greens are falling into disrepair every year. Walking past my local bowling green recently, it occurred to me that if new people don't take up the game, it will eventually cease to exist. (I'm nothing if not perspicacious.) And so here I am, inappropriately dressed, on a sunny Saturday afternoon, ready to do my bit to stop the slide.

---

[20] I listened to *The Bed* – or most of it anyway – about six months later, when I finally tracked someone down who had a CD player. The old boys had a lot of fun reminiscing – that much is audible.

I'm hardly given a warm welcome. 'Are you lost?' says Jacinda, wife of the captain, when I breach the perimeter and dare to approach. I explain my interest in the sport and put across my readiness to do whatever I can to halt its inexorable decline. Jacinda nods appreciatively, finishes her espresso martini, then hands me over to Barry, whose job it is to check out the newbies.

But before Barry's prepared to examine me, he wants paying. It's five quid, which is fair enough, but the problem is I'm not carrying any cash. 'There's a cashpoint in the village,' says Barry. 'Lad like you should be back in a jiffy.'

There isn't a cashpoint in the village, so I buy a bottle of prosecco in Tesco and get some cash back. When I get back to the green, Barry accepts the cash and doesn't question the booze. Perhaps this has happened before. 'Stick the bubbly in the fridge,' he says, indicating the clubhouse, 'We'll pop that open later.' I'm starting to smell a racket.

Barry doesn't bowl anymore. It's his groin apparently. It's 86 years old and can't do what it used to. Which is why Barry oversees the debutants. When he tells me to grab a mat and lay it down two metres from the overspill, I worry Barry's going to start us off with some yoga. After establishing that I'm right-handed, Barry tells me to put my right foot on the mat and my left foot forward, about a metre or so. Then he tells me to place my left hand on my left knee (which is by now bent), and to bring my bowling arm forwards from the rear, keeping it straight throughout. Barry says I'm to release the wood when my right hand is roughly in line with my right knee. Clear as mustard.

'As you probably know,' says Barry presumptuously, 'the bowls are biased, meaning they're heavier on one side. As they slow down, their bias becomes more evident.'

'Like my grandmother.'

'By the end of its journey, the wood gets tired and practically falls over.'

'Ditto.'

'Now off you go then. Let's see what you've got.'

Turns out I've got quite a lot. Barry likes my delivery. Says I get down well and follow through nicely. And he likes my line and length. Says that, with the exception of one or two that went off towards Tesco, my woods appear to know where the jack is. My favourite element of the bowling action is the final one. I like holding my finishing position – statue still, right arm extended – and watching the wood's shapely progress towards the jack. I like watching the stages of its journey: its initial burst forward, its late leaning, and its final sideways fall. It's a good-looking thing. It's a becoming arc.

I also like where I am. I like my situation and its constituents: the lawn, the benches for spectators, the surrounding parkland, the clubhouse, wherein Jacinda is no doubt enjoying a glass of prosecco with the treasurer. Another thing I like about lawn bowls is the frame of mind it puts me in – attentive, calm, intent. Most of all, though, I like talking to Barry, getting a potted version of what he's been up to for 80-odd years. He tells me that he used to be a postman and that he married young – Sandra, the love of his life, who he misses every day. He tells me that he used to have a couple of pints after work, go to the football on a Saturday, do overtime if he had to, and have a short holiday in Scarborough every Easter. That was life for Barry, and he didn't mind it one bit.

'Anyway,' he says. 'Less gassing. You've got one left, and I want you to give it everything you've got.'

'Okay.'

'I want you to apply everything I've taught you.'

'Righto.'

'I want you to really concentrate.'

'Got it.'

'And if it's a good one we'll crack open that champagne.'

'Prosecco.'

'Whatever.'

'And I think Jacinda's already drunk it.'

'Off you go then. Send her away.'

I deliver my final wood. There's a solemnity to the moment, as the pair of us study the bowl's slow journey towards its target, me down on one knee, holding the finish, and Barry at my side, bent at the waist and using his hand as a visor.

It's a shocker. The wood ends up in the overspill. It's my worst delivery yet, and by some margin. Barry laughs. Can't stop himself. He pushes my head away with his hand, which must be what men from North London of a certain age do when they're amused. The gesture almost knocks me over, which only makes him laugh more. Once he's settled down, and composed himself, and we've gone around the lawn gathering up all the woods, Barry says: 'Going forward, Ben, I reckon you might be better off not concentrating.'

7

A pair of trousers that I would instantly remove in the event of finding myself in them

Wherein the author invites people over, quickly wishes he hadn't, steams a pair of dungarees and is introduced to bridge.

21 April

I'm hosting a dinner party. Italian themed. The plan was for the labour to be neatly divided between Megan and me, though you'd be forgiven for thinking otherwise. As things stand, Megan is making a papier-mâché meatball helmet, while I'm roasting seven duck legs, resting a cake, proving some dough and (not for the first time since I took up fun for a living) swearing profusely under my breath.

I bit off more than I could chew. That's where I went wrong. Imagine a Venn diagram with one circle containing skill and the other containing ambition. Typically, where the two overlap is where you'll find a dinner party. Although not this one. This one you'll find in the cleavage of folly and incompetence. I'd never baked a loaf of bread before, and I'd never baked a cake before. So of course it made sense to do both for the first time on the same afternoon.

You should have seen the focaccia an hour ago. The dough was meant to be resting but in truth it was erupting. Catalysed by yeast and a desire to take over the world, it had breached the terms of its parole and taken up residency on the counter. (I forgot to cover the bowl with clingfilm.) All was not lost. I channelled my Mary Berry, waited for the bread gremlin to calm down, then got stuck in. I kneaded. I pummelled. I manhandled. I did whatever it took to bring the mixture to heel, and in the process managed to prove myself as much as the bread.

And while all of that was going on, I was also poaching oranges for the cake. I cut open a poached orange now. Ah, the smell! I swear to God, if I could only smell one thing for the rest of my – sorry, what's that, Megan? You're moving onto helmet number two? An olive stuffed with an anchovy? And we'll be serving these when the first guests arrive, will we? If they dry. I see. Splendid.

Speaking of guests, one's just cancelled. The reason they're giving is Covid, which is a bit passé but whatever, it happens. The show must go on. Then, while transferring the bread to the oven and the cake mixture to a tin greased with butter paper, another guest cancels. 'It's actually a bit far to come,' they say. Isn't it lovely when people have helpful realisations just in time? I open the limoncello. Treat myself – in both senses – with half a mug. Stressed? Yeah, why not. We can use that word. I don't often lose my cool, but when I do, it tends to be in a vehicle or in a kitchen. So you can imagine how cool I was when I worked in a kitchen that was in a vehicle. But it's alright because Megan's finished the olive helmet and is now blow-drying the meatball. It's at this point that it dawns on me that this dinner party, if it's going to be fun at all, is going to be fun of the second type – i.e. not for a long time yet; on reflection only. Did Mrs Dalloway get worked up like this when she threw her party? Maybe she did. Maybe that's why she wrote a memoir about it all.

I check the duck ragu for sticking and seasoning. I 'knock back' the dough. (Or have I already put it in the oven? See. I'm really losing my grip here.) I blend the cake into a gorgeous goop while selecting an outfit, then cherry-pick the juiciest olives and put them to one side, to be enjoyed tomorrow. I'm gaining the upper hand. I can feel the hormonal scales tipping in my favour – dopamine taking the lead from cortisol and so on. Nigella would be … if not proud then at least unalarmed.

Another guest cancels. It's going to be just me and meatball head at this rate. The doorbell goes. They're early, the bastards.

Nope. It's a Deliveroo order for the flat above. I get changed, put on some appropriate music – 'Shake It Off' by Taylor Swift. Another dose of limoncello, put the pasta on, seek out the blasted balsamic vinegar, adjust the ambience until dim but flattering.

'Meg!'

'Yeah?'

'What time is it?'

'It's gone half past but don't worry because Tom and Dinita just cancelled.'

'Please tell me you're kidding or I'm going to punch you in the anchovy.'

She was kidding. Tom and Dinita turn up. They are absolutely thrilled with the meatball and olive helmets, but say next to nothing about any of the food placed before them. They were both supposed to arrive with 'something Italian'. Tom brought some breadsticks and Dinita just said 'ciao' when she arrived. To add another twig of fun to the evening's bundle, I instigate a period of reminiscence during the ragu. I ask my guests to share a memory of Italy. Dinita says she had a great holiday in Corsica once (sic), while Tom tells us all about Mussolini and national populism for half an hour. By the time I serve up dessert, my vagal tone has recovered, my mood regenerated, and my humour rebooted. For the next ten minutes, I can honestly say that it's a genuine pleasure to be hosting a dinner party.

To round off the evening, we play a game. It's a version of Balderdash. You take a novel, show everyone the cover, read the blurb, then everyone has to invent the first sentence. The invented first lines are then mixed up with the real first line, which has been written down by the person who selected the novel. The task is twofold: to guess the real first line, and to have others think the real first line is the one you invented. On paper, a spot of fun indeed. In reality, barely worth the paper it's written on. Some people can't remember how to use a pen, for a start. One highlight, however, is when someone proposes the first line of *1984* to be 'Trevor had been a barber for 9 million years.' Clearing the table, I get a message from someone who wasn't invited to the dinner party saying they can't make it. Just about sums it up really.

All in all, was the dinner party worth the investment? All the stress and strain? Nah. Don't get me wrong: dinner parties are wonderful; so long as they're other people's.

22 April

No sooner have I taken up my station at the library than a lady is pushing a small boy towards me. The kid's got his chin on the lending desk; he's perfectly placed to be stamped on the forehead. His nanny (forgive me for assuming) encourages the boy to get something off his chest.

The boy looks at her, at me, at her again, then says, 'I want—'

'Not "I want", Stanley,' says the nanny. 'You must say "Please can I have". Remember?'

Stanley gives the nanny a look (that conveys, to my mind, the basic idea that he's got this and she needn't interfere), then turns to me, puts a hand on the desk (to solidify his negotiating position), and says, 'Please can I have what I want, please?'

I issue Stanley what he wants – one book by Oliver Jeffers and, oddly, another by Michelle Obama. I get Stanley to stamp them for me – saves me the trouble – and get told off by Maureen for doing so. Apparently a kid had an accident once. Went to stamp a book but came down on his finger and broke it in two places.

There's a nice coincidence later on, if you don't mind me sharing. It started while I was shelving a book of poems by A. A. Milne, *When We Were Six* or similar. Before returning the book to the shelf, I flicked through the poems, and enjoyed one in particular called 'A Thought', which is essentially an experiment in putting oneself in another's shoes – and then taking them off.

> If I were John and John were me
> I'd be six and he'd be three
> If John were me and I were John
> I shouldn't have these trousers on.

No sooner had I returned the book to its rightful spot, than a man walked in wearing a pair of trousers (lime green with pink pinstripes) that I would instantly remove in the event of finding myself in them. The man wanted to become a member. Said: 'I want to become a member.' I told him about Stanley, about his 'Please can I have what I want, please?' We both had a laugh about that. The man's name was Juan, as it happens, which I believe is John in Spanish. Really – you couldn't write this stuff. (Or shouldn't, perhaps. One of the two.)

25 April

Because a few people had mentioned the card game bridge, and all of them favourably, I thought I'd give it a go. A bit of digging led me to a friend of a friend with an interest in the game – a chap in his early thirties called Rollo. By developing an interest in bridge at this stage of his life, apparently Rollo is 'investing in his future'. (Someone might want to tell the guy about premium bonds.) When I approached him online, Rollo said he was happy to introduce me to the game so long as I did some homework in advance. So over the next week I attempted to pick up the basics – or some of them anyway. Here's what I picked up: the game involves four players, playing in pairs, with one team the defence, and the other the declarers; one member of the declaring team is a designated dummy (that'll be me, I thought); each game involves a contract and starts with an auction; during said auction players are encouraged to communicate to their partner whether they have a good hand or not, which they are to do non-verbally, which suggests that bridge might be a tiny bit like charades. All things considered, and despite doing it in the bath, I can't say doing my bridge homework was especially fun.

And I can't say playing the game is much of a laugh either. Throughout the evening, Rollo does his best to elucidate and encourage and so on, but he's fighting a losing battle – if it wasn't for the lamb chops he's promised for dinner I would have walked out ten minutes ago. I have no idea how to non-verbally communicate the strength of my hand, not least because I don't know the strength of my hand. The final nail in the coffin is when Rollo says, rather casually, that based on what he knows about life and the various ways a person might amuse them-selves, bridge's barrier to entry is higher than just about any other barrier to entry he can think of, and he can think of plenty. That is to say, when it comes to bridge, you have to learn a hell of a lot before you can even *enter* the game, to say nothing of enjoy the damn thing. When I'm done with my chops, and we're about to resume, I ask Rollo a straight question: is bridge worth the effort? He says that the game has plenty of virtues, certainly enough to justify the groundwork, but if it's a decent fun to effort ratio I'm after, perhaps I should give skipping a go. Cheeky git.[21]

26 April

I'm at the charity shop, and let me say this off the bat: there's no need for the gym if you've got a rack of clothes to steam. While the bulk of the steamer – which is really a large kettle on wheels – doesn't need to be lifted, the steaming handle does, and it's flipping heavy. On top of being lifted, the handle needs to be carefully contorted this way and that in order to make an impression on the creases, of which there are – not unreasonably for something that's spent the last fortnight in a bin liner – plenty.

Within a few minutes, the muscles in my upper arm (insofar as there are muscles in my upper arm), start to complain and whine. There must be a pint of lactic acid in the right one before I've finished steaming a set of dungarees.

Though I must be grateful for small mercies: at least I can *identify* the dungarees, which can't be said for the majority of the garments before me. 'Now just what the Mary Poppins is this?' is a question I ask myself on numerous occasions during my steaming stint, usually of an item that looks too irregular to be bearable, or too scant to be of use.

With time, I start to get the hang of it, and start to enjoy having the hang of it. Steaming clothes almost becomes fun, or if not fun then one of fun's uglier, less photogenic relatives. My new dexterity gets me thinking – about whatever I want, really. One thing that can be said with confidence in favour of steaming

---

[21] I did give skipping a go. And it was much better than bridge.

clothes is that after a certain amount of skill has been acquired, the mind is permitted to wander. I continue steaming and day-dreaming for what feels like an hour, then pause for a well-earned rest only to discover that I've been at it for less than ten minutes. Fair to say that time is not flying. When Natasha comes down to check on me, I ask if I can be redeployed. She just smiles at me benignly, as a parent might smile at a child who has just asked if they can carve the turkey.

8

The gap between who we habitually are and who we actually are

Wherein the author embarks on a pilgrimage, is diverted by butterflies, learns that it's better not to concentrate and is ordered to laugh.

27 April

I wasn't up for a pilgrimage in Galicia. And I said as much to Meg, who was. Nothing against Spain, of course, and nothing against Saint James (who stuck his neck out for the cause, and was duly beheaded by Herod Agrippa), but I didn't see why, if it was a long schlep she fancied, we couldn't just do it in the Peak District or the Cotswolds, rather than through nondescript Spanish towns towards a cathedral that meant nothing to either of us.[22]

But Megan was insistent and I'm nothing if not scared of her sometimes, and so here we are in the town of Santiago de Compostela, fresh off the boat. (Well, plane.) The name Santiago de Compostela, roughly translated, means Saint James of the starry field, and the story behind the name involves the discovery of Saint James in a field on a starry night by a Galician shepherd about 1,400 years ago. Or something like that. Reports vary.[23]

---

[22] Saint James was an apostle of Jesus, and the first to put his head on the line for Christianity. His remains are held in a cathedral bearing his name in a city doing likewise, the trek to which has been a pilgrimage for Catholics since the Early Middle Ages.

[23] How did the remains of James find their way to Spain in order to be discovered and accurately identified by an uneducated shepherd? Depends who you ask. According to one legend, after James was unreasonably beheaded in Judea, a couple of his mates set about transporting his body to Galicia. (Don't ask me why. They just did.) The ship ran into trouble off the coast of Spain, and the late James was lost at sea. About a week later, however, his body turned up on the beach covered in scallops (which is why pilgrims to Santiago de Compostela attach a scallop shell to their luggage). For unclear reasons, the encrusted body was taken to be buried in a field a hundred miles to the east. About 800 years later, a shepherd or similar spotted a star above that very field. Correctly interpreting this utterly unremarkable bit of celestial activity as a major tip-off about something important, the shepherd or similar ran and told the bishop, who followed the star

We board a bus to Sarria, a town about 80 miles to the east, and where our Camino will begin. Sarria to Santiago is the last stretch of the Camino Frances (the French Way), which is the oldest, and most undertaken, of the various extant routes to Santiago. It starts in France, traverses the Pyrenees, drops into Spain, then heads west through Pamplona and León to Santiago. About 500 miles all up.

'I saw a film about the Camino,' says Megan.

'Yeah, you said.'

'*The Way*.'

'That's right. Starts on a golf course or something.'

'Charlie Sheen's dad is playing golf and he gets a call from the French police to say that his son is dead, so he drives the golf buggy to France—'

'He drives the golf buggy to France?'

'Yeah.'

'Christ.'

'At least that's how it looks in the film. He drives off in the buggy and the next thing he's in France.'

'Right. And then?'

'And then he's given his son's ashes and he does the Camino.'

'Naturally. How did the son die?'

'Doing the Camino.'

'Great. Can't wait.'

'In a storm.'

---

as if it were a satnav and duly dug up old Jimbo. How the bishop knew it was James that he'd unearthed, God only knows. Maybe because he was covered in scallops. The German word for a scallop, incidentally, is Jakobsmuschel, which means Jacob's clam. Don't say I never tell you anything.

'Ideal.'

'And on the way to Santiago, Charlie Sheen's dad meets a crazy Dutch guy and a crazy American woman and a crazy Irish writer who used to be in *Cold Feet.*'

'Speaking of cold feet.'

'What?'

'Well, I've got them now.'

'Why?'

'Because I don't want to die on the Camino, Meg, that's why.'

'There's more chance of you dying on this bus.'

'Is there?'

'Yeah.'

'Well that's reassuring, I must say.'

'By the way, don't look out the window. Otherwise you'll spoil the surprise.'

The bus makes a stop in Portomarín, where we'll be staying the night. I've booked a nice room in a hotel with an outdoor pool, and the idea of travelling another twenty miles eastward on the bus in order to walk twenty miles westward in sweltering conditions strikes me as the quintessence of folly, so I propose getting off here and checking in to the hotel *rapidement.*

'Hey, honeypuff.'

'Honeypuff?'

'How about we get off here?'

'What?'

'You know, check in, dump the bags, dip in the pool, long lunch. Rather than walking twenty miles through the desert just to get back to where we are now.'

'Are you joking?'

'No.'

'In which case you disappoint me.'

'It was just an idea.'

'You should *want* to walk a long way. The amount you've to atone for.'

'Are you implying I've more sin than you?'

'I'm not implying, I'm stating plainly.'

'Nonsense.'

'Look what you had for breakfast.'

'So what?'

'Beef madras and cauliflower cheese.'

'I was being resourceful.'

'And on average you get out of bed at half past ten.'

'Anything else?'

'Sloth.'

'Sloth?'

'Yeah. You're sloth-like.'

'Am I now?'

'And here's your chance to make amends.'

'Those trees are nice.'

'Stop looking.'

* * *

When we arrive in Sarria, it is plain that we are not alone in seeking both salvation and weight loss: the town is bustling with *peregrinos*. When we're deposited at the bus station, a period of bickering commences, to do with the distribution of weight between our backpacks. Mine is smaller, and therefore lighter. Meg's is larger, and thus heavier, which she is suddenly furious about. When I ask if she has room for the sun cream she just about blows her top. She says I shouldn't always expect her to deal with my 'excesses'. I point out that it was she who sent me to the shop to acquire the cream. She says that's not the point; says the point is that I'm never prepared, never organised. I offer to carry her pack, but she declines the offer because she prefers her pack because it has special straps. 'Fine,' I say, and set off alone and at pace in order to make some kind of point.

I retain the upper hand for about five minutes, but surrender it when I ask if we can stop for a *bocadillo* and maybe a small beer at an attractive side-street café, to which she replies, 'There you go again. With your sloth', before promptly sitting down and placing an order for *pan con tomate*. Note to self: when you go on holiday, you don't get to leave yourself behind. That is, your relationship travels to Spain with you, where it's as liable to blow up as it is at home, because the fundamental features of any 'escape' or 'getaway' – even a pilgrimage – are still the pair of you.

When we depart the café, the waitress shares with us her hope that we find some answers on our journey. I tell her I'll be happy to find a few questions.

* * *

We walk up and out of town. Past a prison on Mercy Street, and into the countryside. We're quickly overtaken by a practically naked pilgrim wearing little but a cockle shell. We cross a stream, go over a railway, pass beneath a bridge and between some fields – and as we walk the amount we are carrying lessens, and the going grows beautiful. The deep breathing. The steady exercise. The simplicity of intent. The clarity of direction. The novelty and variety of what's around. It doesn't take long, it really doesn't, for the Camino to become a friend, for it to soothe and offset.

We continue through villages, hamlets, tiny towns, following a well-trodden ribbon and rough rural lanes, through fields of juvenile corn, and beneath a steady natural canopy. The views may have the shape and palette of the British countryside, but they are new to me, and so their effect is soothing. They alter what I'm looking at, both actually and inwardly. Perspective is twofold: at once exoteric and esoteric. It is outward to Coruña, Santiago, the end of the world; and it is inward to the burden I bring, to those dark butterflies that flutter through everyday thought without rest. I catch one now: it is about neglect. I catch another: it is about death. I catch another: it is about failure. My understanding is shallow, but wouldn't a Buddhist ask me to acknowledge these butterflies and then let them go free? And wouldn't a psychoanalyst ask me to clutch them, inspect them, and study their roots and effects?

'What's wrong?' says Megan.

'Nothing.'

'You look confused. Concerned even.'

'No, I was just— I'm feeling good, actually. Feeling better already.'

'Good.'

'It must be the scenery, the fresh air, the walking.'

'Whatever it is, I'm grateful because you were starting to wind me up.'

'Was I?'

'You can be so stroppy.'

'I know.'

'Such a moaner.'

'I'm sorry.'

'So cynical. So negative. So *deflating.*'

'I do love you, Megan.'

'Are you chafing yet?'

'Yeah. You?'

'Majorly.'

'Beer stop?'

'*Fine.*'

* * *

On that first afternoon, the best thing I see is two butterflies dancing. They must be courting, flirting, sussing each other out – a kind of flight of fancy. Both butterflies are alike in fashion: green and orange with a black dot on each wing. They dance between us, above us, and then swoop and soar and strike off towards the Cantabrian sea, remaining visible while aloft and metres away, reduced to specks but in themselves unaltered, before diving once more, always as a pair, and swooshing past us, between us, deep in ancient ceremony, answering a timeless call. Their play – or foreplay – is genuinely captivating. It goes on for some minutes – quite a display of stamina. Wouldn't catch me dancing coquettishly for as long as—

'Ben.'

'Mm?'

'Are you going to just stand there all day?'

'Sorry.'

'I'm actually sweating my tits off here.'

'Right.'

'Are you holding in a fart or something?'

We come to a bridge, on the other side of which is Portomarín. I can smell the chlorine of the hotel pool. The past few hours have been hard and hot and taxing, and I yearn to be submerged in its icy tonic water; to be at one with the glistening piscine that will eviscerate all sores and obliterate all sighs.

The bridge is long. It spans the Rio Minho, which is shallow here and barely drifting. Crude rockeries puncture its surface – the peak remains of the old town, which was flooded during the construction of a dam. Only the church was saved from drowning: it was slowly dismantled and then lugged up the hill.

We cross the bridge and a short climb brings us to the hotel. We're here. We made it. I turn to look at Meg, who is leaning against a wall in the late sun. She's glistening. I've never seen her looking so – I want to say luminous but I'm going to say damp. I smile, and laugh silently, and feel assorted *qualia* (that is, emotional qualities that can't be pinned down or defined), which are the fruit of a day's exertion, a day's exploration, a day offline and out-of-office. To walk all day (well, for seven hours including two breaks) in a staggering furnace (30-degree heat) is to close the gap between who we habitually are and who we *actually* are; is to take a step (or several thousand) closer to the prime version of ourselves. I do hope there's a lilo.[24]

28 April

I do some stretching in the morning. Megan is beside herself watching me limber up. She goes so far as to take a snap behind my back (or posterior in fact) and share it online for a dozen people to be faintly puzzled by. Why are we compelled to snap and share? Is it because we are already, in the midst of the moment, scared of it being forgotten? By snapping and sharing, are we subconsciously trying to negate the vulnerability of all things in

---

[24] There wasn't. In fact, there wasn't even any water. In the pool, I mean. It was dry. And I was distraught. The oasis on the horizon, that had kept me going all day, had been a mirage. So it goes.

the face of time? Are we vainly raising a middle finger to our eventual demise? I ask Megan. She says: 'I just think you look so ridiculous that it deserves to be seen.'

* * *

An hour into our walk, we pass an old man. A Spanish sage. Sitting by the wayside. He calls us over. Presents Megan with a walking stick, clearly handmade. Meg thinks he wants money for it, but my Spanish being what it is, I'm able to figure out that the man wants Megan to take the stick to Santiago for him, to *do* the Camino for him, because to be frank he can't be arsed and there's something good on the telly tonight. She accepts the assignment.

* * *

At midday, we come to a fork in the road. The Camino splits: one route is labelled 'original', the other 'complementary'. No sooner have we chosen the original way and set off along it, than an old woman is off her doorstep and ordering us to retreat. The woman is dressed all in black, and her face carries the ample handwriting of Time.[25] She tells us to stop, to turn around, to go back and take the other way. Her reasoning isn't obvious, but we pay heed, we turn back, we display faith in Galicia's version of Google Maps. I thank the woman profusely – for caring to intervene. She dismisses my thanks. Waves them away. Tells us to be gone. Such people are the true waymarkers. It is our elders

---

[25] The phrase, I believe, is Grace Paley's.

that truly show the way. Unless they're talking categorical gib-
berish of course, which is often the case.

We follow a woodland path for an hour, which returns
us to the main route. We trudge roadside for a while, along a
hard shoulder, uphill and uncovered. It's pleasantly punishing.
There is little traffic to speak of, so although we're roadside
the experience isn't in any way oppressive. We are frequently
passed by pilgrims on bicycles. One cyclist, roughly in his 80s,
has a music player in his pannier, and is currently listening to
Robbie Williams. Because the hill is steep, and his gear is high,
the old man progresses at the same rate as us, despite his frantic
pedalling. I reckon our equality is instructive, though I'm not sure
how. At the end of 'Angels' he pulls over to vomit.

It is hot again. At a guess, 30+. The sheer fact of exercising
in this heat, at this incline, is both exhausting and exhilarating.
Conversation has dried up. For most of the morning we were
talking about Megan's earliest memories (being attacked by a
crab, a cow giving birth) but now I am alone with my thoughts.
They aren't crisp or logical. Instead, they are irregular and vague,
more like scraps of psychic sediment than anything neat and
cohesive. What do the scraps amount to? What purpose do they
serve? It's hard to tell. They're too bitty and incomplete to interpret. My instinct – and bear in mind that I'm speculating wildly,
not having the tools or diction for this sort of mind-reading – is
that they are faded former feelings, echoes of earlier emotions, slight traces of key moments in life, that would usually be
obscured and silenced by the radio of everyday thought.

In any case, as we approach the crest of a hill, the stench of
manure becomes so intensely suggestive of ancient parmesan
that my spaghetti junction of thought is ruptured and my attention is brought back down to earth.

'That's what you smell like,' says Megan.

'You've had two hours to come up with something meaning-ful or nice or charming or insightful to say and you go with that?'

'It's true.'

'It's clearly not true, Megan.'

'It's true to me. It's my truth.'

'Anyway, what have you been thinking about?'

'I was thinking about my old science teacher for a while. And Padrón peppers. And my stick. I like it; it's growing on me. I was worried about splinters at first, but not anymore. You?'

'Robbie Williams mainly.'

'So you've been thinking about Robbie Williams and I've been thinking about Padrón peppers?'

'It would appear so.'

'Wasn't this meant to be spiritual?'

'We should ask for our money back.'

* * *

We stop at an *hostería* – a hostelry. Sitting down has never been so much fun, I swear to God. Walking the Camino, you earn your respite. I've said it before and I'll say it again: value alters. Here I am sitting in the shade, with a coffee and some cold water, feel-ing wealthier than I have ever done in my life.

'Just watching that man eating his salad is making me feel relaxed,' says Megan.

'Yeah?'

'He just seems so *present*.'

'Oh calm down, Meg.'

'What?'

'How absent can someone be eating their lunch?'

'You'd be surprised. I'm often very absent when eating my lunch.'

'When?'

'All the time.'

'Well I've never noticed.'

'That's because you're not paying attention.'

I wish Megan hadn't mentioned the man eating his salad making her feel relaxed because now I can't stop looking at him, and thinking about positive feedback loops. The man is eating his salad in a relaxed manner because he is relaxed. Megan notices him eating his salad in a relaxed manner because *she* is relaxed. Noticing him eating his salad in a relaxed manner makes her *more* relaxed. Her being more relaxed makes her more likely to notice other people eating salad in a relaxed manner, which only promises to make her even *more* relaxed. You can imagine this going on and on inexorably until the entire world consists entirely of people eating salad in a relaxed manner while appreciating others doing likewise. Yikes. This has got to stop. This is getting ridiculous. I can't keep thinking like this. I need to get back on the internet. I need something to worry about.

* * *

A few miles beyond the *hostería*, we come to a natural plateau that offers a panoramic view of this portion of Galicia. We can see where we're going, where we've been, and where we won't go. You think you can see the horizon, but then you look closer and see that it's deeper, that it's further still. I get down on my haunches to look at a dandelion. What a change it goes through! From a garish juvenile yellow, to a pale, wispy, near nothingness, that begs to be whisked away on the wind like ashes. At which point is the flower best? At which stage is it most beautiful? At no point. At neither stage. It is the life course that is finest. It is the whole thing that appeals.

* * *

We reach Palas de Rei, our stop for the night. We dump our bags at the hostel and then go searching for food. I pop into a small, unassuming place just around the corner, to ask if the kitchen is open. Waiting in line, I watch the kid of a customer playing a sort of basketball game that the proprietor's put up on the counter. Basically you have to hit a big orange button in such a way that a small plastic ball (which is tethered to a bit of string, and therefore unlikely to go far) is propelled with just the right amount of velocity to go through the small plastic hoop. The kid's really trying hard at this game. He's busting a gut to get this ball through the hoop. I've been in here about five minutes and he's been at it nonstop. He's so intent and determined I swear his anterior cerebral artery is about to blow up. I'm worried for the kid. It sure doesn't look like he's having fun. Anyway, when his mum is served her coffee and turns round and clocks that I'm a pilgrim she asks where I'm from. Before I've finished saying 'I'm from Portsmouth in England', her son turns to me and says, utterly uninvited, 'I'm from Long Beach, California.' The way he says it, you can just tell this kid's super proud of being from Long Beach, California. But that's not the point. The point is that while the kid is telling me where the hell he's from, he absent-mindedly hits the big orange button and the ball sails through the hoop. He can't believe what he's done. What appeals to me about this incident isn't the sight of the kid chuffed to bits with himself, rather the fact that he finally got what he wanted when he stopped caring about the process. I say to the kid, 'Look what happens when you don't concentrate, huh?' Doing so, I think of old Barry my bowls instructor, who said words to that effect when I focused real hard on my final delivery and fucked it completely. The lesson here: stop trying, people. And move to Long Beach, California. The kitchen is closed.

* * *

We find a table on the terrace of a restaurant by the main square. No sooner have we sat down than a group of four Irish women we overtook this afternoon are saying, in unison: 'Ben! Megan! Get your backsides over here this instant. Are you having a pint?'

Over the next two hours, we hear quite a lot from Josephine, Margaret, Mary and Denise. Between them, they've got more crack than the Grand Canyon. For the most part, we hear about Denise living next door to Sally Rooney in Mayo. According to Denise, Sally's books are too raunchy for the Irish sensibility, which I find hard to believe, based on the way this lot have been carrying on this evening.

Other topics of conversation over the course of the evening include original sin, self-fertilisation and laughing yoga. I'm intrigued – and sceptical – about the latter. Mary explains how she was down in the dumps after her divorce and tried a bunch of things to perk herself up. She chanced upon laughing yoga, which basically involves meeting up with some like-minded (i.e. equally dotty) people and taking it in turns to *pretend* to laugh. Apparently if you really commit to the pretence the brain can't tell the difference and issues emotional rewards as if you were genuinely creasing up – something to do with mirror neurons.

Besides, Mary says that nine times out of ten the sight and sound of someone pretending to laugh is enough to set her off authentically. She can tell I'm deeply dubious and goads me to give it a shot. I refuse. Of course I do. I'm not flipping mad.

'Come on! Let's hear you laugh!'

'No.'

'Come on. Stop being a spare part.'

'I'm not being a spare part.'

'Well fecking prove it then.'

'You want me to laugh?'

'That's right. But properly mind you.'

'Now?'

'Yes now, you eejit.'

'You want me to pretend to laugh right now?'

'He's sharp your fella, isn't he, Megan?'

I do it. I throw caution and decorum and reservation to the wind and pretend to laugh as heartily and emphatically as I can manage, for as long as I can bear it. And strike me down with a stick if my performance doesn't have everyone pissing themselves. Which of course just encourages me to keep going, and at some point the fake laughter becomes genuine and there are tears in my eyes. Who would have thought it? It was in my gift this whole time to absolutely crack myself up. Astonishing.

It all calms down sufficiently for me to finish my dinner and for Margaret to call a taxi, only for Mary to go and say, dead casual and matter of fact, 'No it's been grand the laughing yoga. I do it first thing in the morning as I'm waiting for the kettle to boil', which sets me off again. Just the image of it. That's what gets me. The image of Mary clutching the kettle while cracking up on purpose.

When the taxi comes, the ladies have had a change of heart. They order another round of pints, including one for the driver, and they tell him they won't be going anywhere until he's drunk it. Denise lifts her fresh pint and, looking at Megan and me, says: 'There's always time for one more. Even if there isn't.' It is for such lessons that one travels.

9

A perfect harmony of despair and delirium, all wrapped up in glee

Wherein the author continues to walk, befriends a pair of Mormons, is taught by a Spanish teenager that sadness is a constituent of everything good in the world and gets absolutely effing drenched.

29 April

Dressing for the day, I learn from previous mistakes and tuck my shirt into my shorts and pull my shorts up a bit so the beltline isn't rubbing against the same spot as yesterday. Megan stirs. She must have a monster hangover because she starts the day by saying something unkind and untrue.

'You look like Humpty Dumpty,' she says.

'Pardon?'

'You look like Humpty Dumpty.'

'Meg. Humpty Dumpty is an egg.'

'And your point is?'

30 April

Somewhere between Ribadiso and O Pedrouzo, we join up with a pair of Americans for a stretch. They're from Utah, old school friends. Jaydon and Whitney. Mid-twenties. They grew up on the same street, met on their first day of school. On the bus, in fact. Jaydon was terrified about what lay ahead, and so decided to live his truth and throw up everywhere. All the kids in his vicinity switched seats, as you'd expect – except Whitney, who stayed where she was, opposite Jaydon. When Whitney says, twenty years later and by way of explaining her refusal to budge, 'I just like the smell of food', it's easily one of the grimmest things I've ever heard in my life. When I ask the pair what they do for fun, Whitney says abseiling and Jaydon says 'leaving a highly demanding religion'. And he's not joking. Jaydon is a lapsed Mormon, and for the next hour or so, as we continue westward to Santiago and a sense of completion and fulfilment, between fields of cabbage and corn and under a copious canopy of cumulonimbus, he fills me in on the detail. It takes him nearly six miles, and causes me to wince and smile and scratch my head in equal measure. Good stories will do that.

Only towards the end of our conversation do I notice how much Jaydon's carrying. His pack is twice the size of mine – maybe even thrice the size.

'Do you want to switch for a bit?' I say.

'Nah. You learn to ignore it. I'm fine.'

'Sure?'

'Yeah. It was even heavier before. I left a lot of stuff in Pamplona. Is that seriously the only bag you've got?'

'Yup.'

'You're basically carrying a purse.'

'A man who is not satisfied with a little, is satisfied with nothing.'

'Is that from *The Simpsons*?'

I don't know what to say to this, and Jaydon can tell.

'Ben. Honey. I'm kidding you.'

For another half-a-dozen miles, the four of us walk and talk. We talk about the rise of James Corden and the temper of Gordon Ramsay. We talk about what animals we are (apparently I'm a kangaroo). We talk about what celebrities we resemble (apparently I resemble the guy who plays Saul in *Better Call Saul*, who is also a kangaroo). We talk about *The Office* ('Wait, you have that?' says Whitney. 'Honey,' says Jaydon, 'they don't have that. They *made* that'). We talk about American idioms ('On a fishing expedition' is one I quite like, which is said when searching for something without really knowing what it is you're searching for), and we talk about what British cuisine is exactly (though not for long). We talk about Donald Trump, Venezuela and the importance of curiosity. We talk about baseball, cricket and the island of Bermuda (which is where we agree to rendezvous in the future, it being a geographical compromise).

And at the end of all the talking, as we approach the outskirts of O Pedrouzo, our stop for the night, it occurs to me that there are two types of escapism: one being pretty vacuous and not solving ever so much, the other promoting a kind of self-expansion and solving a fair bit. The last few hours, I decide, have been somewhere between the two.

Our escape is halted when I spot some writing on a wheelie bin and want to know what it means. It's in Spanish and Jaydon translates.

'It says: "if you read this you will die".'

'Shut up.'

'No, it does. So basically you just killed me.'

'Who would write something like that?'

'I actually quite like it.'

'What?'

'It's quirky.'

'So Whitney likes the smell of sick and your favourite author's someone who writes "if you read this you will die".'

'And your point?'

'Get me a ticket to Utah.'

'Attaboy.'

* * *

We secure a room in the hostel the Mormons are staying at, then eat simply around the corner (*caldo gallego*, a local soup of cabbage and potato, that can stay local for all I care). Afterwards, while Megan takes advantage of the hostel's bathtub, I nip out for water and some cigarettes (not once in this journal have I hinted or suggested that I am anything but a complete and utter fool). I stop in a bar for a beer. When I ask to borrow the lighter of a young Spanish pilgrim, I fall into conversation with him and his schoolmates – all doing the Camino.

They're all roughly seventeen, and go to an international school in Madrid, and are easily the most impressive quartet with a combined age of 68 I've come across in some time. It's not just the quality of their English (they're using words like 'hefty' and 'ambivalent'). And it's not just their knowledge (they're telling me about Galicia, and Cervantes, and Shakespeare). And it's not just their manner (they're courteous and charismatic and curious). It's their *wisdom* that gets me. One lad tells me to give the local soup another try, and says that if I keep in mind the struggle of the Galician people for centuries as I eat it, the soup will taste better. What sort of teenager tells you that? Another lad, when I tell him I'm writing a book about fun, is absolutely *insistent* that I include a chapter on sadness, owing to 'the relational quality of all things'. They're not all wise old men, mind you. One of them is a bit more on my level. He says the book I'm writing needs only three chapters – money, drugs and sex – and that he's happy to ghost-write them if I can't bring myself to do it. Not one of the lads thinks I'm especially wise when I tell them that the Camino has been the most fun thing I've done so far this year.

'Get real man – why?'

'It has it all. Novelty. People. Nature. Exercise. Learning. A sense of adventure. Peace of mind. Octopus.'

'Octopus!'

'Yeah. There's tons of it round here.'

'Ah man, I'm going to *send* you some octopus, okay?'

'Suits me.'

'And then you're going to take it to a goddam nightclub, alright?'

'Deal.'

'By the way, Benjamin.'

'Yeah?'

'Is your girlfriend still in the bath or what?'

'Good point. I better run. *Buen Camino*, lads.'

No, a delightful group of young people. As I said, very impressive. And yet, for all their erudition and wisdom and self-awareness, and their poetic eulogies to Galicia, and their knowledge of Shakespeare, and their appreciation that sadness is a constituent of everything good in the world, they all want to be bloody lawyers.

When I get back to the room, Megan's reading in bed. She's got some news.

'I've got some news.'

'Oh yeah?'

'You might not like it.'

'Oh yeah?'

'We're getting up at 4.30 a.m. tomorrow.'

'No we're not.'

'Yes we are.'

'Why on earth would we do that, Megan?'

'So we can set off when it's dark.'

'And why on earth would we do that, Megan?'

'Because that's what everyone else is doing.'

'Oh, in which case count me in.'

'It will be novel.'

'Well, I grant you that.'

'And fun.'

'Says who?'

'Well, no one, but.'

'4.30? I'm flipping shattered, Megan.'

'Well, you shouldn't have gone out gallivanting.'

'I haven't been out gallivanting. I was talking to some very impressive—'

'We're leaving at 5.'

'Fine.'

'It'll be nice.'

'Can't wait.'

'Don't be like that.'

'No, really I can't.'

'Well I'm sure you'll manage to wait. Because it's only four hours away.'

1 May

I'm shocked to discover that we're not alone. Despite the rain, and despite the dark, there's about a hundred pilgrims walking out of town on the main road at this ungodly hour. I can't get my head around it. You can excuse one inexplicable decision, but a hundred such decisions? It's upsetting. It's worrying. It suggests – it suggests a cult.

There's no talking. Which makes things even eerier. A hundred lost souls, drifting silently in the damp darkness towards their – salvation? Demise? It could go either way. That's how it feels. We enter a wood, which does nothing for my nerves. The pack begins to split and spread, and before long it's just the four of us. Jaydon has a small torch. The beam is weak, but a little light can go a long way when it's as dark as can be. I try to get some chat going with the Americans, but they're not responsive. It must be a rule. No talking before dawn. Megan's poking me. Is pulling at my sleeve. She wants my attention.

'What is it?' I whisper.

'I'm worried.'

'About what?'

'I think it might be a trap.'

I stop. She stops.

'What are you on about, Megan?'

'I think the Mormons are going to kill us.'

'Right.'

'And then take us back to Utah in their big backpacks.'

'Uh-huh.'

'And then take us down to Jaydon's basement to be exorcised.'

'You know what, I think you're on to something Meg – should I go ask?'

An hour later, and we're still in one piece. The Mormons are talking again, there's daylight, and we appear to be out of danger. But not out of the rain. It's relentless. Biblical even. My trainers are completely out of their depth. Meaning my socks are sodden. Fatigue kicks in. And in. And in. I should still be in bed. Stirring. Drawing the curtains and thinking, 'Blimey. What lousy weather. Better go to a café for a long breakfast until it clears up.' Our reward for setting off early? We'll get to Santiago several hours before we can check in anywhere, and will have to just mope around feeling totally and utterly fulfilled – with rainwater.

We are no longer four abreast. We are in file, with a safe – and telling – distance between us. My mood is in step with the elements: dismal. In the context of the pilgrimage, and of my year of making merry, this is a slump. This is a wet trough. If I was going to write a chapter on sadness, I should do it now.

I should dictate it to the damp, uncaring sky. I distract myself from self-pity by fantasising about a room, a shower, a bed. How quickly and based on so little do our requirements change. Yesterday, on the road, I craved paella and illumination. Now my needs are basic – shelter, warmth, sleep. When I reach the promised land – a hostel – I will be happy, gloriously so, and forever. I don't care what the science says about hedonic adaptation, I swear to God that once I'm dried off and warmed up and tucked up in bed, I will be unswervingly and unstoppably happy for the rest of my life. I shall want for nothing so long as I live. (Except maybe lunch.)

Two hours later, and we're just a couple of miles shy of our target, our beacon. We're so close, and yet I'm ready to give up. I want to get a bus, or a taxi, or a donkey – anything that will deliver me (and just me, screw the others) from this sodden torment. Some fishing expedition this.

'What's up?' says Megan.

'Nothing.'

'Come on. Speak up. I'm not going to judge you.'

'I can't go on. I'm done.'

'Stop being a complete and utter wimp.'

'It's my feet.'

'Your feet?'

'They're wet.'

'Think of my uterus. The lining of which is breaking up and falling out of me as we speak.'

'Okay. You win.'

'It's not about winning.'

'No. You're right.'

'It's about who's losing the most. And that's me.'

'Okay.'

'So stop whining and give me a big voluntary laugh.'

'A what?'

'A big voluntary laugh. Like you did with the Irish women the other night.'

I do as I'm told. I summon all the bogus bonhomie hidden within me, and then I let it all out. And it's one of the weirdest sounds I've ever generated. A perfect harmony of despair and delirium, all wrapped up in glee. It cracks the atmosphere, it makes Megan laugh, and it makes the Mormons turn around and say, 'What the actual fuck?'

We reach Monte do Gozo, or Mount Joy. A massive hill overlooking the city, and also a massive misnomer. Ordinarily you can see the cathedral from here, but not today. Today you can barely see what's right in front of your face; today the finish line is veiled by inclement weather. In Spanish, the word for weather is the word for time – *tiempo*. There must be something insightful and intelligent to be said about those two things being the same, but for the life of me I can't think what it is.

I'm in the city now. Alone. Megan got tired of my fatigue and pushed on with the Americans, who were eager to join the queue to collect their certificates. I'm being overtaken by other pilgrims, left, right and centre. They're checking the maps on their phones to pinpoint the ending, despite the towers of the cathedral looming over them. You've come all this way and you still can't see a thing, I think uncharitably. My pace is sluggish; I'm sliming along like a half-arsed abalone.

I turn a corner and – there she is. The cathedral. My reason for walking. Pilgrims huddle for group shots, smile for selfies, appraise the church for a few minutes and then wonder what to do next. You're not allowed in the church.

Not until noon, and only then if you started queueing last autumn. I'm cynical because I'm dead on my feet, and cold to the bone.

I withdraw to an arcade, in front of the town hall, opposite the church. I sit on a stone bench, remove my shoes and my socks, dry my feet with my T-shirt from day one, put on plimsolls. A busker is singing that song of Leonard Cohen's that contains the line about there being a crack in everything so the light can get in. So the rain can get in more like.

'Finally!' says Megan.

'Hello.'

'We thought you'd drowned.'

'I've missed you too.'

'The Mormons are getting their medals.'

'Have you delivered your stick?'

'Oh fuck!'

'Where is it?'

'I think I left it in the woods when I went for a wee.'

'Are you joking?'

'No.'

'You absolute numpty.'

'Do you think it matters?'

'Do I think it matters? I think the old boy's probably keeled over already.'

'Shall we go back and get it?'

'Absolutely not.'

'His life might depend on it.'

'I don't give a toss.'

'Oh, I'm really annoyed!'

'When can we check in?'

'2 p.m.'

'What time is it now?'

'10.30.'

'You know, I'm actually about this close to having a meltdown.'

'In which case you're lucky.'

'Why?'

'Because I phoned the hostel and the girl said we can check in whenever we want because of the weather.'

'There is a god.'

'You're welcome.'

'And she works in a hostel.'

'Now cheer up.'

No sooner have I stepped into the dormitory than I'm in the shower. When I climb into an available top bunk, the sensation is indescribably blissful. There's no two ways about it: today was Type 2 fun – the reward coming after the event. Provided, that is, that I don't contract pneumonia while I'm dreaming.

10

Fishing is essentially a satirical activity

Wherein the author fails to catch a thing, considers the fifty shades of fun, tries to talk to a stranger and pretends that a child has gone missing.

3 May

If there are 50 shades of fun, then one of them is surely just sitting down and watching the world (though not on a motorway etc.). It's not a high-octane shade, and nor is it high-adrenaline. It isn't likely to change your life, and can't really be done as a team, and yet it's definitely a kind of fun. (In my book, anyway.)

Sitting on the bench can throw up just about anything. And it can also throw up just about nothing at all. For a long time today it looked like it was going to throw up the latter. For about half an hour, nothing happened. My bench session was still diverting and relaxing and full of unpredictable elements – but it was, on the whole, pretty bland.

Then a couple of things happen in quick succession. First, a child on a scooter enters the scene. Without looking over his shoulder, the child asks a question of his father, who is trailing by a few metres and has just appeared in shot. 'Why can't some people see?' asks the boy. When his father starts to a give a thoughtful answer, the boy says 'whatever' and scoots off disdainfully.

No sooner have the pair turned the corner onto Sharples Hall Street, than a man sits down next to me. His stillness is striking. He doesn't get out his phone, or pull out a packet of cigarettes, or check his watch. He just sits there, staring ahead, as if copying what I'm doing. After a few minutes, I turn and ask the man if he's had a good day so far. He looks at me and laughs, then says, 'Have *you*?' As far as opening exchanges go, it's not an auspicious one.

I say something about working from home, and being worried about my posture. What I say must be pretty damn banal, because after I'm done saying it, the guy just smiles at me kindly, nods a couple of times, then gets up and leaves. Boy, does that tickle me.

Perhaps fun is the wrong word to describe what I get out of sitting on the bench. Or perhaps it's sometimes the wrong word, and sometimes the right one. Perhaps that's it.

6 May

The first time I went fishing was under duress. My brother was into it, and so I was dragged along. When I saw the flounder being put out of its misery with a mallet, I seriously considered asking my dad to just do me a favour and knock me out too.

Since that fateful day, not much has happened to challenge my opinion that fishing is essentially a satirical activity, undertaken by good-natured stooges to demonstrate how society is capable of duping us into doing preposterous things with our disposable time and income.

So, when the brother of a friend, having heard of my fun agenda, reached out via text message to say that fishing was the nation's preferred pastime and he was willing to prove it, I was both highly cynical and irresistibly curious.

I meet Dominic at a busy tube station in South London. This is a hectic, built-up area – 'vibrant' if you're an estate agent, 'chaos' if you're not. At any rate, hardly a spot for fishing. I reckon Dom's having me on.

'Alright, Ben.'

'You 'avin a laugh, Dom?'

'Eh?'

'What are we going to catch around here? Bronchitis?'

'It's a little London secret, mate. Did you bring the snacks?'

A short walk leads us to a slender, freshwater river – just 50 metres from an M&S. While Dom sets up camp, I make a start on the mini samosas. He doesn't appear to have brought an awful lot of gear. Just a rod, a net and a little stand to rest his pole on. Pretty accessible stuff.

'Not much to it, Dom.'

'This is as raw and simplistic as fishing gets.'

'And you thought that would suit me?'

'Try to keep it down a bit, yeah?'

'Sorry.'

I take out the tea towel I've brought from home and spread out the snacks. A decent range from the M&S yonder. But to be candid they don't look half as good as the marinated pork that Dom's brought along.

'What's the marinade mate?'

'Paprika, cumin, dash of oil.'

'Nice. And the meat?'

'Luncheon meat.'

'Really?'

'Sh. Yeah.'

'Bit retro. About 98 per cent collarbone that stuff.'

'Yeah, but they like it.'

'Who does?'

'The fish.'

'The fish?'

'Did you think it was for us?'

'Well …'

'Are you pretending to be utterly clueless, or is it coming naturally?'

Dom hooks a marinated pink cube onto – well, a hook.

'Smoked paprika, huh?'

'And cumin.'

'Rather aspirational, these trout, aren't they?'

'Barbel.'

'Pardon?'

'And chub. Maybe some tench if we're lucky. Anything but eel.'

'I see.'

'They're a nightmare. They can swim both ways so unhooking them is chaos. You end up covered in slime.'

'Olive?'

'No it was vegetable oil.'

'No I mean do you want an olive?'

'Not yet. Work to do.'

Dom gets to his feet and launches his faux pork into the River Wandle, a chalk stream that rises in the south at Carshalton Beeches and empties into the Thames at Putney. He means business, this kid. He's not messing about. He keeps his eye trained on the end of his rod at all times – watchful for the type of tell-tale tugs and twitches that are imperceptible to the unschooled. He tells me about the watercourse as he stares at his pole.

'It's chalk-based, as I said, which is why it's so clear. Didn't used to be, mind you. There used to be a load of factories along its course, dumping all sorts of crap into the river. It got so bad that it was officially renounced, had its river status annulled.'

'Cancel culture gone mad.'

'Now look at it. Now it's very clean. Still showing signs of South London life, mind you.'

'That shopping trolley?'

'By way of example. Ah, crap!'

Dom's alarm pertains to a dog that has spotted a duck and is presently charging through the river in hot (and wet) pursuit, very much to the detriment of Dom's chances of filching a chub.

Dom's mood doesn't stay soured for long: soon he spies an otter in the river and is beside himself, only for it to become clear on closer inspection that it's actually a squirrel in jeopardy. Thankfully, the squirrel is able to skilfully extricate itself via a dangling branch of a willow tree. When the squirrel reaches dry land, there is a look on its face that unmistakably (or rather potentially) communicates something along the lines of, 'Well, I certainly didn't expect to be doing that this afternoon.'

We've been here five minutes and something is already obvious: fishing comes with a host of stuff on the side. Experiential paraphernalia, if you will, like mallards and squirrels and willow trees and chalk-based watercourses. If you get into fishing, you get an unplanned education in botany, geology and the natural sciences. The same can't be said if your hobby's Candy Crush or Sauvignon Blanc.

Dom reels in his hook, line and sinker. The bait's gone. He reloads with enviable swiftness and dexterity, always one eye on the river, for signs and omens and auguries. By no means is this guy relaxed. Instead, he's focused, intent, determined – and experiencing as much flow as the river.

When I say as much to Dom, he whispers something about the world being easier to cope with when it's reduced to a river and a fish, then tells me to turn the volume down another notch, lest I scare the latter away. I'm starting to realise that for Dom scaring the fish away is a fate worse than castration.

'Silly question perhaps, Dom.'

'Go on.'

'But do fish have ears?'

'Are you taking the piss?'

'No.'

'Massive ears mate.'

'Really?'

'No.'

'Then how do they—'

'They sense vibrations. Including sound waves.'

'Cool.'

'Not really. If they were deaf, they'd be easier to catch.'

'And you'd be having fish for your tea every night.'

'I don't eat them.'

'What?'

'I throw them back.'

'Throw what back?'

'What I catch. I throw them back.'

I say nothing. Just look at Dominic with extra intensity to ascertain whether he's winding me up. He's not. I'm convinced of it.

'So, if you don't mind me asking, Dominic, just what the hell are we getting out of this?'

We're getting a lot out of this, as it happens. Or Dominic is, anyhow. And he has been for some time. Got into fishing as a kid. Would spend evenings after school and entire weekends experimenting with his rod. Putting new and untrialled things on the end of it, etc. Used to play matches, against other anglers. The best anglers of his age, around the same lake, each given six hours to catch as many fish as possible, the winner winning the right, presumably, to be sprayed with champagne while throwing all the pilchards back into the lake ceremoniously.

He loved the sport, the game, the chase. Still does. It appeals to the hunter in him, to his basic instincts. Perhaps his ancestors were snipers, or archers, or riflemen, or kestrels. He tells me he once caught a 30-kilo tuna in Majorca. He was fifteen. Weighed about the same as the fish. It took him about a week to reel the so-and-so in. Because social media didn't exist back then, all

Dominic could do was kiss the tuna on the mouth, cradle it for a while, then send it back whence it came.

'Doesn't it, sort of, *annoy* the fish?'

'In a sense.'

'Even traumatise them?'

'I get your point, Ben, but you need to remember two things: 1) fish probably aren't cerebral enough to experience trauma. 2) Is it better for the fish to be wounded or eaten? 3) [sic] I'm not sufficiently high-minded or enlightened to put the mental health of the fish above my own.'

'So you'd say fishing is good for mental health?'

'I guess. I was out here a lot during the pandemic. And even before the pandemic, when things were really stressful at work, I'd come here three or four evenings a week, even in winter, sometimes staying past midnight.'

'Past midnight? In winter?'

'If I hadn't caught anything, yeah.'

'What did your girlfriend think?'

'It took a while for her to understand.'

'I should have thought it did.'

'When it first started happening, she did some internet searches to see if I had a condition.'

'Fair enough.'

'Then she suspected I was having a fling.'

'With someone called Rod.'

'But I enjoy it. It's better than being in the pub. Or in front of the television. I like the pub and television but not at the expense of everything else.'

'And I guess it must take your mind off other things.'

'Yeah. I suppose so. By accident.'

'Because you're focusing on the end of your rod.'

'Exactly.'

And at that very moment, as if by magic (or, more likely, as chance would have it), the end of Dom's rod abruptly lurches northward. In one lightning-fast action, Dom springs to his feet, takes the pole from its dock and yanks the damn thing southward, the better to convey to whatever's after his meat that there's no such thing as a free lunch. Or free luncheon.

Only sometimes there is such a thing as a free luncheon. Because when Dom reels in his tackle, it bears no trace of bait or fish, and every trace of a thick wodge of river cabbage.

We move downstream. To a new spot. Where we give it five minutes and then move again. This happens several more times in quick succession and I don't mind telling you that all the moving is starting to grind my gears a touch. After all, it's not straightforward transporting the picnic each time. I can't just shove it all in my backpack, because there'd be olive oil and falafel and chicken wings and salmon flakes everywhere. So each time Dom indicates we're off, I have to hastily stack up the open containers and proceed like an awkward waiter in pursuit of Crocodile Dundee.

Here's the thing: I thought fishing was going to be *relaxing*. I thought it was essentially waiting + beer, which I fancied I would both be able to manage *and* profit from. And I thought Dom and I would be getting to know each other. Having a long chat, full of confession and banter. I thought we'd get a chance to play that parlour game, I'm in Business, wherein you have to invent a business you're running (say tailoring), and then give an assessment of how the business is going that is somehow a play on words (it suits me). I even brought travel Scrabble with me. I thought fishing basically amounted to Socratic dialogue followed by a monkfish supper. When I mention this to

Dom – my preconceptions and so on – his response is typically muted and aphoristic.

'Ten per cent of fishermen catch 90 per cent of the fish.'

'Meaning?'

'Meaning I'm part of the 10 per cent.'

'Are you sure about that, mate?'

'Hm?'

'I mean, you could have fooled me. All you've caught so far is some curly kale.'

'The first is always the hardest,' he says, turning away from me.

There's no two ways about it, his impotency is getting to him. His errant rod has put his nose out of joint, if that's not too angular an image. Dom reckons either we're talking too much or the fish have cottoned on to his marinade and are giving his meat the cold shoulder.

'You mean they're suspicious of the bait?'

'Every fish in this river has been caught before.'

'Not by you, they haven't.'

'Ben. Seriously. Would you pack it in?'

'Sorry.'

'The fish put two and two together. They learn from experience that if they nibble such and such, there's a chance they'll be hauled out of the water and made to pose for an Instagram shot.'

'Which they're not into?'

'Look at that!'

'What is it?'

'Can you see it? Over there.'

'Looks like a goldfish.'

'It's a koi carp. They're bred for garden ponds. It's an ornamental fish.'

'An ornamental fish?'

'It must have escaped somehow.'

'Really?'

'It doesn't stand a chance in this river. You just wait till the other fish clock it.'

'Will they give it some grief?'

'Let's just say that before long it will be wishing it hadn't ventured out for the evening.'

'And it won't be the only one.'

'Are you flagging?'

'Nah, I'm good.'

'Here we go!'

'You got something?'

'Sure have.'

'You've caught that goldfish, you bastard.'

'Nah, this thing's hefty, mate.'

'Yeah?'

'Hopefully – touch wood – it'll be a lovely barbel.'

'Nice.'

'Beautiful fish.'

'Cool.'

'Sexy as hell.'

'Settle down, Dom.'

'Oh, she's hefty alright. And a fighter. A warrior even. Come on sweetheart, come to daddy ...'

'Do you always feminise them?'

'No, but you can tell. This a lovely massive girly barbel.'

'Can't wait to see it, Dom. It really makes all the waiting worthwhile – don't you reckon? No pain, no gain, and all that. I'll tell you what, I'll get my camera ready. We'll stick her up on Twitter, shall we? Get ready to say cheese, Dom. Dom?'

Dom's gone quiet. Dom's gone still.

'What is it, mate?'

'It's a sodding eel, that's what.'

7 May

Silly moment in the changing room at the gym. Barely worth mentioning but I do so because I've got this hunch that it might be the small things that make the biggest contribution to well-being. Basically, having been swimming, a small boy was playing a game of hide-and-seek with his dad in the changing room. I'd say the pair were onto their third or fourth game of the kid hiding in one of the lockers and the dad pretending to have no idea where the kid was when I turned up. I could sense the dad was losing enthusiasm, while the kid was only just getting into his stride. It was at this juncture that I got involved. It wasn't much of an intervention. To be honest I was just trying to help the dad out a bit, and maybe give the kid something to think about. Basically, what happened was this: when the kid got in the locker for the umpteenth time, and the dad counted to ten and started saying things like 'Oh dear, where *has* Charlie gone?'– you know the sort of stuff I mean – I joined in the roleplay by saying, to the dad, but loud enough for the kid to hear, 'Charlie's gone home, mate. Yeah, I saw him. He hopped on the bus.' The dad – thank God – cottoned on pretty quick and said, with Charlie now starting to lose his shit in the locker, 'Is that right? Gone home, has he?' And then when I said, just to clarify matters, 'Yeah, he just walked straight out of the changing room, picked up a milkshake from the café, and then hopped on the bus. He'll be at home by now I would've thought,' and the dad replied, 'Well he could have *told* me …', well I don't think I've ever heard a kid laugh so much in solitary confinement. And I have to say it felt quite nice, in an odd way, being a small part of the above. Just making someone's afternoon a touch better, even the afternoon of a kid I don't know from Adam. Not the sort of thing you can organise, mind you. But that's often true of fun, I'm learning. It's a pretty ad hoc phenomenon when it comes down to it. Not the easiest to schedule, to stick in the diary. You sort of just have to watch out for it, listen out for it, and then take your chances when they arise. Fun's more like humour than happiness, I suppose. In that you have a *sense of it*. A sense of fun.

11
The psychic benefits of novelty

Wherein the author oversees the production of marmalade, learns about the necessity of boredom, is acquainted with g-force, weighs up some goats and is promoted to manager.

9 May

I'm sitting on the bench having a chat with a consultant from Vienna. The chat doesn't prove life-changing, or mind-bending, but it's certainly an improvement on silence. I learn that her idea of fun is to walk for miles and miles in terrible weather while breathing deeply.

You don't have to be a detective to work out that fun for this lady is essentially *relief*. Is respite. Is a moment of calm amid the storm. This notion – that the lack of something (work, strain, concern, pain) can be something in itself (relief, pleasure, maybe even a type of low-key fun) – is not unfamiliar to me. I recall a fisherman from Plymouth once saying that heaven was a place where every day was landing day. That is, where every day provided the emotional gorgeousness of two weeks at sea coming to an end.

For many, periods of calm, of stillness, of peace, wouldn't qualify as fun. They'd need more – more action, more energy, more drama. But for the lady next to me, fun is whatever brings about the cessation of discomfort.

And on that note, I'm off, because my backside's starting to hurt.

11 May

It's the Comics' end-of-season club dinner. Over the course of the evening, various awards are handed out – but none to me, alas. It hasn't just been a dismal year for me personally. It's been a dismal year for the team. A record number of points (one); a record number of goals conceded (119); and a record amount of bookings (six). For all that, it's been a blast, and even as I'm toasting the season that was, I'm looking ahead to the season that will be. I'm determined to pull my socks up. I'll do some hard work pre-season, get my fitness up, get in the gym, improve my skills, so that next year might be victorious as well as fun.

At the end of proceedings, the gaffer has a quiet word in my ear.

'I'm stepping down, Ben.'

'Really? That's a shame.'

'I can't carry on. Not after the year we've had. It's time for a new pair of hands.'

'Why are you looking at my hands, gaffer?'

'We want you to be the new manager, Ben.'

'You must be joking.'

'We've seen how you play and think it makes sense. Will you consider it?'[26]

15 May

I'm returning a book to the library. *How to Be Bored* by Eva Hoffman. In short, the author reckons too many of us are hyperactive these days – too much to do, to consume, to choose from. What's more, the author reckons we've become *addicted* to being hyperactive: thousands of tiny micro-doses of dopamine have got us hooked on clicking and booking and looking and

---

[26] I did consider it, and reached the conclusion it was probably a terrible idea, and so said yes. On top of the intrinsic allure of being in charge of twenty extra-mature bus drivers, one of the reasons I took the job – and this will sound daft – was to pay homage to serendipity; to doff my cap to the delightful way that one thing can lead to another. I admit that being romantically subservient to propositions of all kinds will eventually end in tears; but until then – and perhaps even thereafter – I will continue to dance to the tune of chance.

ticking. It all adds up to an illusion of being full, says Hoffman; a sleight of mind that tricks us into thinking we're fulfilled and engaged and purposeful and prospering, when in fact we're running on fumes and in someone else's shoes. Sit down, for heaven's sake, says the author. Take a breather. Be bored a while. Be idle a bit. Because your inner life needs feeding as well as your outer one.

23 May

On a whim, I decide to go to Alton Towers – a theme park just up the road from Derby. It's not exactly par for the course to visit such places alone, but what are norms for if not to be transgressed? When I arrive at the park, it's quickly apparent that the chief financial officer of Alton Towers is less enamoured of spontaneity than I am: the price of admission is about double what you'd pay if you booked in advance, which is an unfair punishment of whimsy if ever I saw one.

Having neither a map nor much of a clue, I decide to just do a lap of the park in an anticlockwise direction. The first ride I come to is a rollercoaster called the Smiler. There's a special queue for single riders, which is a nice consolation for having no mates. That said, I might have benefitted from having a bit more time to steel myself for the impending g-forces, which do all they can to dislodge my breakfast. (G-force is short for 'gravitational force equivalent', and is basically a measurement of the size of any given force that is acting against you. For the purpose of illustration, the ideal amount of g-force in my opinion is the amount you get when you sit down.) It's fair to say that me and the man next to me don't have much of a conversation on our way round, which I think is reasonable given that we are for the most part upside down and hurtling along at six-months-a-minute. In lieu of talk, I produce a series of noises like 'aaaaah' and 'errrrrrr' and 'ohhhhhhhhh'. By the end of the Smiler, I'm 100 per cent grimace and practically fluent in non-lexical vocalisations.

Because I got shafted at the gates, I'm after value for money. So I eschew the park's more sylvan elements and bag a couple more rollercoasters in quick succession. On both rides, I get photographed on my way round. Like someone drawn to the wreckage of a car crash, I can't resist having a look at the pictures at the end of each ride. I look the opposite of elegant in both. With the size of my face accentuated by propulsion, and my forehead gleaming like an arctic shelf, I look like a vast turkey escalope, unbreaded. Ah, cameras! You've done my levels of self-awareness untold wonders!

Next up, the Wicker Man, which is possibly the most off-putting looking rollercoaster I've ever seen. It's made of wood for a start, and parts of it seem to be on fire. One thing that looks okay is the lack of a queue (God bless diligent parents who refuse to absent their children from school). I get to the front in just a couple of minutes, where I find myself in a sort of dark antechamber. I'm ushered forward dramatically by a ride attendant, and then a projected Wicker Man tells us we're all about to be burnt alive to atone for the sin of some farmers from Somerset. It all feels a bit juvenile, to be honest – until, that is, we're strapped in and the Wicker Man takes off. Let me say this: the ride might look like a piece of A-level coursework, but it certainly shakes off the cobwebs. In terms of audio, I issue the same set of noises as I did on the Smiler, only this time I'm good enough to decorate them with obscenities. At the end of the ride, I turn to the lad beside me and apologise for my language. I exit the carriage enlivened, despite having had the life scared out of me – a paradox that probably warrants consideration.

There is this to be said on the matter of lunch at Alton Towers: if you're wanting something healthy, I suggest you start nibbling the grass, because there's sod all else available. I consider taking a seat in the Rollercoaster Restaurant, but it's totally rammed, and to be honest I'm not convinced by its USP. Essentially, each table incorporates a mini rollercoaster that stretches from the table up to the ceiling. You order your grub and then when it's done the food descends from ahigh, down a twisting track on wheels. I'm all onboard when it comes to the psychic benefits of novelty, but what if your hotdog's rubbish and you want to send it back? And since when did g-forces improve a salad?

I give the Rollercoaster Restaurant the cold shoulder and plump for a portion of 'saloon fries' from a quirky food truck. I eat them at a lakeside picnic table, in front of the park's eponymous 'towers'. There's a stage nearby, upon which a pair of singers called Lemon and Lime are going through their set for the 963rd time this year. The duo are really going for it, despite only having me and my chips for company. No, I tell a lie. A family of four have just sat down nearby, and the daughter, maybe five or six, has raced towards the stage to dance. She's soon joined by her younger brother, whose way of dancing reminds me of my own, it being less like dance and more like a kind of cautious, hunched-over spin. But he doesn't care. And neither does his sister. Instead, they're swinging each other around joyously, the embodiment of unselfconscious euphoria. They're really spinning fast now. In fact, they might want to slow down a notch. On the face of it, the brother has reached the same conclusion as me, but unfortunately for him it's his sister controlling the merry-go-round. The brother's disquiet is getting louder by the second. He doesn't like the speed he's going at, or the lack of control. And he's noticed the look in his sister's eye and he doesn't like that either. He's seen it before and last time it spelled disaster. He tries to pull away but his sister won't let him. He wails. She laughs. He screams. She gleams. Then – suddenly acquiescent – the sister lets her brother go mid-spin and the poor boy goes flying – towards the corner of a picnic bench, which he duly introduces himself to, just above the eye. At this point the parents stop filming. I've said it before but it bears repeating: how flimsy euphoria, how fragile fun!

After my lunchbreak, it's back on the tracks. Boy, does Rita take me by surprise. For such an unassuming amusement, Rita doesn't half pack a punch. We go off like a proverbial rocket, doing 0–60 in about a second, which is the sort of spurt that will dislodge your endoskeleton. The sudden, incomparable, and in my case unanticipated haste is indisputably fun, however. You could argue that one way to measure something's fun factor is the amount of time you allow to lapse between instalments. Consider, for example, the fact that I haven't seen my Great Uncle Patrick for 24 years. Consider, also, the fact that as soon as I'm off Rita, I'm on her again, but this time with my eyes closed, curious to know what this sensory deficit will do to the experience. I'll tell you what it does: it *amplifies* it. The best ten seconds of Alton Towers? Doing Rita with my eyes closed. Without doubt.

Having had enough Gs for one day, I seek out something calmer. I chance upon just the thing – the Congo River Rapids. It's for kids, really, but they'll let anyone on. You climb into a circular dinghy and then just go with the flow. As far as I'm concerned, the ride's chief attraction is that it promises some quality *me* time. After a hectic few hours, I'm keen to just close my eyes and feel nothing more abrupt and anomalous than a breeze. When I reach the front of the queue, I go to hop into a dinghy on my own but am prevented from doing so and ordered to join the dinghy of three men from Sheffield in their fifties, who don't look any more pleased about the fact than I do.

It's awkward. That's the thing. They don't know what to say to me, and I don't know what to say to them. I'm not often lost for words, but this new situation has caught me off guard. It strikes me as wholly absurd, which, coming from a grown man on his own at a theme park, is really saying something. We proceed in silence for about five minutes, feigning interest in the scenery, trying desperately to dissociate ourselves from the inconvenient truth that we're all sat in a dinghy at Alton Towers on a workday. Eventually I just fold my arms and close my eyes, and pretend the whole thing isn't happening. At which point we go over the edge of a small shelf, and one of the blokes gets soaked. His mates are in stitches, and the atmosphere onboard improves no end. We spend the rest of the ride comparing notes: I tell them about Lemon and Lime, and they tell me how they got their tickets for fourteen quid on eBay. I ask them what they do for fun when they're back home. Their answers – pigeon racing, Doncaster Rovers, and researching the history of Sub-Saharan Africa – confirm what I've suspected all along: that there's nowt so queer as folk, and that fun really is a funny thing indeed.

Then – as it will – rain halts play. I turn on my heels and head for home via Derby, clutching a picture of myself in the midst of Rita, looking like a petrified gammon. I've had a great day at Alton Towers and would definitely go back, though not on a whim. Sixty quid to have your organs reorganised might represent value for money at some point in the future, but it doesn't yet.

26 May

Kentish Town City Farm was founded in 1972, on the site of a disused timber yard in a densely populated and somewhat rundown part of North London. It claims to be both the first of its kind – i.e. a farm where you'd least expect one – and also the oldest, the latter point surely tautologous on account of the former.

But I shouldn't be churlish, or in any way negative, because it's a terrific place, it really is. As well as the farm's attractions (goats, pigs, café etc.), the sheer *incongruity* of the place pleases me greatly. There must be local residents who get eyeballed by goats each time they pull the curtains or step outside to hang the washing.

The randomness of a city farm adds to its charm, and thereby elevates the experience of visiting it: more evidence, were it required, of just how contingent and unstable are such things as value and quality. Serve me an omelette in a restaurant and I'll take it in my stride. Serve me one on the moon and I'll never forget it.

It's not a vast farm, and nor is it orderly. Its floorplan is higgledy-piggledy, to use the academic term. When I enter (which one can do freely and every day between 9 a.m. and 5 p.m.), I'm greeted by a quartet of sizable white chickens, each sporting – or flaunting, or suffering from, or living with – flabby red wattles and flabby red whatever you call the things they have on their heads.[27]

I move on to the goats. They've got a decent square-footage going on, that's for sure, and their realm is cheek-by-jowl with

---

[27] You call them combs. And these chickens were Rhode Island Whites, if you're interested.

the railway line, so the views are pretty good, too. In terms of accommodation, they've lucked out. Potted biographies of each of the goats is displayed next to their enclosure. 'Rosie isn't a morning person,' reads one. 'Hendrix can't stand Rosie,' reads another. Of all the goats, my favourite is Alan, who worries about the future apparently. Get the kid some therapy.

Each goat has been allotted a boulder – a sort of granite plinth or pedestal which they will climb onto with unexpected ease whenever they fancy a change of perspective. You can't read much into their expressions. They don't give much away in this regard. They're inscrutable, stoic, almost Zenlike. Kind of enlightened looking. They're quite inspiring, really. Then one goat starts firing poop-pellets out of its backside and the effect is lost, or if not lost then altered.

On top of the goats, the farm boasts a communal garden (overseen by volunteers), a café (where I have a cup of tea), a trio of donkeys, a couple of pigs and a cow. It's the pigs that get me. That hold my attention I mean. Pigs might not look as clever as goats do, but they're pretty smart at any rate. An information display tells me that pigs have a 'theory of mind', meaning they have the capacity to deceive other pigs. Show a pig some hidden food and it will keep this info to itself, knowing that other pigs don't know what they do. Basically pigs know how to bullshit. Pigs also get bored. Apparently they get massive ennui. Because of their relative intelligence (they're on a par with human toddlers), they have moments and days when they're just like, 'Oh my God I'm so *bored.*' I think that's wonderful.

As well as boredom and deception, pigs are also capable of empathy. For example, when a pig gets excited about something it's familiar with – a piece of music, say – the other pigs will get excited as well, even if they've never heard the album in question.

Pigs are emotionally *in tune*. I just love the idea of one pig getting its jig on to something by Amy Winehouse and the others slowly coming round to the idea and eventually throwing some shapes themselves, if only in support of the enthusiast rather than from a genuine appreciation of the music itself.

Speaking of genuine appreciation, I'm now full of the stuff for Kentish Town City Farm. The farm offers a provocative and educational mini-break that promises to lift the spirit and tickle the funny bones. More importantly, it's an important and under-valued community resource. There ought to be one on every corner, and I don't care how impractical that is.

27 May

There ought to be a bench on every corner as well. I'm back on mine now, reading a stray copy of the *LRB*. Very interested to learn in said publication that the utilitarian philosopher Jeremy Bentham (1747–1832) devised what you might call a fun calcula-tor. Bentham's 'felicific calculus' – to give it its proper name – was a means of ascertaining whether something was worth indulging in, all things considered. The units of measurement preferred by Bentham when weighing up something's pros and cons were 'hedons' and 'dolors', the former linking etymologically to pleas-ure, and the latter to pain. For example, a piss-up in Derby the night before a whimsical trip to Alton Towers might score highly in hedons, but it might also score highly in dolors (on account of the subsequent hangover and the financial damage incurred), meaning its overall fun factor would end up being quite modest. Optimum activities are those which issue huge sums of hedons while costing very few dolors. Watching goats is an example, albeit one not mentioned by Bentham.

30 May

There's something awesome and humbling about the ethereal and unthinkable intelligence that is behind so much of what we complacently rely on – a jar of instant coffee, say, or the small intestine. By unravelling the complexity of one thing, we remind ourselves of the unnerving complexity of all things, and are given a useful kick up the wonderment thereby. For a variety of reasons, it matters how marmalade is made.

And jam, for that matter. We shouldn't neglect jam, it being the principal outpouring at Wilkin & Sons' Tiptree factory in Essex. The Tiptree brand is iconic. It's been around for over a century, and the company has supplied the Queen with all manner of spreads since she was knee-high. I'll get this off my chest up front: my visit to the Tiptree factory is enormous fun. It's better than Alton Towers. No great rushes of adrenaline, I grant you, but a steady release of feel-good hormones that do wonders for my mood. The discovery, the novelty, the unlikeliness, the characters, the perfume! Massive hedons indeed.

I enjoy having an introductory coffee with Peter Wilkin, the chairman, whose great-grandfather got the whole thing rolling back in the day. I enjoy hearing about the time an episode of *Midsomer Murders* was filmed at the factory, wherein a key character drowned in a boiling jacuzzi of rhubarb and ginger jam (in mysterious circumstances, needless to say.) I enjoy hearing about the houses Mr Wilkin built for his employees and how he incorporated his workforce into the business by giving each member a stake in the firm. I enjoy telling Mr Wilkin that if his employees had any sense they'd preserve him at once, and I enjoy being ushered out of the boardroom and onto the farm, the better to see the raspberries, the damsons, the greengages, the plums.

I enjoy learning about the clever and careful innovations that make the farm sustainable, like the new polytunnels that catch the rainwater and send it back to the farm's reservoir to be redeployed. I enjoy the sight of the strawberry plants in their tabletop beds, and I enjoy studying their tiny white flowers, from which come the berries, pale and timid at first but growing red and bold with time. I enjoy standing amid a group of mulberry trees and learning that the phrase 'caught red-handed' has its roots in the picking of mulberries, which stain the skin something rotten. I enjoy seeing the farm's camp, where seasonal workers live in chalets and play ping-pong and have BBQs after long sessions picking in the fields. (One regular picker, Magda, can pick three times as quickly as the second-fastest picker, which is rather astonishing.)

I enjoy being told about the time Michael Portillo – he of the salmon jackets and citrus chinos – visited the farm for an episode of *Great British Railway Journeys*, and I enjoy, in turn, recalling the time I met Portillo, backstage at a travel book festival, when I was wearing a pair of bright red trousers that he clocked instantaneously. 'Now that is a pair of trousers,' he said, by way of introducing himself. 'I put them on with you in mind,' I said. 'Oh, stop it,' he said. (Which I did. Because when Portillo tells you to stop it, you stop it. Something to do with his imperial manner. Nice bloke though.)

I enjoy going around the factory and observing the various stages of production – the poaching, pulping, boiling, cooling, jarring, capping … I enjoy the sight of several gallons of jam going mad in a gargantuan pan, and a thousand lemons being peeled by a circle of employee-owners, each sitting on a stool and nattering away. I enjoy watching the jars of marmalade being steamed and spruced prior to labelling. (From certain angles, and with some sleight of mind, it's quite possible to anthropomorphise the jars of marmalade as they wriggle along, rubbing shoulders, tinkling appreciatively as they go on their way.)

I enjoy some of the science, some of the nerdy titbits regarding pectin, and anti-foam agents, and the favourable properties of copper over steel, and the company's ongoing development of a strawberry-picking robot. I won't ever put any of this knowledge to use, of course. A lot of it won't even be retained. And yet its acquisition is unquestionably pleasurable, for the simple act of learning something, if only for a moment, can occasion a tiny boost of morale, and serve as a gentle high-five to the soul.

I enjoy some of the accidental – or industrial – beauty. Like the sight of a hundred pallets of marmalade patiently await-ing collection, each stack formidable, each jar gleaming, each spoonful of marmalade set for an equally sticky fate. I enjoy talking to some of the workers on my way round, like Neil in the pudding room who says the factory is a nut-free zone if you don't include the staff. Christ, I even enjoy wearing a beard snood.

And I particularly enjoy being sent home with a bag of good-ies. Not at all does it bother me to take the 16.20 from Kelvedon to Liverpool Street – past the flat but bountiful fields of Essex – with a clattering bag between my legs containing strawberry gin and lemon curd, tomato ketchup and blood orange vodka.

When I get home, I'm full of it. I reckon myself a right jammy so-and-so, and don't mind who knows it. I'm phoning this person and that, telling them about my day out at the factory, about the lifecycle of a greengage, about the manufacture of quince jelly.[28]

Perhaps my day out in Essex was better for having come out of nowhere. Perhaps it was more enjoyable for being unplanned. The only reason I got invited to Tiptree was because I wrote a book with marmalade in the title that Mr Wilkin happened to notice in a bookshop in Colchester. Going forward, I'm not taking any chances. I'm not going to leave it to Fate to return me to Tiptree – no, siree. Instead, I'm going to write as many books as I can with preservable fruits in the title. Don't believe me? Well, consider this: up until a few weeks before the publication of this book, its title was *Here Comes The Plum*.

Factories, huh? Who would have thought it? I'm not so naive as to think they're all a picnic; but nor am I so cynical to think that they can't be entirely marvellous.

---

[28] Come to think of it, counting the number of times we mention an experience might not be a bad way of measuring its fun-factor. By this metric, the most fun I had during my year of making merry was spotting Keira Knightley at Waterloo station.

12

The invisibility of what's constant

Wherein the author superintends a toilet, face-plants on several occasions, drops a clanger at the charity shop and suggests that writing about fun is like dancing about architecture.

3 June

Hove lagoon, on the south coast of England, is a manmade basin filled with seawater, whereat one can practice (and perhaps even master) such unlikely endeavours as windsurfing and wakeboarding. I'll be giving the latter a stab, which I'm somewhat nervous about, because this sort of thing is hardly my cup of tea. I can honestly say – as I squeeze into a wetsuit – that I'm not looking forward to it. When did I last do something like this? Something counterintuitive involving propulsion and water? I've *never* done something like this. Indeed, I've never been in a wetsuit. Which means I've never felt quite this snug and apprehensive at the same time.

I watch from the edge of the lagoon as fearless youngsters take to it like ducks to water. Their youth is an advantage. In terms of synapses, their brains are less stuck in the mud. Their heads are basically tubs of cerebral playdoh – total plasticity. Mine isn't. I've had 30 extra years getting used to not strapping my feet to an ironing board and being towed by a motorised seagull across a vast puddle.

I'm issued an impact vest and a helmet by Jack, my instructor, who then sits me down and runs through the basics – i.e. relax, let the cable do the work, don't face-plant. Getting the board on isn't easy. I get abdominal cramp trying to fasten the straps. I lower myself off the pontoon and into the water. I get hold of the handle on the end of the tow line. Jack counts down from three, and then we're – face-planting.

We try again. Jack counts down from three, and then we're up and cruising (for about a second and a half and then we're not). It hurts when you headbutt the water. And it hurts more when there's a crowd watching you do it. Jack asks if I'm alright. I tell him about the escalating cramp in my toes and the salt in my eyes. He just starts counting down from three again, which is my cue to grab the handle and get myself in position and relax and let the cable do the work and not – face-plant again.

For crying out loud. I've literally been in the water less than a minute and I've experienced more pain and trauma than I had done in my whole adult life up to this morning. I've got another half an hour of this. Which means on paper I've got roughly another 90 more face-plants ahead of me. What a prospect. I wasn't kidding about the cramp in my toes, by the way. And it's back in the abdominals. My muscles are literally like, 'What the Mary and Joseph are you up to?' We go again and I stack it again, but this time I forget to let go of the handle, and so I get dragged along on my face for a few seconds, with my nose as a rudder. Sexy.

We take a break. Jack reels me in gently, helps me up onto the pontoon, tells me I'm the first person to request a stoppage within five minutes. I buy myself some time by asking Jack about his life. He falls for my trap – goes on for ages about the time he broke his fibula on Lake Windermere. Then he tells me about his journey to becoming a world-class wakeboarder, which came to an end when he quit competing because the pressure was sucking all the fun out of it. He says that as soon as there's a goal, some of the magic is lost. I make a note.

'Maybe that's why I'm not enjoying this, Jack.'

'How's that?'

'Because my goal is to survive.'

'You'll be alright. Finish your tea and hop back in.'

After a few more false starts – which are bothering me less and less, I must say – I'm up and running. I'm sailing, even. I'm cruising, in fact. I'm veritably standing tall. And then I'm not, because you're not meant to stand tall, you're meant to have your knees slightly bent, especially when cornering. We go again, and I'm up and running again, and I feel a burst of pleasure knowing the previous occasion wasn't a complete fluke. In the last minute or so, I've come on leaps and bounds. In the last minute or so, my performance has improved by about 140 per cent. There's a strong chance I'll never get better at anything at a faster rate so long as I live. It's an argument for trying new things: the gains you can make from a position of utter crapness are seismic, and the brain isn't dumb to the fact, meaning you get rewarded with a swift surge of positive hormones.

Said surge of hormones is useful in taking the edge off the cramp, I must say, which is only getting worse, especially in my abs. It's like they're – rattling. It's like my abs – in so far as I have any – are *rattling*. I call for another break. Jack concedes but says that I'm not getting another one until I've done a complete figure of eight; that is, until I've cornered successfully at either end of the lagoon. I tell him there's more chance of Keir Starmer pulling up in an ice cream van. Jack asks who Keir Starmer is. I briefly worry about the credentials of Generation Z, then grab the handle and tell him to fire her up.

I'm pretty much getting up every time now. I'm feeling increasingly confident on the straight and narrow, but cornering remains a nuisance. It's the 'cutting' that's a problem. No matter how loud Jack screams 'Look at the bench!' or 'Bend your knees!' or 'Lean back!' or – my personal favourite – 'Bend your knees, lean back and look at the bench!' I just can't resist standing up, leaning forward and looking at my feet.

But we persevere. We really do. We even persevere for five minutes longer than we're meant to. To be honest I'm desperate to stop by this point. Because the last ten minutes have been awful. I seem to be getting worse. I think it's because Jack has given me more to think about, so now I've got more ways to trip myself up. Learning isn't linear, that's for sure, not if my progress chart is anything to go by. Indeed, I just had my biggest crash of the lot. Got my knickers in a twist and almost went straight into one of the fibreglass ramps. I could have cried, I was that distraught. Instead I screamed at Jack from afar. I screamed that my eyes have changed colour, that I've got rigor mortis in my toes, and that my abdominals are rattling around like two split peas in a jerry can. 'One more time,' says Jack. 'You can do it,' says Jack. 'One more time,' I say. 'But I definitely can't do it,' I say. And do you know what? I was right. I couldn't. So Jack relents and calls it a day. He hauls me out of the water like a massive sack of scampi. I'm spent. Jack has to take my board off for me. I can barely move.

'How do you feel?' he says.

'Dead,' I say.

'Sorry to hear that,' he says.

'Don't be,' I say. 'Because it feels great.'

What doesn't feel great is when I pull an intercostal muscle trying to get out of my wetsuit.

5 June

Library. There's a party in full swing around the corner on the square – for the Queen's Jubilee. The library is open for the duration of the party so that people can pop in to spend a penny, and I've been roped in to manning the facilities. What's more, I've been asked to get as much change out of the needy as I can – to top up the library's coffers. The things I do for my Queen, eh? I don't mind, though. I'm sure she'd do the same for me.

It's not much of a chore. I just sit behind the issue desk with a book, occasionally asking anyone who enters for a donation. You can imagine the range of responses I get. Some people are literally bursting and can't stop to chat, which is fair enough. Some dutifully fish out a piece of silver. Some – those who've spent a bit of time at the Pimm's stall – make a show of pretending to put something in the box, giggling as they do so. One guy – for whom the invitation to make a donation comes as something of shock – asks if I'm taking the piss, which is quite amusing given that it's he and not me running such an errand.

About an hour or so into my lavatorial obligation, the weather takes a turn for the worse, and all that was out is suddenly in, with the result that the once peaceful lobby is now throbbing with monarchists. If it wasn't already, my supervision of the dunny is now a total waste of time. People are filling their boots willy-nilly. I couldn't charge them if I wanted to, because I'm now busy handling the sundry enquiries that are being fired at me left, right and centre, like 'Do you have any strawberries?' and 'Can you turn my child into a member?'

The library is now the centre of festivities, which I don't mind. It's certainly an improvement on me on my tod plus whoever needed the bog. A lady – farthest along in terms of drunkenness – is wearing an inflatable crown. A man – farthest along in terms of nuttiness – has accessorised his flat cap with

Union Jack napkins. A pack of children – farthest along in terms of restlessness – have been given a box of coloured chalks and invited to embellish the pavement outside. (One kid is halfway through a sketch of what appears to be Charles I without a head.) And still the enquiries come: 'Have you got a bag?', 'Do you live in the village?', 'Have you seen Brigitte?'

At around 5 p.m., things quieten down, and the party draws to a close. The weather has changed once again and everyone is back in the square, where an orchestra has started up. Whenever the stars align and there's a moment of complete stillness in the library and on the street outside, a gentle, uncertain version of 'Jerusalem' is just about audible from my position behind the lending desk. Such moments of stillness are rare, however, and all the better for being so. I swear to God if it was quiet all the time you wouldn't hear a thing.[29]

At the end of the song, a lady enters in a state of enthusiastic annoyance. She's lost her brolly. No she hasn't – here it is, in the vestibule of the ladies'. She looks at me on her way out – closer this time, in less of a hurry – and says, 'Are you a republican? Please God tell me you are, because I've been looking for one all day. I'm Irish, you see, and by rights I should loathe the monarchy but as it is I merely get bored with the lot of them on a regular basis. Not that Cromwell was much better. Regarding the Irish I mean. Is there any cake left? There is? Ah, that's grand. Will you come and have a look at the music? The orchestra is deadly. I've put a request in for 'Danny Boy' and because the conductor's an agreeable sort he said he'd do it.' She leaves me to it, and you have to smile.

---

[29] Still not quite sure what I meant by this. Something to do with scarcity inflating value, and the invisibility of what's constant.

9 June

I try another class at the gym. This time it's Barre Fitness, which advertises itself as a range of 'ballet-inspired' strength and conditioning exercises. Because it advertises itself in such a fashion, I'm apprehensive about pitching up. Not because I think ballet isn't for the likes of me, but rather because I just can't imagine behaving in a way remotely balletic. When I booked the class, I immediately went to cancel. I managed to resist the urge, only for it to return a few hours later. For one reason or another, I was clearly far from comfortable with the idea of giving barre a go. Which, of course, was all the more reason to give it a go. Feeling uncomfortable about something can be a paradoxical hint that you're onto something good, that you're on the right track. (Though it can also just be a hint that you're not.) So, yeah, I was nervous. Indeed, I still am nervous. And I think the guy next to me – who's also arrived early for the class – can tell.

'You alright mate?' he says.

'Kind of.'

'Yeah, I know what you mean.'

'I'm just a bit worried about the "movements derived from ballet" bit.'

'Nah, you'll be alright.'

'You reckon?'

'Yeah.'

'What are you basing that on?'

'How's your *demi-plié*?'

'My what?'

'I'm kidding. You'll be fine.'

'And if I'm not?'

He shrugs. 'If you're not, you're not.'

In the event, the class is great. Despite my early nerves, and my inability to understand a lot of what the instructor is saying (at one point she admonishes me for having a bad attitude, which puts my nose out of joint until I learn that an 'attitude' is a ballet position), I find the class oddly compelling and surprisingly accessible. Compared to yoga anyway. In yoga, I still feel like I'm years away from the starting line. In barre, I feel like the benefits are more readily available – until, that is, I'm asked to do an arabesque with arms *allongé*, and I'm like, 'Say what?' Nonetheless, I'll be a regular at the barre going forward, I fancy.[30]

15 June

Someone once said that writing about music is like dancing about architecture. Well, I'd say that writing about fun is a bit like dancing about architecture, too. In short, the two things are ill-fitting. For example: you're halfway down a log flume and you're wondering what it is exactly about gravitational force equivalent that tickles one's funny bones. Not helpful.

When fun is doing its job, when it's hitting the nail on the head, it's meant to stop you thinking, not get you thinking more. It's meant to be about freedom, not deliberation. It's meant to be about escaping the self, not reflecting on it. It's meant to be about evading the typical burdens and stressors we're all routinely subjected to, not dwelling on them. To borrow the words of Michael Foley, fun is about escaping the 'self-imposed tyranny of the project'. And to think I've made a project out of fun! The joke's on me, alright.

---

[30] I never went again.

But I have a solution, and that's to switch off during, and switch on after. (I know – genius, right?) It's to just dive into the salsa (for example), and then think about it when I'm back on *terra firma*. So far it hasn't worked though. So far, I haven't once been able to remain thoughtless in the midst of fun. But even if it never works, even if I never manage it, even if I'm never able to leave consideration in the car while I do my thing on the trampoline, hopefully this diary will still have some value. Why might it? Simply put, because if I'm having fun while overthinking the damn thing, then the chances of you having fun while not giving a monkey's are pretty high. In fact, I reckon you can add roughly 40 percentage points (or the qualitative equivalent) to any of the verdicts/appraisals offered in this book. If I like it, there's a good chance you'll love it. If I loathe it, there's a good chance you'll like it. If I emerge from a year of fundertakings feeling more confident and alive and curious and playful, there's a good chance you'll emerge feeling godlike. Although do keep the receipt because that's not a guarantee.

21 June

I almost drop a massive clanger at the charity shop by flogging a Prada coat priced at £999.99 for £99.99. Fortunately, the customer is kind enough to point out my sizable oversight. Good job Natasha's downstairs, else she would have had my guts for garters (and got a good price for them as well). She's a good manager, Natasha. Shelter are lucky to have her. Great with her staff, friendly with her customers, and she won't flinch in the slightest when it comes to pricing a pair of Gucci socks at half a million pounds. She knows what she can get for things. Multiple times a day she gets it in the neck from customers who accuse her of daylight robbery/behaving uncharitably, usually when the customer's attempt to get 50 per cent off the asking price has failed spectacularly. 'If you really want 50 per cent off,' Natasha once said to a punter in pursuit of a pair of Armani wellies, 'then just buy one of them.' Nice.

Anyway, Natasha's all about getting the most money for the charity, which is why she doesn't let me value anything other than the books. The book section has sort of become my domain. The first thing I'm asked to do each shift is to refresh the shelves, which basically involves taking off the shelf anything that's been hanging around for too long (*A Practical Guide to Racism*, for example), and putting on the shelf stuff that's recently been donated.

Today, among the latter, I discover a Norwegian phrase book. Being a conscientious bookseller, I give the item ample consideration before making a decision whether to shelve it or not – which is to say I kill twenty minutes downstairs committing a few everyday phrases to heart. *Egget mitt er for mykt*, should you be interested, is Norwegian for 'my egg is too soft', useful in the event of finding yourself – well, I'll let you decide in what event such a phrase might be useful.[31]

After I've refreshed the shelves, Natasha tells me to mind the till for a bit while she eats her lunch. Doing so, a customer comes in with an American Bulldog looking more disillusioned than me. While its master is perusing a rack, the dog decides

---

[31] Note to self: I really should have stopped volunteering at the charity shop much earlier than I did. I was having, I now see, a negative effect on the shop's performance. For a start, I was getting in the way of someone (another volunteer, for example) who might have been prepared to actually do a decent job. In effect, by wasting time learning useful Norwegian phrases, I was probably actually making more people homeless.

on a whim to take the umbrella of another customer into its mouth and keep it there for the next ten minutes – as you do. The dog's best friend tries her best to move the dog outside, so at least the commotion isn't carrying on inside the shop, but the umbrella is longer than the doorframe is wide, meaning the dog can't fit through it with the brolly in its gob. I don't often put my hand over my mouth when in a state of disbelief but on this occasion I do.

In the midst of this melee, Natasha reappears from downstairs apparently having a heart attack. She can't talk, just keeps gesturing to her mouth and suggesting heat and so on. She's sweating. Copiously. And her lips have trebled in scope.

'What the hell's happened, Natasha?'

'Chilli. Sauce. Might. Need. Ambulance. Can't. Breathe. What's. Going. On. With. That. Dog.'

All in all, the most fun shift I've had so far.

25 June

The highlight of my shift at the library is probably when an ancient member called Malcolm Dick comes up to me and – apropos of nothing – launches into a speech about why I oughtn't pursue a career in dentistry. The lowlight is when I'm press-ganged into taking over the 'Rhyme Time' sessions the library runs on Wednesday mornings. Apparently the slot has been vacant since the previous incumbent had a nervous breakdown and returned to Canada.[32]

---

[32] Rhyme Time is the bane of my life.

HERE COMES THE FUN

13

A chance to re-evaluate what we value

Wherein the author sets sail for the Baltic, gets his pants in a twist playing bingo, gets his pants in a twist learning Welsh, gives ABBA the cold shoulder and offers a thought on Hamlet.

2 July

In a spirit of daring and contrariness, I'm off on a cruise. Despite having travelled with my elders before (see *The Gran Tour*), and despite having survived a series of lockdowns all but tethered to an unfamiliar 85-year-old (see *The Marmalade Diaries*) – I arrive at Tilbury Town train station (twenty miles east of central London) unhelpfully apprehensive, for the simple reason that cruise ships aren't the conventional home-from-home for solo blokes in their thirties.

Walking the mile or so from train station to cruise terminal – where new British line Ambassador's refitted flagship *Ambience* is purring impressively – my nerves are dealt another blow when I learn that Margaret Thatcher used to be the ship's godmother. One consolation regarding this Thatcherite ill-omen, however, is the prospect of buying my cabin outright at the end of the cruise.

I spend ten minutes in my cabin approximating someone unpacking, then head up to the top deck to admire the unassuming landscapes of Kent and Essex. I'm not alone up here, that's for sure. The ship's entertainment team are currently making a song and a dance of our departure. It's all very uplifting, although when they do 'Enjoy Yourself (It's Later Than You Think)', I can't help thinking the lyrics might be a bit close to the bone for the average passenger. When I'm asked during a Rod Stewart number to put my hands in the air, I decide to call it a day and head down for dinner.

* * *

When I enter the ship's main dining room (known as The Buckingham), I'm sat at a table occupied by seven other people travelling alone. It's a round table, and potted biographies are

HERE COMES THE FUN

presently flying back and forth across it. There's Derek from Cornwall, 86 years young but somehow looking like George Best at 40. There's Sarah from Nottingham, an ex-teacher who won't reveal her age but does mention once voting for Churchill (presumably in an election, rather than *Britain's Got Talent*). And there's Alasdair, a former bank manager from the Highlands of Scotland, whose stated mission in life is to extract value for money.

I'm sitting between Sally and Michael. No sooner have I said hello to the latter, than he's telling me about his recent divorce. He says it came as a shock. Says he thought things were okay. Says – passing me the basket of bread rolls – that her new bloke's an OBE *and* a CEO. (And a complete and utter knob as far as Michael is concerned.) But all is not lost, says Michael. The new bloke is *totally stressed out*, says Michael. He's about to blow a gasket and isn't as much fun to be around as he used to be. Michael knows all this because he hired a private investigator. He provides this last piece of information with a self-satisfied wink, then turns to talk to Alasdair and Derek, who are discussing the size of their cabins.

I turn my attention starboard (or is it portside?). To Sally. Like Michael before her, she's quick to unload. (It would seem that preoccupations are used to break the ice around here …) Her husband has Alzheimer's. He recently moved into a care home and doesn't know who she is now, not really. The pandemic was hard, she says. It seemed to go on forever. Her husband (John) was still living at home then, and there was nobody around to lessen the load, or to just pop in for a chat and a cup of tea. Conversation with John wasn't exactly *ideal*, as she's sure I can imagine. Not least because he was entertaining a range of delusions. Chiefly that a man was coming over to the flat all the time to have dinner with Sally behind his back. Needless to say, it's not nice to be accused of such things, but Sally knew it was just John's mind playing tricks on him. It broke her heart though, tricks or no tricks.

'How's your sushi anyway?' she asks.

'It's good.'

'I'm not really into fish. Not since my dad brought one home and made me gut it. Put me right off that did.'

'A dodgy early encounter then?'

'Not half.'

We eat silently for a while.

'I've got a son, but he disowned me,' says Sally abruptly.

'I'm sorry to hear that,' I say.

'I had him when I was young, and his dad cleared off pronto. I had to work two jobs which meant my mum had him a lot. She spoiled him. I was the one who always said no, because we couldn't afford anything. I suppose our relationship was always a bit rocky, but then five years ago he made it clear that he didn't want anything to do with me. He got married last year and I didn't even get invited to the wedding. But I sent his girlfriend a text anyway, saying I hope it goes well, and that all I want is for him to be happy.'

You won't be surprised to learn that there's a pause here, as Sally takes a moment. 'I hate to say it but sometimes I feel I'm better off without him. He used to give me a fair bit of grief. Used to call me some awful things. I'm not going to finish this pork – do you want it? Here, have this bit. I've not even touched it.'

'Thanks, Sally.'

'You're alright.'

3 July

After ten minutes on the top deck reminding myself what the North Sea looks like, and then a three-course breakfast down in the Buckingham, I attend the ship's 'book club' in the Botanical Lounge. Apparently we were meant to read a book in advance, though it hardly matters because today all we do is go round the table saying hello and what books we like, that sort of thing. Sixty per cent of the group (twelve of twenty) mention Richard Osman, which is refreshing. It's intriguing how long it takes some people to say their name and an author they like. Took one bloke over ten minutes. It will always amaze me how some people will go around with such confidence in their interestingness, while others will go around believing they are anything but. Have a bit of a laugh when it's my turn to introduce myself. 'Hello, I'm Ben, and I have to admit, I thought this was the bingo.'

* * *

At midday, there's a cocktail party for all the solos on board. I spot Sally from dinner last night, so make a beeline for her. She's in the middle of making an interesting point about balconies. In short, she wouldn't want her cabin to have one in a million years, no matter how long it was. Why? Because she saw on the news that a girl got murdered in her cabin once, and it was via the balcony that the murderer broke in. So in Sally's mind, a balcony is basically an accessory to murder waiting to happen. Has a very keen sense of danger, does Sally. She says she's more than happy to take a look at the likes of Copenhagen and Stockholm, but wouldn't 'be seen dead in public after dusk if you paid her', which is a scenario that takes me a while to get my head around.

We all go through to the Buckingham for lunch. I'm sat next to Paul and opposite Prue. The former is from London, and the latter from Yorkshire (Hull, to be precise, though Prue prefers not to be). As soon as she was able, Prue headed down to London for an adventure. What she got instead of an adventure was a job teaching I.T.. Says that a lot of her students were tradesmen who had been encouraged to modernise, and not all of them took the technological revolution in their stride. She remembers one guy – a plumber from Basildon – throwing a computer out the window, presumably in anger.

Paul, on the other hand, used to work in imports and exports. He says that while he may be retired from work, he's by no means retired from life. He loves to travel, and doesn't mind doing it alone, not one bit. I ask Paul what his favourite travel memory is, and he says it was sleeping under the stars while cruising down the Euphrates River in Syria.

'The Euphrates is in Turkey, Paul,' says Prue.

'It's in Syria, Prue,' says Paul.

'No, I think you'll find it's in Turkey.'

'It's Syria.'

'Turkey.'

'Prue – *it's Syria.*'

'Paul – *it's Turkey.*'

'Syria.'

'Turkey.'

'Syria.'

'Turkey.'

'How about we move on?' I say.

'Fine,' says Paul.

'Fine,' says Prue.

We return to our chicken kievs.

'Turkey,' whispers Prue.

'Syria,' says Paul, getting up and leaving the table.[33]

* * *

After lunch, I return to the Botanical Lounge for a Welsh language lesson. It is chiefly curiosity that motivates me, though doesn't the science suggest that language-learning reduces the risk of dementia?[34] There's a fair number of people in attendance, which either says something about the appeal of learning Welsh or the reality of spending a fortnight on a boat. Our teacher, Cerys, hails from Wrexham, which she says isn't as fantastic as we've all heard.

We start with the alphabet. I can just about manage to pronounce the letter 'a', but 'rh' is beyond me. Each time I attempt it I just attract concern. The same is true of 'ch', which – spoiler alert – does not come out as it does in church or cheese. When we move onto numbers, as Cerys counts from one to three, I jot down a rough phonetic version that makes sense to me (namely: Ian, die, tree), and then come up with a little mnemonic to help the info stick (namely: my stepdad falling out of a cedar and not surviving.) The number five in Welsh – *pump* – is quite fun for the record, while the number six – *chwech* – is so problematic to pronounce that I reckon I'll just avoid it going forward.

Cerys then introduces us to the days of the week, before moving on to certain key phrases, like 'Did you see the rugby on

---

[33] It's both. But that's hardly the point. The point is that it was fun watching them disagree.

[34] Broadly speaking, it does – but with the exception of learning Welsh, which I'm told actually increases your chances of going bananas.

Saturday?' I continue to jot down phonetic approximates, or little personal aide memoires. For example, April in Welsh is 'a brick' said with a scouse accent (*Ebrill*). Red is 'coke' in Geordie (*coch*). And very well thanks is 'Diane Diok', the Welsh-Serbian tennis sensation (*da iawn diolch*). At the end of the lesson, there's a little competition to see who's made the most progress. *Nobody wins.*

In any case, it's been a diverting hour. It got the old cognitive cogs moving, and it's always good – and humbling – to be reminded of the extent of one's ignorance. I'm all for coming back in a few days for round two, until Cerys mentions that the next lesson will focus on train stations.

* * *

From the Botanical Lounge I sashay across to the ship's pub, the Purple Turtle, for some bingo. The caller is full of adlib and whimsy, which I like to see. That said, when he says 'We're about to start, ladies and gents, so eyes down and hearing aids out', the remark is a bit presumptuous for my taste. The first game is for 60 quid, with just one line required. I make a sluggish start and know early on that I'm not on to a winner. The second game is for a hundred-odd quid, with two lines required, and I do so badly that I'm actually embarrassed. The final game is for two-hundred-odd quid, with a full house required. I get off to an absolute flier, enjoy a steady middle third, and am well in the mix coming down the stretch – and if you were sitting next to me, you would be in no doubt about it. I can't sit still for one. And I can't keep my mouth shut for two. Can't stop whispering hostile feedback to the bingo gods each time a number is called that I don't have: 'Just my luck', 'That'll be right', 'For the love of Mary and Joseph what have I done to – yep, that'll be right, just my luck, haven't got that one either'. This might sound odd, but it appears to me that I am more emotionally demonstrative playing bingo than in any other area of life. The sport just gets me going. It just fires me up. My heart's going like the clappers. If I played bingo full-time I'd be slim in a week (if that's how weight loss works). Anyway, I manage to nail three numbers on the trot, meaning I only need the number seven and I've won. In terms of synaptic activity, I'm on fire – '72!' I'm living proof that bingo is edge of the seat stuff – '18!' And just think, if I win I might be able to afford the onboard wi-fi – '47!' I'm literally about to burst with apprehension – '16!' – when some other sod, on the call of eleven, makes a triumphal noise that is so muffled and half-hearted as to be disrespectful to the sport. It is not a crisp 'bingo!' or 'house!' or 'yep!'. If it sounds like anything, it sounds like the number six in Welsh. I'm angry. I'm genuinely wound up by the man's success and his unintelligible claim. I leave the Purple Turtle and head up to the top deck to let off steam, more in love with bingo than ever. She is a curious mistress.

* * *

After enjoying a roughly twelve-course dinner alone at Borough Market (the ship's buffet option), I head up to the Observatory bar on deck fourteen to check out the disco. There's an ABBA cabaret in full swing, and the dancefloor is rammed. As inviting as that sounds, I opt to watch from the sidelines, my one concession to 'letting go' being a slow tap of the foot.

Dancing has always conflicted me. I get it and I don't. Dancing at weddings – fine, you're buzzing and among friends. Dancing when youthful at a disco – reasonable, you're pumped on alcopops and are under the spell of Cupid and Eros. Dancing independently among strangers on a Sunday night at sea – not convinced.

The fact that I'm not convinced isn't lost on Margaret. She's spotted me on the edge of things. I met Margaret this afternoon, at the solos cocktail party. She's a combination of Pat from *EastEnders* and Nessa from *Gavin and Stacey*.

'You doing your impression of the most boring person in the world?' she asks, charmingly.

'Hello, Margaret.'

'Well? Are yeh? This isn't a library, pet.'

'I know, I know.'

'You're putting me off me drink.'

'I'm actually a pretty fun guy.'

'Are yeh fuck. You're sending emails during an ABBA cabaret, pet.'

When Margaret says 'pet', two things happen at once: 1) 'Dancing Queen' comes on, and 2) Margaret seizes the moment – and me with it. In giving me no choice in the matter, Margaret teaches me something about fun. Namely: sometimes we go towards it happily and under our own steam, and other times we go kicking and screaming and under someone else's.

Finding myself on the dancefloor, I do everything I can to not look out of place. It's more difficult than it sounds. For a start, everyone else seems to be handy with their feet. And there's also the fact that I can't stop wondering about the songs and their lyrics. I mean, just what the hell is 'Waterloo' all about? Is it about the train station? Is it allegorical? When I pose these questions (at the top of my voice) to Margaret, who's got some moves alright, and is about as self-conscious as a bar stool, she's disbelieving.

'You can take the boy out of the office, but not the office out of the boy. Let your hair down!'

'As I said, Margaret, I'm actually a pretty—'

'You've got to FEEL the music, Ben. Not bloody THINK about it.'

Then Margaret helps me feel the music by casting herself as Gepetto and me as Pinocchio and proceeding to manipulate various parts of my body until I resemble someone thoughtless and rhythmic. Having got me going, she lets go and stands back – to see if Newton's first law of motion (that once something is set in motion it will remain so until a force acts against it) applies to a stiff fella on the dance floor of a cruise ship.[35]

4 July

Waking up on a boat is an odd – but not unpleasant – occurrence. One feels happily unmoored, and nicely adrift. Sort of uprooted, sort of non-domiciled, but helpfully so, healthily so. Disengaged from thither and then, re-engaged with hither and now: it is a chance to re-evaluate what we value. To see the wood *and* the trees.

In any case, it's nice having something different to look at each time you draw the curtains in the morning. This morning when I draw the curtains, it's Denmark staring at me, and in particular a castle which was once home to Kenneth Branagh when he played Hamlet in *Hamlet*.

Not the most fun character, was Hamlet. Liked to dilly-dally, if I remember correctly. Not one to just 'go for it', to give things a crack. Not sure what Margaret would have made of the Prince of Denmark on the dancefloor last night. She would have had a job getting His Majesty to throw caution to the wind, to *feel*

---

[35] It doesn't.

rather than think. And I would have been on Hamlet's side, I fancy. I would have defended his conscientious objection. Why? Because when all things are considered, it's better to think too much than too little.

Or is it? I'm not trying to be funny or awkward – I genuinely have mixed thoughts on thinking. It's easy to have one's head turned on the matter. You look one way and it seems inarguable that procrastination is the thief of time and that you ought to just crack on. But then you look the other way and it appears for all the world that the unexamined life isn't worth living. It rather leaves one in a muddle regarding thought, and yearning to be put on factory settings for a while.

* * *

After breakfast, I head to the theatre at the back (or aft) of deck eight for a talk about the Mona Lisa, to be delivered by Helen Pointer, a professional caricaturist. Waiting for Helen to begin, I feel unmistakably happy. It's not often that I'm able to put my finger on a feeling and say with complete confidence, 'Yep, that's happiness.' But I'm able to do it now. Which is odd when you think that I'm alone, on a boat, approaching Copenhagen, and potentially about to be bored to tears.

Or perhaps that isn't odd. Perhaps *happiness* is odd. In my experience at least, happiness has certainly been liable to turn up at some unlikely moments, and without an invitation, and on some very flimsy pretexts. I remember being briefly and distinctly happy a few years ago when I missed a train to Margate, for example. Work that one out.

Perhaps fleeting bursts of happiness – which are about all we can ask for – are the outcome of positive pressure that has built up over a period of days or weeks – a bit of luck last Thursday, a touch of fun on Saturday, some good news on Tuesday, a chance reunion this morning. Perhaps the fleeting bursts are like tiny happiness storms, the roots of which are scattered elsewhere, all but impossible to trace. It's a nice thought.

Anyway, Helen's on stage. She asks if anyone's ever been to the Louvre, and some bloke shouts out that he's been twice this morning already. Helen brushes off the man's attempt at toilet humour, and proceeds to give a swift lowdown of Da Vinci's most famous painting. Put simply, some time after the artist's death, the painting ended up in the hands of Francis I, then king of France. The Mona Lisa remained a possession of eminent Frenchmen until 1911, when she was pinched. The robbery turned out to be her lucky break: the painting's value was elevated by the scandal; its 'worth' rocketed on the tides of media attention and gossip. Parisians started going to the Louvre in droves to *see what was missing*. 'You don't know what you've got until it's gone,' says Helen, which is one way of looking at it. Another is that people will stare at nothing if it's been in the papers. In any case, the Mona Lisa turned up two years later, in Italy. The Italian authorities seized the painting and returned it to the Louvre, though not before sending her on a national tour of Italy's galleries.

Speaking of tours, I'd better go and have a look at Denmark's capital.

* * *

The tour of Copenhagen basically involves being shown the sights for a couple of hours and then dropped off in the centre of town for some 'free time'. When the latter period is upon us, our young guide encourages us to spend our free time wisely – by mooching around the Isle of Power, where Parliament and several other important buildings are situated. I give the Isle of Power a wide berth, and follow my nose instead.

It's telling where instinct takes you when you're dumped in a city and given only an hour to explore. Mine takes me to get something to drink (fermented honey and water), to consider some statues (including one of Christian IV, who became king aged eleven), to peruse the window of a souvenir shop (where the complex phenomena of a nation are reduced to a mermaid), to have a chat with a local teenager about his favourite thing to do in the city (swim in the Baltic), and to then go and do that thing (which does two things to me: gives me a new lease of life, and makes me late for the coach by seven minutes).

When our guide announces that there's time for a quick stop at the Little Mermaid statue before returning to the ship, a Mexican wave breaks out on the coach. Fast forward ten minutes, and not everyone's so happy. Trying to get a life-changing selfie with the eponymous mermaid, Peter from Ipswich accidentally (one assumes) backs into Rhonda from Halifax and sends her tumbling. Stunned into action, our guide gets out his megaphone and asks everyone to be aware of their surroundings, which is a sentiment that ought to be shared publicly on the hour every hour, as far as I'm concerned.

When we're dropped off back at the ship, I pay heed to our guide's advice and go for a little walkabout. Not 50 metres away from where the *Ambience* is berthed, on the other side of a complex of offices and flats, I discover *another* statue of the Little Mermaid. This one might have been put together by Picasso, and is to my mind superior to the one up the road by some margin. Apart from its abstract nature, another difference between this one and that one is that that one receives about a million visitors a year and this one receives, at a guess, roughly four. As with the Mona Lisa, maybe it needs to be stolen before it can be prized. Just a thought.

* * *

After dinner, a group of us head off to the theatre to see a comedian do his thing. He's pretty decent, I'd say. Brings to mind a cross of Andrew Marr and Harry Hill. His set is going down really well until he asks, in the build-up to a punchline, if there are any Elvis fans in the crematorium. And he probably loses a couple more fans when he explains how, at the height of the pandemic, and in a reversal of what he'd normally do, he started farting to cover a cough on public transport.

My highlight of the evening comes about an hour later, up in the Observatory bar. I'm enjoying a band on stage when I notice the suburbs of Copenhagen sliding past in the background. The visual interplay of this here and that there gets under my skin somehow. I've never felt so in the moment and in the process at the same time. It's like we're sort of magically killing two birds with one stone. When you cruise, there's no checking out or checking in as you go along, no connecting trains or onward planes. All the dots are joined behind your back, while you're playing roulette or dancing to Barry White or reading the latest Anthony Trollope. (Just checking you're awake.)

I'm labouring a simple point, and that is that it looks and feels good to have the city going by as I'm standing here listening to 'Rio' by Duran Duran. It is a moment to savour, and were I given a cast-iron guarantee that nobody could see me, I would move to the centre of the dancefloor and truly make the most of it. But I can be seen. I know I can because a bloke called Ron from Newcastle has just nudged me with an elbow and said, 'Not bad them lot, are they?'

When we get chatting, I try to explain to Ron my feeling about it seeming like we're being and going at once, and he says, 'Don't be daft, it's just like when you're in the car listening to the radio'. By way of explaining his being on the cruise alone (some people feel they have to), Ron says he's recently divorced. He says he tied the knot too early, that he married a narcissist before they even existed. Then he says he'll have just one more drink before calling it a night. And then, over the next couple of hours, he says the exact same thing several times more. And I don't mind a bit. I like talking to him. I appreciate his candour. His openness. His willingness to tell me that things haven't always been rosy for him. His willingness to be vulnerable, to put himself out there. Ron's admissions encourage some of my own, and before long we're having what you'd call a heart to heart, sitting on a pair of bar stools, by the side of the stage, to a Motown soundtrack, on our way to the Danish island of Bornholm. It may not be fun, but it's not a million miles off.[36]

5 July

Just a bowl of porridge for breakfast, because if I keep doing what I've been doing, the ocean's going to find me unbearable. I jest, but there's a serious point to be made here: in the face of

---

[36] A recent set of studies undertaken at the University of Mannheim in Germany identified something called the 'beautiful mess effect', which suggests that opening up to a stranger, being honest about our frailties and setbacks, our flaws and anxieties, is more likely to prove attractive to whoever we're talking to than repellent. Good news for intimacy, people.

a buffet – whether experiential or culinary – you need to take it easy. You need to resist FOMO, and you need to squash your inner gannet. You need to know that more isn't always merrier. If you want to fill your plate, fill it with *balance*. If you want to fill your diary, fill it with *moderation*. (I swear I could write a self-help book if someone just gave me the chance. I've already got the knack of *italicising* down to a tee.) So yeah. The perils of wanting too much. The need – in front of a dozen ways of stuffing yourself – to bear Epicurus in mind, who reckoned the person not satisfied with little is satisfied with nothing. The necessity, now and again, of biting off *less* than you can chew. The wisdom that's inherent in a humble bowl of porridge. (And a croissant, if I'm honest.) It is all food for thought. And I'll scoff the lot, if you don't mind.

6 July

Nexo is a tiny former fishing town on the island of Bornholm, which sits some way east of the rest of Denmark, with Poland due south and Sweden due north. I walk inland, away from the harbour, towards the *sommerfuglepark* – or butterfly park to you and me. When I get there, the first specimen to catch my attention is the Monarch. A display tells me that the Monarch butterfly undergoes a 4,000-kilometre migration every year from the north of America to somewhere in Mexico. But here's the thing: it takes *several generations* of the Monarch butterfly to complete the return journey. That is, one butterfly makes it a quarter of the way, runs out of steam, breeds and then dies. Then a second generation Monarch flies another leg of the journey, runs out of steam, then breeds and dies. And so on until the great-grandchildren of those butterflies that set off a year earlier finally make it back to their preferred summer hangout. It's a tantalising spin on multi-generational travel.

The greenhouse is choc-a-bloc with butterflies. It's fun to watch them land on the flowers; to watch them settle, gradually slow their fluttering wings, then rhythmically plunge their cutlery into the belly of the flower to extract their liquid lunch. Some take their meals gracefully, pictures of composure, while others feed frantically, going at the flowers' sweet spots like pneumatic drills, dipping and double dipping their frontal straws.

I do a lap, and am pleased to discover a pond full of koi carp. I'm reminded of the one that Dominic and I spotted in the River Wandle that had escaped from a back garden. That wouldn't have happened if I hadn't gone fishing. That association, I mean, that connection. An obvious point to make, of course, but the way dots join in this way has a more profound, less obvious aspect to it, I feel. Experience creates memory, which in turn allows association and reference and the joining of dots. This natural process thickens and complicates our webs of been and being, done and doing, here and now and then and there. It prompts revision, reflection, reminder. It alters the fabric of the everyday. It is an advert for – and ramification of – trying, searching, asking, learning. We are the sum of what we pay attention to – and what we *paid* attention to. The more we look, the more we see, the more we see again. It's the again I like. It's the chance recurrence. It's things reappearing and their being richer for having a precedent. It's seeing a koi carp in Denmark and being taken back to a moment by a river in London. Having said all that, I'm now giving my full attention to a boy picking his nose, and remembering how I used to do likewise for hours on end, so what do I know?

I spot my favourite butterfly. I watch it hop from leaf to leaf, as if in play, as if struggling to choose. Its wings are transparent – as mesh. I can see the green of the leaf through them. The wings' colour is the colour of what is beyond. The wings' colour is the colour of what they encounter. The butterfly is called a Postman. It delivered me something, alright: a hit of wonder.

Walking back to the harbour, I realise that a bit of random fascination goes a long way in my book. The butterfly park was no rollercoaster, but measured in volume of smile and degree of agog and extent of marvel, it's deserving of a podium finish in the fun Olympics. (Assuming there's enough room on this podium for twenty-odd things.)

Back onboard, I bump into Paul, he who slept under the stars in Syria or Turkey. He tells me that, while I was gawping at butterflies, he was riding a public bus around the entire island. Did a whole lap for six quid. Is rather pleased with himself.

'No sense getting old without getting crafty,' he says.

'Quite right, Paul.'

'The bus was half price. The driver wanted me to be over 70 and Danish, but I told him that I was nearly 70 and European and that would have to do.'

'And you liked the island?'

'Oh, it was wonderful. It really was. Fields of wheat. Little fishing villages. The ruins of a medieval castle and not a hedge-row in sight. It reminded me of Kent.'

'Did you get something to eat?'

'Yeah, I had one of those open sandwiches they go in for.'

'Yeah, what's going on with those?'

'How do you mean?'

'Well, is it forgetfulness or what?'

'Oh Ben you are funny.'

'Cheers.'

'I'd throw you off this boat if I wasn't somewhat disabled.'

* * *

Down for dinner in the Buckingham. Sit next to Derek, who, in terms of keeping up appearances, is doing about as good a job as me. He's got a bit of a mullet going on, which you don't often see on an 86-year-old.

'You're never 86,' I say, buttering my roll and Derek at the same time.

'I certainly am.'

'You look good for it, Derek.'

'I better do. I've paid a lot of money to look like this.'

'Have you?'

'Whatever 50,000 pints of bitter costs, yeah.'

As we chat during dinner, I learn that Derek's passionate about bicycles. Watching them, riding them. He was still racing well into his sixties. Picked up a few minor injuries along the way, of course – broken leg, shattered collarbone, skull fracture, that sort of thing. He fractured eleven bones playing rugby once, as well. He received a high ball and got absolutely clattered. Derek reckons it had been that sort of week.

'Did you bother with work?'

'I worked in a little corner shop for many years. But then my wife at the time got a job in Gibraltar and so we moved out there. Then after we got divorced I came home and started running a pub. That was no picnic neither. There was this big dispute between me and the brewery (who I was renting the pub off) about fixtures and fittings.'

'Sounds exciting.'

'I'd paid for the pub to be tarted up, you see, so when the brewery wanted to move me on, but said they wouldn't pay me for the work I'd done, I wasn't best pleased.'

'So what did you do?'

'Refused to budge and stopped paying the rent.'

'And what did they do?'

'They stopped supplying the beer. So I just went to Tesco instead.'

'You kept trading?'

'Yep. Made a fortune. Eventually they wrote to me to say that the bailiffs would be round at this time on this day, so I got my brother and some of his dodgy mates to, you know, secure the place. A picture of them having a ruck with the bailiffs ended up in the local paper.'

'Yikes.'

'It ended up going to court. And the brewery had this top-end barrister working for them, and I had nothing, just me. Not only did they want me out, they also wanted about 50 grand for lost earnings. And their legal fees of course.'

'And what happened?'

'I was found guilty.'

'Shit.'

'But I'd seen the judge give their barrister a sort of thumbs up, just before he gave his verdict. Now I don't need to tell you that a judge is meant to be impartial. And here he was basically winking at the prosecution. Good job I spotted it.'

'I'd say it was, Derek.'

'Fast forward a few months and I got off scot-free.'

Derek starts laughing. And he's soon wishing he hadn't, because now he's coughing. And choking. He's having a full-on coughing and choking fit.

'You alright, Derek?'

Derek gives me a signal, a hand gesture, suggesting that it will pass, that he's been here before, that he just needs a second.

'Throat cancer,' says Derek, when he's back from the dead.

'Throat cancer?'

'Three years ago. It's harder to swallow these days. Things get trapped. I'm only meant to have soup, really.'

There's blood on his tissue. He puts it in his pocket.

'What's for pudding?' he says.

'Tomato soup,' I say.

'I'll have it in a cone then,' he says.

Pudding comes and pudding goes. And so does coffee. By this point it's just Derek and me left. The others have gone in search of amusement. He's telling me about where he used to live.

'It was a three-bed semi near Plymouth. Lovely it were. Sold it for a third of its value to my daughter and her husband.'

'That was good of you.'

'I had an annex, you see, and the plan was that I would move into that. But as soon as the deal was done, they kicked me out.'

'I hope you're joking, Derek.'

He's smiling and shaking his head.

'Bloody hell, mate.'

Derek keeps smiling, as if it's a laugh, but the smile starts to break, starts to falter, so he reaches for a bread roll that isn't there.

'When was this?' I ask.

'About five years ago. Not heard from them since. I'm in a flat now, housing association. Nice enough place. But it's not the same.'

14

A bearded man with an axe

Wherein the author continues to cruise, joins a choir, takes a line dancing class, celebrates aimless wandering and asks if beauty can be fun.

7 July

I'm enjoying the view up in the Observatory when Derek limps in and asks if I'm here for the line dancing as well. I tell him I'd rather plunge a knitting needle into my liver, but he reckons I'd be daft not to give it a go. I plead incompetence, but he's not having it.

'Being incompetent is half the fun. Up you get.'

'Look. Derek. You've got a ropey knee, and I've got the wrong attitude. Why don't we just watch? Have a cappuccino?'

But he doesn't want to hear it. He's off. Towards the dance-floor. And he's using his trailing hand to send me a signal that he's disappointed, that he thought better of me. Which does the trick, of course. Which gets me on my feet. Nothing like a guilt trip to bring out the best in us.

Or the worst in us. Because before the warm-up is over, it's clear that I'm not a natural line dancer. And if I'm bad, then I'm not sure what Derek is. It looks like he's doing an impression of someone lost in an elevator. After learning some 'basic' steps, like the grapevine and the slosh, the instructor wants to bring our hips into play. This is a nice idea in principle, but the trouble is mine don't seem to want to play ball. Whereas the instructor is clearly used to communicating with that part of her body, I don't think my brain's ever sent a message to my hips in my life.

Nonetheless, we combine some grapevines with a few kicks and turns, throw in a bit of thigh slapping, and before long we have, in theory at least, something resembling a routine. We repeat the routine over and over again, facing a different direction each time. With each rotation, I start to grow less dependent on the instructor for my cues, and begin to move from one element of the routine to another with less panic and more, dare I say it, fluidity.

Don't get me wrong, I'm still not dancing well. Not by a long chalk. Doing the steps is one thing, but doing them well – that is with grace and rhythm and vim – is another thing again. If you put me next to the instructor, you'd be forgiven for thinking we were doing different dances. My steps resemble her steps in the way a piece of cheese resembles a fountain pen. But that hardly matters, because I'm having fun, and so are those around me (apart from Derek, who is by now sat down rubbing his sore knee). The experience is certainly better for being collective. Were it just me and the instructor, or me at home and a virtual tutor, it would be fun but not *as fun*. That's my hunch anyway.[37]

Towards the end of the session, I'm even getting a bit cocky. Sort of embellishing the steps, adding some extra pep to them and so on. Which is when things start going wrong, of course: I've had just enough education to perform, but not enough to showboat. I almost trip myself up at one point. They say that the only thing more dangerous than having no knowledge is having a little bit, and they don't say that for no reason. When my line dancing debut is brought to a close and I return to my table, Derek says I was better than the bleeding instructor. Talk about a flirt.

'I even took a video of it,' he says. 'Or tried to, anyway. I think I might have ended up filming a close-up of my face for five minutes.'[38]

---

[37] In an interesting piece of research into how having other people around can affect one's experience of something, prominent anthropologist Robin Dunbar showed that while doing something alone can issue a fair amount of serotonin and endorphins (can be fun, in other words), doing the same thing with another person can issue twice as much.

[38] He had.

July 8

In the 1950s, Finland was one of the poorest countries in the world. Child mortality rates were lamentable, and the nation owed pots of money to the Soviet Union in war reparations. (Finland had collaborated with Germany during the war, believing their enemy's enemy to be their friend etc.) Cue 70 years of enlightened development and governance, with a focus on education and social equality, and now you have the happiest country in the world according to the United Nations. But also a country that prescribes more anti-depressants than just about anywhere. Go figure.

I go – with my figure – to a public sauna. The municipal complex – which includes a few outdoor pools and a rooftop restaurant – is bang in the middle of Helsinki, down by the harbour, in the shadow of a whopping redbrick orthodox church, and next door to a vast Ferris wheel, one of whose cabins is a sauna, which provides a clue as to just how important the art of sweating is in Finnish culture.

By way of a warm-up I have a quick dip in a pool full of seawater – and strike me with a yardstick if it's not absolutely Baltic. I was expecting frigid, but this is freezing. It was warmer in Copenhagen. Much warmer. I'm instantly transported back to the men's pond on Hampstead Heath in winter, which is a shame, because I didn't like it there. Climbing back up the ladder, I slip on the penultimate rung (which has acquired a useful covering of algae), bash my shin painfully, and fall back into the pool, which if nothing else provides a bit of fun for the woman behind me.

When it comes to the sauna, I've got options: male, female or unisex. I go for the former, and soon wish I hadn't, because all the chaps in here are seismic and brilliant. You wouldn't describe the atmosphere as especially social. In fact, it's dead silent. Until, that is, one man throws some water onto the boiling hot stones and the steamy feedback causes me to yelp. It's fair to say that I'm struggling to unwind.

I cook myself for ten minutes at 100 degrees Celsius then transfer myself back to the sea pool (as if my vital organs didn't already have enough on their plate). When I return to the sauna, I'm pleased to discover that it's now just me and one other bloke. I try to say good afternoon in Finnish, knowing that, when it comes to breaking the ice, getting things wrong can sometimes go a long way. My plan works. When the bloke finally works out what I'm trying to say, he practically wets himself.

We get chatting. About sauna mostly. The man tells me that the iron basket in the centre of the sauna is full of granite stones, which are being heated by electric resistors. He tells me that the application of water to the stones is crucial because it cranks up the humidity, and gets you sweating. He tells me that he was delivered in a sauna and that such an occurrence isn't unusual. He tells me that his dad smokes sausages in the sauna and that such a pastime isn't unusual either. He reckons the Finnish prime minister probably executes much of her work in the sauna; that the sauna might be considered the crucible of Finnish nationhood; that all manner of injuries and ailments can be ameliorated in the sauna, including lunacy and broken ankles; and that when a Finn is in a certain mood (and in a sauna), they like to whack themselves with a bunch of birch branches called a *vihta*, just to add a certain *je ne sais quoi* to proceedings.

'And we have sauna competitions as well,' he says.

'Oh God, really?'

'It's basically who can stay in the longest.'

'I thought it might be.'

'A guy died once.'

'I'm not surprised.'

'Japanese guy. He was on holiday here in Finland and thought he'd just give it a go.'

'Did he win?'

The man says nothing. He seems perturbed by my question.

'He *died*,' the man says eventually.

'Yeah, I know, but, I – it was a joke.'

'Seriously? This was a joke?'

'Er. Yeah.'

'This was the famous British humour?'

'Er. Yeah.'

'You should show more respect.'

'I'm sorry. My bad.'

And then the man starts laughing like he did when I said good afternoon.

'I'm kidding you, man! I'm kidding you!'

Ah, the Finns. What jokers. Though there's a serious point to be made here regarding the passing of the Japanese tourist in the sauna: if you can't stand the heat, for the love of God get out of the kitchen. Don't just stick around trying to be cool. It doesn't work.

And on that note, I get out of the kitchen and wander back to the boat, feeling like I'm going to pass out.

9 July

Before and after dinner, I've taken to just sitting on the back deck for an hour or so. I like to watch our long tapering wake, and to listen to the sounds we make as we go. The sheer scenario – that I'm aboard a vessel cruising at a rate of knots across a vast, immeasurable body of water – is spellbinding.

You can look at it two ways. The water I mean. When I look at it vaguely, my mind goes places: to what's inside, what's beyond, what's in store. And then when I look at it closely, the water appears so unbearably complex as to be stressful. Watching the sea's gazillion split-second alterations makes my cerebral cortex feel like it's about to break. Which is when I usually call it a day, and go and watch an abridged version of *My Fair Lady* or similar.

A cruise is fun for many reasons. The pleasure it affords can come in many forms. It can be energetic, comic, intellectual, conversational, gastronomic. It can also be visual. Indeed, it *will* be visual, often and reliably. A case in point was this morning at dawn. I'm up on the top deck, leaning against the railing. The ship is at rest in Stockholm harbour. The water is like silk, and a group of distant gulls are flying so low, and in such numbers, that they seem like mosquitoes. About them is the city in silhouette, its shape and scale and scope showing signs of industry, communication, diversion – a telling, and ascending, sequence. Eastward, towards Finland, things are lighter. Half of the sky is a rainbow: red and orange and yellow, rising to violet and black. The sight of Stockholm harbour at this hour – at this moment – is more than the sum of its parts. The spectacle stands for something else. It is not just what it is, but what it points to. It points to nature and beauty, and things beyond our control, beyond our ken. In its light, we are humbled and lifted at once.

The question I want to ask is: is the experience of beauty fun? And the answer I want to give is: yes, absolutely, chuck it in there with everything else. Because something happens to the brain when we look at beautiful things. Something good. I don't care what it is exactly. It's enough that it happens. I don't want to know how the magic works.

10 July

As Stockholm slowly recedes, I stand at the back of deck ten and admire the thousands of woody islands that make up its famous archipelago. Each island appears to be incontrovertibly idyllic – until you look a bit closer, and the sight of a bearded man with an axe all but confirms that there's also something incontrovertibly sinister about this paradise, about these verdant isles with their charming seaside bothies. After all, it's not for no reason that Scandi Noir is a ubiquitous genre of television and literature. Dark things happen in Scandinavia, and I wouldn't be surprised if they happen in the most angelic of places – like over there, where that man with the axe lives.

Speaking of things angelic, check out this guy. He's just emerged from his little summer house, strode down to his private jetty, and hopped onto his private jet ski. So far so mainstream. Now he's racing the ship, overtaking us with ease, his dark locks dancing as he goes. I get out my binoculars and ascertain that he's wearing an unbuttoned white linen shirt and black leather trousers. Fucking hero. From what I can tell, the young man is at this moment almost certainly one of the happiest beings on the planet. Although there's always the chance he does this every evening and is actually craving a change. After all, not everything that glitters is gold. In any case: time for dinner.

11 July

I wake up in Visby, the capital of Gotland, a sizable Swedish island stranded in the Baltic Sea. I head into town on foot. After fifteen minutes or so, I reach the town's famous medieval wall, which is thick and handsome, and a sign of insecurity if ever there was one. What's quickly obvious upon breaching the wall and ambling

HERE COMES THE FUN

along Shopping Street (*Adelsgatan*), is that there's no traffic, no vehicles. Instead, there are low-rise buildings painted in pastel shades with semi-octagonal roofs, and more ruined churches than you could shake a Swedish herring at. The ruined churches are evidence of the status and affluence the town accrued in its past life as a maritime trading hub. They haven't been levelled, and they haven't been restored. They've been left alone, to wane and age, and are better for the fact. They add a striking feature to the town's look, its personality. Beauty can be ruinous.

I duck into a bakery for a spot of *fika*, which entails a cinnamon bun and a chat with the Norwegian baker (bloody immigrants). I take a pew at a high counter on the terrace, which offers a view of the main square, which although main is hardly bigger than a couple of tennis courts.

You see more when things are small. You see Ron from Newcastle in a T-shirt that would stop traffic. You see the girl that played Eliza Doolittle choosing a souvenir. You see Ellen and Cathy, sisters from Southend, who have two pints of lager a night and not a drop more. You see Derek trying to tie a shoelace and being helped by a stranger. My view is restricted, and yet what I see appears endless, appears eternal.

I go down to the seaside, to a million silver pebbles, and a stone jetty jutting into the Baltic. I enter the water. It is warm but choppy, so I don't venture far lest I'm dragged out and washed up on one of those spooky islands in the Stockholm archipelago. I'm no Braveheart yet. In my book, discretion remains the better part of valour.

After my swim, I eat a crepe. I take the waiter's advice, and order something the size of a beach towel and lacquered with butter, brown sugar and lemon. It is one of the finest things I've ever eaten. It is a balance of simplicity and indulgence, a harmony of sweet and sharp and savoury. The brilliance of each mouthful is exaggerated and prolonged by the chewiness of the pancake, which acts as a support vehicle for the butter-sugar-lemon cocktail that's stealing the show.

All in all, and pound for pound, I reckon I've just had one of the best 90 minutes of my life. It's my kind of fun. I love the aimless wandering. I love the clueless ambulation. I love losing myself amid the thick and limitless variety of life. I love what it gives me, and what it takes away. I love how it makes me *feel*. In the right frame of mind, it can be such a sensory endeavour, just wandering around, and so emotionally various. It is food for thought and it is filling for your boots. It is how things look and how things sound. It is how things were and how things are. And – if you eschew the crepe and avoid the bun – it needn't cost you an arm and a leg.

Walking back to the ship, in a residential area, I pass a couple of old Swedes having a natter in the street. They give me a wave, and I give them one back. I say 'how are you?' in Swedish, which amuses them greatly. Then I point to the ship in the distance, and try to explain with the eleven Swedish words at my disposal that I'm a passenger upon it. I fail to get my point across, I fear, but they're all smiles in any case, and by the time we're saying our goodbyes we're practically mates. Before I'm out of earshot, the two women begin to discuss what's just happened – in an appreciably different tone. I wouldn't be at all surprised if their outward friendliness had concealed a profound inner suspicion of everything I stood for – and stood in.

'Did you see what that English turnip was wearing, Ulrika?'

'I did, Fanny. I may not be able to see much these days but I could see that he was dressed like an ice-cream.'

No matter what the women made of me, I feel really pleased to have met them. Which I'm sure you'll agree is a wildly disproportionate reaction.

12 July

I'm convinced I can't sing, and so I don't. But I'm also convinced that being convinced about something is rarely a sign that you're right – a hallmark of science is doubt, not conviction – meaning there's a chance I might not be as bad as I think. So I join the ship's choir.

I've missed a couple of sessions, so when I arrive in the piano bar (which is packed), the group is already split into subgroups, according to singing style presumably. I ask a couple of ladies where the 'badly' group is. They ask what I am – bass, tenor, etc. – and I have to tell them that I seriously haven't a clue. This is the first singing environment I've been in since I was at school. Granted, I was in a boyband as a teenager, but they never switched my mic on. It was to save money on batteries, I was told, though I've always had my doubts. I spot Sally, and decide I'll join her group and just hope for the best. 'But we're sopranos, love. Can you sing soprano?' I think of the pizzeria up the road from where I live, and then the television series, and try to deduce from those two cognates what the answer might be. 'Yeah?'

The conductor of the choir – Thiago from Brazil – hands me a sheet of music and sends me downstream towards the tenors. There're three of us, and I'm quite sure that makes us the three tenors, who I've heard of – so that's promising. Before we crack on with the song – 'Love Changes Everything' – we warm up our voices, which involves Thiago playing some scales on the piano and us sitting up straight and doing lots of elaborate yawning. I don't mind this part: it comes quite naturally. I've yawned before, and I don't mind doing it on request.

When Thiago's convinced that no amount of warming up is going to make a blind bit of difference, we make a start on the song. At this stage, it's still not been made clear to me why I've been made a tenor on looks alone, so I keep schtum for a few bars, in order to gauge how the other two are going at it. They seem to be middle of the road, so I give that a shot – and miss. Personally, I reckon tenor is too high, but persevere in any case. After all, I'm hardly belting it out. And even if I was, I don't think anyone would notice. There's this to be said for choirs – the weak and apprehensive can take cover behind the others, and then share the spoils. In this sense, joining a choir is a very undaunting introduction to singing. There aren't many other pastimes that allow for such camouflage. Dancing? No chance. If you've got three left feet and as much dynamism as a baked cauliflower, you'll be found wanting within seconds. Football? Ditto. Although you'd still get in my team. Four-hundred-metre relay? There'd be no hiding the fact that it takes you twenty minutes to run a hundred metres, and you'd be swiftly (or slowly in your case) ostracised.

'Sit up,' says Thiago. 'Breathe in,' says Thiago. 'Tenors!' says Thiago. Somehow, in my panic, I attempt all three at once – that is, to sit up, breathe in and start singing at the same time, and very nearly choke while falling off my footstall. This blows my cover: one of the other tenors, a bloke called Damien, who's already lost all patience with me, non-verbally communicates that I should join the fat blokes over there, half of whom are asleep.

On top of all the lovely people like Damien, another good thing about singing in a choir is that there are lots of moments when it's not your turn, especially in rehearsal. Which means you can just enjoy the sound of other people singing, or simply relax. That said, I do get told off by Thiago when I order a cappuccino during our first full run-through.

All things considered, I'm enjoying myself. It's good to get the singing monkey off my back, so to say. And it's good to get some stuff off my chest. The whole experience is cathartic somehow, and energising. I won't use the word joyful, because I'm too awkward and at odds, but I will use the word cheerful, which is not to be sniffed at. I can't say it's been ever so social up to this point – there's a fair scattering of jobsworths about, I'd say – but not all gratification is instant and entire.

At the end of the session, after a few run-throughs that bode ill for the public performance on Friday, Damien asks me to stay behind for a second. In short, he's deeply suspicious about my ability and wants Thiago to ascertain whether I'm worth keeping or not. It's quite a bold intervention, I must say, but I acquiesce nonetheless. Thiago says that he can't really as he needs to be somewhere else, but Damien won't take no for an answer, insists that Thiago puts me through my paces. This small – and wholly unnecessary – bit of drama has caught the attention of a soprano called Angelica, who I reckon is a bit put out by what Damien's up to. Maybe he's plotted against newbies before. Given little choice, Thiago gets me to sing the first few lines of the song unaccompanied. As I do so, Damien looks confirmed in his opinion while Angelica appears quietly optimistic. I'm only doing one thing, but it's producing two very different results. It's suggesting to Angelica that with a bit of practice and encouragement I'll be fine to perform on Friday, and it's suggesting to Damien that my vocal folds aren't worth the name and that for the greater good I ought to be expelled. As it stands, it's a stalemate. We all look at Thiago. He closes his eyes, slowly shakes his head, and sighs. 'Ben,' he says. 'Would you be prepared to sing *very* quietly?'

13 July

Skagen, Denmark. Because storms are forecast, instead of venturing out alone on foot, I hop on one of the organised tours. If it's going to chuck it down, I'd rather be in some sort of container. The tour only lasts a couple of hours or so, but in that time we see and learn a fair bit. We see the low yellow buildings of Skagen, with their terracotta tiled roofs. We see the sandy peninsula which marks the meeting point of the Baltic and North Seas. We see scores of fishing boats heading out to Iceland and Norway for herring and cod, and twice as many cargo ships anchored at bay, waiting for work.

The best bit of the tour, if you're asking, is the unadulterated fun of running up a vast sand dune, and then down the other side, and then turning around to see Derek, of all people, at the summit. He'd been warned by Svend (our guide) not to even attempt climbing the dune, certainly not all the way to the top. And yet here is, or there he is, at the peak, waving, looking like a rickety combination of Dudley Moore and Lawrence of Arabia. And now here he is, or there he is, sort of wading down this side of the dune. And now there he is on his arse, having stacked it. When I get to him, he's totally unharmed. I ask him what he was thinking. 'Not much to be fair. Which might have been the issue.'

* * *

Dinner is nice. It's been labelled a 'gala' dinner, meaning everyone has dressed up. Even Derek has got a tuxedo and bowtie on. I'm not dressed up because I didn't bring anything to dress up into. I make sure to ask the others, before I sit down, if it's alright for me to do so, on account of my appearance and so on. Derek says sure, but so long as I face the other way. Cheeky git.

Full crowd tonight. So there's Derek and Alasdair, both looking like the grandfather of James Bond, if you can imagine such a figure. There's Sarah, who does wish I'd at least packed a suit. There's Michael, who's mentioning his ex-wife much less at dinner these days, and especially since Sarah first dragged him up onto the dancefloor. And there's Sally, of course, who's currently inspecting her first course distrustfully.

Sometimes you're not in the mood to have someone relatively strange on either side of you during a meal, and a serviette placed on your lap, and five courses followed by coffee. Sometimes you're in the mood to sit alone, and watch the sea, and just have some pasta and spill some on your trousers. But tonight I'm in the mood. It's because we're approaching the end, I suppose (the sense of an ending will do wonders for something's appeal). And it's also because we're much more comfortable with each other now. No one stands on ceremony these days. Instead, they lean across the table and say, 'Now who's going to top me up because I've run out of merlot?'

It's nice talking with all of them, but it's nicest talking to Derek. First about his tumble this afternoon – a few of us essentially had to pull him back up the dune by his arms, as if he were a bluefin tuna – and then about what's in his diary for next week, and then finally, though not for the first time, about his grandson, who he's been estranged from since all that business with his daughter and the three-bed semi.

Derek's telling me about his grandson's first mountain bike, which Derek got for him when the lad was five or six. He's telling me about the look of ecstasy on his grandson's face when Derek rode the bike up the garden path and told him it was his. He's telling me about going to every single one of his grandson's races for years, and about watching him climb the rankings before finally becoming a regional champion at the age of fifteen. And he's telling me how he hasn't spoken to the kid for five years. He still follows his progress though. He uses the internet at the library to keep up with the results. And he goes to watch him compete whenever the race is within 100 miles of Plymouth. Always keeps his distance. Doesn't want to ruffle any feathers. When Derek shares with me this last detail, about going to the races but keeping his distance, it breaks my heart a little bit, if I'm honest. The thought of him proudly watching his grandson, but not being allowed to talk to him, to say hello, to say well done.

Our conversation comes to an end when the Baked Alaska parade begins, which basically involves a large slab of ice cream baked in meringue being given a tour of the dining room. It's a cruise tradition, and everyone is loving it. Passengers are clapping and waving their serviettes in the air, all in honour of a dessert. And they're playing that song again, 'Enjoy Yourself (It's Later Than You Think)'. At least it feels more appropriate this evening: disembarkation is nigh. Looking around the room, I wonder which of the new friendships will sustain, and which of the seeds planted on board (swing dancing, ice sculpting) will flourish in the real world. My guess is that most will fall by the wayside. But there's no shame in that. What matters is that they happened at all.

After dinner, I pop in the Purple Turtle for a cheeky digestif. There's a 'gameshow' going on, as there is most evenings around about this time. The gameshow is called Mini Me, and involves children around the age of five or six answering questions about their parents, and then the parents having to guess what answers their children gave. The first kid – Terrence, if you'll credit that – doesn't seem to know his dad at all. When he's asked what his dad's job is, he just has a wild guess and says 'farmer'. (It turns out he's an accountant.) The other kid, on the other hand, knows more than perhaps she ought to. When asked who her mum has a crush on, she gives her supporters a quick glance (her dad, nan and brother are all sitting nearby), then dips her face into the microphone and says, 'Alan next door.' There it is again: a little knowledge is a dangerous thing.

14 July

After breakfast I head off to the final choir rehearsal, which goes smoothly enough, and then onwards to the ship's main atrium, for our first and only performance. I have a little chat with some of the basses as we wait for Thiago to sort out a technical issue. It turns out they're all in choirs back home. One joined to get over the loss of his wife. One joined to get away from his wife. And one's been at it since he was in nappies and has just never bothered to stop. There's more than one reason for doing something, I guess.

By now the atrium – known as Centre Court – is packed to the rafters. Thiago arranges us on the main staircase, the better to be marvelled at/pummelled with tomatoes. I try to hide away but Thiago puts me in the centre. Maybe I've got a voice after all. 'You'll be less obvious here, Ben. Acoustically I mean.'

No sooner have I spotted certain familiar faces in the audience – Helen the cartoonist, the girl who spends all her time at the back of deck ten looking for dolphins – than the performance is over. It truly whizzes by. Maybe Thiago was playing really fast on the piano to get it over with. Or maybe time speeds up when you're having your moment in the sun. Either way, I get an appreciable buzz from the performance, despite hardly contributing to it. I get a few of the words wrong – singing 'glove' instead of 'love' on one occasion, having spotted a nice pair on a lady in the front row – and there's an awkward moment when I come in on an instrumental section, though nobody seems to notice.

When we finish, the crowd are certainly appreciative, which can be looked at one of two ways. Several people were so taken by our performance, that they even started filming it, which *must* mean it was good. I feel a bit undeserving at the end, a bit of an imposter. But not sufficiently to temper the swelling of warmth and pride I experience when the crowd start calling for an encore. It's a feeling I could get used to. And it's a feeling I could get used to helping others get used to. By being supportive. By expressing respect and appreciation. By giving them a standing ovation when they've hardly done anything at all. That sort of thing. You know what? I might make it a resolution. To make others feel warm and proud whenever – and however – possible. What harm can it do?[39]

* * *

The rest of my final day at sea is fairly uneventful. I do a bit of packing, nip to the gym to see if I can't shake off some of the timber I've put on this past fortnight, have a quiet dinner alone at the back of the boat, and then head down for the show in the Palladium, which is a medley of songs from West End musicals. The songs from *The Lion King* are my favourite. When Thiago, playing Simba, advances on all fours to the edge of a promontory and sings the lines, 'There's more to see than can ever be seen /

---

[39] Like the majority of resolutions, this one lasted two days.

More to do than can ever be done', it's the first time in my life I've been able to strongly identify with a lion.

A cruise has plenty of strings to its bow. For a start, there's the simple magic of living on something that has a rudder. There's the blessed disengagement from the 'real world' that a cruise facilitates, especially if you turn down the ship's internet package. There's the array of optional diversions, such as fruit carving, oil painting and lectures on marine biology. There's the endless opportunity to natter with people from all walks of life. There are the miscellaneous pleasures that a cruise will routinely throw up, like the sight of a woman on a sun lounger reading a newspaper article with the headline 'Sister-in-law Banned From Axe-Throwing Workshop'. And on top of all those strings are the ports of call, the itinerary itself, which promise all manner of curios, and any number of delights. A cruise will broaden you in more ways than one, of that I am sure.

* * *

I go up to the Observatory for a final nightcap. As per my routine, I sit alone at a high table on the edge of things. It surprises me, for a split second, just how pleased I am to see Derek limp in. Definitely a kindred spirit, is Derek. The independent streak, the rebellious streak, the adventurous streak, the scruffy streak, the friendly streak. He's basically me in 50 years. Though, having said that, when it comes to our haircuts and dancing, a feather would already tip the scales.

Lots of people are up on the dancefloor. Michael and Sarah are up there of course, the former as determined as ever, the latter as dashing. Margaret the midwife is up there, and so is Angelica from the choir. Even Derek's got up to throw some shapes, which is good going considering he's 86 and all his bones are second-hand. And here's Putu from Bali proposing another nightcap. And there's Cecilia from Peru, trying to make sense of something Ron's saying. And there's Vladimir from Ukraine, leaning against the glass of a window, taking a moment to consider all that is going by. And there's Thomas from Tranmere behind the decks, switching smoothly between Iggy Pop's 'Lust for Life' and 'Standing in the Shadow of Love' by the Four Tops, as if there were nothing between them.

Bonds form more quickly at sea. You're a massive family by the end: in the sense that there's some you'd like to chuck overboard, but many more you'd put in a lifeboat ahead of yourself. And you know what, it moves me. Thinking about it in those terms. Because it's the people in the end. They're the bulk of it for me. The lion's share. Yes, the sailing is great, and the ports of call are interesting, and the diversions are diverting, but just imagine doing this whole thing alone in silence with no bugger on the ship or in the ports. People make it matter. They make places matter, by lending them sense and purpose and depth and vitality. They elevate all experience to another level, from where it stands a chance of making a deep and lasting impression. Though I confess to having second thoughts about my impromptu eulogy to people in general when I turn around and spot a youngish bloke – amid all this – crouched over a laptop sending emails. Tosser.

Derek sits next to me.

'Alright, Derek.'

'Alright, Ben.'

'No surprise to see Michael and Sarah up there putting in a shift.'

'She won't sit down, that one. And he won't sit down because she won't sit down. Have you noticed how he dances?'

'How do you mean?'

'He's got a very economic style. It looks like he's dancing but he's almost standing still. He could go on for weeks like that. And he's going to have to 'n' all, if he plans to wear Sarah down.'

'Have you had any luck?'

'In what sense?'

'With the ladies.'

'They're all widows, Ben.'

'Not your type?'

'They're all nice, don't get me wrong.'

'But?'

'But they all want to talk about their dead husbands.'

'I see.'

'Which isn't exactly my specialist subject.'

'Fair enough.'

'What did you get up to after dinner?'

'I went and had a look at the show. Did you see it?'

'No, I was listening to those Russian girls. In that lounge – you know the one. I've never really listened to that sort of music – classical stuff. But I tell you what, it's not bad.'

'Yeah?'

'I reckon it might catch on.'

15 July

Disembarkation is a doddle. I wish it took longer, to be honest. I quite enjoy just milling about, catching up with a few people, watching everyone lined up and raring to go home. Walking to the train station, the way is lined with low-hanging blackberries. I hadn't noticed them before.

15

The spurious privilege of options

Wherein the author pulls up some spuds, is introduced to Turner and enjoys the spectacle of a small boy having a meltdown.

18 July

Community gardening. The first time I was in Ruskin Park (South London) was during the winter lockdown of 2020. I was living a few miles away and used to go on long walks nowhere in particular (but towards the supermarket if anyone asked). One thing I liked about the park was its association with John Ruskin – the eminent Victorian aesthete who encouraged people to pay more attention to the world. Another thing I liked about the park was its community garden. Like much of the world, it was then dormant. I've been meaning to return ever since, to lend a hand at one of the 'edible gardening' sessions that are held on Saturdays. As far as I'm aware, the idea is that you rock up, get your hands dirty, nibble speculatively as you go along, and then take home some spuds.

The weather is exceptional. When I reach the park, the intensity of the sun is alien. A paddling pool, deep to the knee, is carnivalesque. Parents and guardians (some more watchful than others) linger on the grassy surrounds of the pool, chewing the fat, talking shop, changing bottoms. In the background, against unbroken blue, are a clump of young skyscrapers, their roots significant, their fruits unknown.

At the threshold of the garden, I hesitate. Why? Well, it's fair to say I wasn't born with green fingers. They don't run in the family. As recently as two years ago, I would have struggled to identify a single type of tree. I could pick out a rose. I could point to a daffodil. But beyond that I was clueless. Then I moved in with an 85-year-old widow called Winnie Carter. Winnie loved her garden, deeply so, and had an uncanny habit of remembering that something desperately needed pruning just as I was going out the door. So it was that, over the next year, a horticultural education of sorts fell upon me, one that was boosted every Friday evening by Monty Don, the BBC's primetime composter. My education wasn't exhaustive. It wasn't complete. (What education is?) If anything it made me more ignorant, by revealing how much more there was to learn.

When I think of Winnie Carter's garden, I think of: Japanese knotweed; the ash tree with the magpie nest; the mimosa and cherry trees; the roses and tulips; the acanthus I mistook for lettuce, and the blue tits I mistook for goldfinches; the wisteria, the bay leaves, the kinky hosepipe. Perhaps the key thing I learned from Winnie about gardens is how much they can mean to someone. After that long winter lockdown, and with the arrival of spring, we went to Derby for the weekend. A city break. She couldn't stand it – but somehow enjoyed not being able to stand it. 'The good thing about going somewhere,' she said, when we got home, standing on the patio surveying her plot, 'is that you get to come back.' About a week later she fell in her garden, trying to deal with some weeds. Broke a hip and her pelvis and hasn't been herself since. She should have got me to do it. I should have offered.

The community garden in Ruskin Park is about an acre, but I'm no judge. Could be two, could be a quarter. I'm shown around by Sandy, a senior volunteer.

'That's a shed,' says Sandy.

'With you so far. And who's that in it?'

'That's Justin. He's been here from the start.'

'You make it sound like a cult.'

'Over here you've got the berries – raspberries, gooseberries, some blackcurrants. There's a lot of bramble getting in the way, so if you fancy having a go at that, be my guest.'

'Sure.'

'And here we've got the veggies.'

'Right.'

'We've got about ten beds.'

'In case the volunteers get tired?'

'What?'

'Just kidding. I'm not as naïve as that. For a long time I couldn't tell a radish from a fig tree, but then I moved—'

'These are sweet peas. And – as you can see – they're getting bothered by the bindweed. You could have a go managing that, perhaps.'

'Bit of a pest, is it?'

'It is.'

'Despite these lovely flowers?'

'Despite them. You can't be an aesthete around here. It's not that type of garden. It's a useful garden. Not a pretty one.'

'Ruskin would turn in his grave.'

'Ruskin was nuttier than a fruit cake.'

'Is a fruit cake nutty?'

'Yes.'

'The only thing I know about Ruskin is that he implored people to pay attention and appreciate—'

'When he discovered his wife had pubic hair, he was so perturbed he divorced her the next day.'

'Decisive.'

'She went off with Millais.'

'The painter?'

'No, the decorator.'

'Got you.'

'Here's something worth knowing: everything that's a fruit was once a flower.'

'Is that right?'

'These flowers will become apples. And look at these cour-gettes. Aren't they gorgeous?'

'Sure are.'

'Know what's interesting about courgettes?'

'Nope.'

'The female flowers *stay* as flowers while the male flowers stop being flowers and turn into slightly bitter tubes.'

'What are you getting at, Sandy?'

'Oh, nothing.'

'Well I'll have you know that female octopuses, little flowers that they are, *eat* the male octopuses after the latter have delivered a sperm packet via one of their eight tentacles.'

'Shall we move on?'

'Let's.'

All things considered, the garden is a credit to the park and the local community, and hats off to those volunteers who devote a few hours each week to its upkeep and flourishing. Their efforts don't go unrewarded, I'm pleased to say: they get some beans out of the deal, and some berries, and some veg. And on top of the edible rewards, there's a sense of purpose to be found, and connections to be made (with nature, with others), and some exercise to be had, and an education to be gained (a significant one if you start as thick as me). All things considered, it's not a bad place to spend some time.

Sandy sets me a task: to grab a fork from the shed and then dig out a row of potatoes. The potatoes harvest three times a year, I'm told, and this is the youngest crop – which is why they look like 'new' potatoes, I suppose. I try my best for a few minutes but eventually lay down my tool and call over to Sandy.

'Hey, Sandy!'

'What?'

'Have you not got anything larger than a fork?'

'What?'

'Have you not got anything larger than a fork?'

Sandy stops what she's doing, comes over, looks down on me. She shakes her head. 'Not that fork, you—Justin! Bring us a pitchfork would you?'

Of course I knew that Sandy meant a pitchfork when she pointed me towards the shed, but I thought it might raise a smile (if not a spud) if I went with the domestic version and then bemoaned its lack of utility. And it did bring a smile to Sandy's face, which was nice to see, because by her own admission she hasn't been in the best of moods of late. I ask her why she bothers.

'With the garden, you mean?'

'Yeah.'

'It's nice to have something to look after, for a start. And it makes absolute sense – that's another reason. And you also never know who's going to walk through those gates.'

'No?'

'Uh-uh.'

'Who are you hoping for then?'

'Never you mind.'

'Ed Miliband or something?'

She looks at me oddly – like the Finnish guy did in the sauna that time – then changes the subject. 'This place has come on massively the past few years. The pandemic was a spanner in the works, but, you know, we carry on. We've just got some funding to run weekly gardening sessions for people experiencing poor mental health.'

'That's good.'

'There's just something about gardening that's fantastic for the psyche. Or the soul, as my mother would call it. And when it's a communal garden – well, there's the social side as well. Of course, the social side of it doesn't always work out. Now and again people like you turn up.'

'And you're tempted to run for the hills?'

'Exactly. Are you going to turn that soil or just look at it?'

After an hour or so, everyone breaks for tea. I sit with a couple of international students doing master's degrees nearby. One is studying Global Mental Health, and the other Psychosis. A surprisingly cheerful pair considering. When I ask them what they get out of the gardening, they answer at the same time, with one saying food and the other saying salvation. At this point, Sandy comes round with our takeaways: a bag of snow peas and new potatoes. Nice.

On my way out of the park, I notice a bench. It's glistening and olive-green (albeit with patches of historic bird shit), and it bears a quote of Ruskin. The quote says: 'Tell me what you like and I'll tell you what you are.' It's a nice idea: one that I like sharing with the bartender when ordering a pint and a packet of pork scratchings at the pub around the corner.

21 July

I'm at the Tate Britain, about to be shown some Turner paintings by Sally, who as well as being a guide here, is a fellow volunteer at the library. We did a shift together once and she mentioned that she was in the habit of showing people paintings every other Sunday and invited me to partake. So here I am, ready to be shown, because if someone offers you something and you like the sound of it, and it can be slotted in the diary without ado and won't cost ever so much or require vast sums of energy or more than twenty minutes on the tube – then I say go for it! (Try fitting that motivational sentiment onto a bumper sticker.)

Anyway. Back to the main foyer of the gallery, where Sally has just finished making some introductory remarks about the questionable manner in which the gallery's founder, Sir Henry Tate, made his money (it involved a large number of indentured Asians harvesting sugar in Guyana), and is now leading us through to the Clore Gallery, where the Turners are gathered.

We start with a self-portrait, which Sally says was painted just after the artist had been made an associate of the Royal Academy aged 24, and needn't detain us much, not least because it's on the twenty pound note. The next painting Sally shows us is what you might call – inaccurately – a garden portrait. The garden belongs to the Hesperides (or nymphs of the evening), and to be candid I'm surprised the neighbours haven't complained yet, for there's quite a bit of drama unfolding. The painting's full name is 'The Goddess of Discord Choosing the Apple of Contention in the Garden of the Hesperides', which I'm sure you'll agree hasn't the advantage of being snappy.

Paintings – or certain paintings – might be likened to complicated dramas that have been condensed to one shot, to one frame. It's true of the contentious apple painting, and it's also true of 'The Decline of the Carthaginian Empire', which Sally has turned our attention to. The painting depicts, at first glance, quite a pleasant occasion: a harbour setting, a nice sunset – I mean, it could be Aperitivo hour. But on closer inspection (and with a little coaxing from Sally) it becomes clear that, far from some holiday snapshot, this is an episode of war. In short, the Carthaginians have been going at it with the Romans, and now they're throwing in the towel big time. The painting captures the last throes of the conflict: Rome has won, and the Carthaginian

Empire has fallen. The work was produced in 1817, explains Sally, just after the Battle of Waterloo and the fall of the French Empire. It is not unreasonable, therefore, to feel that Turner wanted the viewer to see in the painting a lesson, a warning, a timeless and universal truth – that all that goes up must come down. Sally loves – absolutely loves – how this sense of timelessness is hinted at by the architecture in the painting, which ranges in style and vintage across centuries. Architecturally, the painting is of all times, all eras. And thus, runs the implication, so are its ideas, its action. So pay heed, says Sally. Don't be building no empire.

I came here alone but the experience is proving connective and oddly fraternal. I'm being acquainted with characters and stories from the past. I'm being *introduced*, if you will. I'm being invited to *attend* – not a party or a gathering, but rather certain historical dramas, and their immanent ideas. When Sally talks about the paintings, I feel like I'm being let in on something; like I'm being told *in confidence* what's going on in the wings, behind the scenes, in the shadows. As a result, the paintings begin to move, to come to life – and provide a sort of company thereby. Yes, I'm here with others, but they're not the reason the experience feels social. The reason the experience feels social is the paintings, and their stories, and their side-stories, which, once told, succeed in elevating the images, and edifying them, and somehow making them more than the sum of their parts, more than the sum of their strokes and pigment.

A tour of this kind, in the right hands, does wonders for even the Old Masters. It can bring art to life, and you with it. It can flesh out a painting's hints, and give voice to its quieter elements. Perhaps somebody less novice and unknowing than myself would object to some of the insights put forward, would cringe at some of the criticism, would take exception to Sally's take on Turner – but there you have one of the small delights of being green, of being fresh, of being impressionable: the lack of cynicism. Cynicism has its virtues (certain societal strides have depended on it), but it can also be a lovely thing to lack. We'll each gain a sizable whack of cynicism over the course of our lives, so let us savour the random patches of wonder, of naivety, of not having a clue, that life throws at us (or we throw ourselves at).

Another timeless truth (maybe) is that all things that start must come to an end. When our time is up, and Sally asks for feedback, I tell her that I enjoyed the tour's scale and extent as much as anything else. Just as a menu of food can sometimes be stressful to behold, so too can galleries, with their entire oeuvres and entire epochs and their sheer embarrassment (and perplexment) of riches. Sometimes, when there's a clear and present danger of such perplexment, it's nice to be led by the hand through a wealth of temptations and introduced to just a few lovely things. Despite a tour of this type involving a loss of autonomy and freedom (which are characteristics often deemed crucial and integral to fun), on this occasion I am happy to make the sacrifice. It might appear paradoxical, but in certain situations (i.e. ones we have voluntarily entered into), having little or no choice can be liberating; it can free a person from the spurious privilege of options and decision-making. What's more, the power of a sample isn't, in my view, inevitably diminished by the fact of its partialness. Just as a few tiny lines can stir the reader in a greater fashion than a hundred pages, and a moment can have more weight than a lifetime, so a glance can have more power than a hundred hours of staring. That is to say: sometimes the smallest feasts are the richest. Sometimes a few paintings will do.

23 July

Bench. A boy, barely larger than a watermelon, is beside himself, is crying his eyes out, is plainly distressed to a fantastic degree, while wearing a jumper that says 'Life Is A Picnic'. When his mum tells him to calm down, the boy shouts, 'You calm down!' After a few more tears, they walk off holding hands.

16

An unfiltered version of everything you are

Wherein the author seeks transcendence on the dancefloor, discusses a Danish novel, consents to the addition of wheels, finds himself in range of Kate Middleton and ends up on his arse.

24 July

Against my better judgment, I go Ecstatic Dancing. According to the website, the three-hour session promises connection, authenticity and, yep, ecstasy. On the plus side (ha!), it also promises there'll be no formal steps or routines to learn – you just go for it, just express yourself, just unleash an unfiltered version of everything you are via the medium of dance.

It's fair to say that I'm hardly champing at the bit. Not the least of my concerns is that, when push comes to shove, I won't have anything to express; that the unfiltered version of everything I am will resemble a man standing awkwardly in the corner watching other people flourish. If I struggle to dance to Rod Stewart after six pints and among kindred spirits at weddings, what chance do I have sober, to something instrumental, among pseudo-Buddhists in East London? Dutch courage is out of the question: this is a strictly zero drugs and alcohol occasion (not unreasonable given that it kicks off at half ten in the morning).

When I arrive at the community centre, the first person I meet introduces himself as a 'vulnerability co-ordinator'. Aidan says he'll be on hand when my emotions spill over. He hands me a business card in case I need ongoing help. The name of his counselling outfit is 'Plight Club'. It even has a clothing range. Yikes.

Aidan asks me to keep my top on at all times, even in the throes of ludic delirium, then directs me to the dancefloor, where there are already a few people expressing themselves in uncertain terms. They're on the deck, connecting with the floorboards, writhing and twisting in a way that is sure to please the caretaker.[40] I stand on the edge, holding my bottle of water,

---

[40] Because they're buffing the floorboards, if that's not clear.

essentially in my P.E. kit. I feel rejuvenated, but not in a good way. I want my mum, and I want to express myself by running away.

There are about 50 of us in total. On my right is a chap wearing sufficient breathable linen to sail a ship to Zanzibar, while on my left is someone who can't be said to be wearing much at all. Sure, they haven't taken their top off, but they might as well for all the good it's doing. Oddly – or odder still – there's also a man wearing a three-piece suit and a bowler hat.

One of the organisers of the session enters the hall. He's a young man with the look and manner of someone who started a degree in Geography before discovering mind-altering substances and deferring indefinitely in order to travel South America. He asks us to make a circle and join hands, should we be happy to do so. I'm not happy to do so, but do so anyway. C'est la vie.

Rufus then leads a warmup – which actually involves chilling us out. I guess you'd call it a directed meditation. When I'm asked to close my eyes, I have no objections whatsoever; but when I'm asked to *embody my ears*, I'm tempted to walk out and embody a pint of lager somewhere. At this point in the session, my level of scepticism is hostile. When Rufus asks for 'a big communal groan on the next exhale', I take the opportunity to say, under the cover of 50 people making faintly bovine noises, 'What a load of absolute bollocks.'

When the DJ-shaman enters and begins casting his spell (starting with a stretch of ambient woodwind), most of the group fall under it without resistance or ado. This lot don't need per-suading that the shaman's method is sound, that his ceremony is good.

I do need persuading, however, which is why I remain on the periphery stretching my hamstrings. When my hamstrings are more stretched than any local council budget, I do a series of hip rotations followed by some squats, only slower than I normally would and with my eyes closed. While everyone else continues to explore the space and themselves using dance as their vehicle, I essentially warm-up for football.

At a bit of a loss, I put all thoughts of movement aside and just focus on the music. It's good. It's *really* good. I like its texture, its beat, its mood. If there was nobody else here, and I could just lie on the floor and throb, I'd be loving this. Just as I'm starting to let go, and my hands are starting to twitch instinctively, something hard collides with my face, and I open my eyes to discover a man cartwheeling in my personal space. The ethereal was beckoning, and now I've got a black eye. *La plus ça change.* (I think.)

I close my eyes again and return to the tempo. Before long, I find that my knees are bent and that I'm moving an outstretched hand from side to side in a sweeping gesture, as if sowing seeds, which could be some kind of subconscious trace of the communal gardening I did recently. Then I raise an arm above my head, and begin to gently rock it back and forth, as if fly fishing, which could be some kind of subconscious trace of the angling I did a few months ago. How curious the subconscious mind is!

By this point I'm unquestionably having fun: in part because of the sowing/fishing, and in part because it's now beyond any doubt that I could do some pretty wacky shit in here and still go utterly unnoticed. Next to what the others are up to, my genteel evocations of pre-industrial labour are pretty vanilla.

I continue to fish in sync with the tempo of the music, which is gradually speeding up. Although I've started to enjoy the licence afforded to me, and to revel in the beautiful peculiarity of the occasion, I'm nowhere near transcending. To be honest, I don't think I've got it in me. Perhaps I'm too incredulous to reach a higher plane, too down-to-earth to soar.

Here's a thought. Those who manage to reach ecstasy at a place like this, turn up needing to do so. What's more, they turn up believing strongly that *they will be able to do so* – by this method, by this music, by this means. Their faith in the method – and the dividend of that method – is to my mind akin to the faith shown by people who step into a church or temple or mosque ready to be visited, to be called, to be healed, to be altered.

Am I yet again scuppering my chances of transcendence by overthinking the matter? Almost certainly. But the reason I'm thinking about the matter is because I've been prompted to do so. It's in the title – Ecstatic Dancing. The epithet is a promise, a goal to be striven for. And as soon as there's a goal, there's self-analysis in relation to that goal. (And as soon as there's self-analysis, there's very seldom fun, alas.)

Signs of analysis are thin elsewhere, mind you. Not everyone's overthinking it, that's for sure. I'd say the majority were currently borderline ecstatic, or doing a great job pretending. The intensity of their emotional experience is plain to see, and obvious to hear. There's galloping and skipping, yodelling and groaning – and barely a jot of self-consciousness in the place (save the bagloads I turned up with, of course).

In case of interest, I've abandoned my fishing manoeuvre and have switched to a sped-up version of a Bollywood dance move I learned at a fundraising event a couple of months ago. The Bollywood move is essentially a version of 'heads, shoulders, knees and toes', and I keep it up for half an hour straight, moving around the space non-stop, making eye contact with anyone that wants it, and sort of humming loudly with the beat.

Despite my tendency to think the fun out of any situation, there's no two ways about it: this is departure, this is escape.

Indeed, I don't think I've thought about my personal inadequacies or the cost of living crisis for nearly an hour. And by the look of it, nor has anyone else. People are jumping, people are reeling, people are grinding – one couple with sufficient gusto to make flour of themselves. (Self-raising, of course.)

When the DJ announces that he's going to take things up a level, and I start to feel like I'm about to buckle under the weight of my own flow, I leave the hall and go and have a cappuccino in the café, where I make some notes about the time I danced like a peasant and got kicked in the face.

31 July

Reading is a mode of transport. It is a means of connection. It is a source of amusement and enrichment. It passes the time, and it does so with quiet, timeless aplomb. (Unless you're reading Wayne Rooney's autobiography, in which case it doesn't.) When reading is turned into a club, the pleasures of reading are combined with the pleasures of being with others. (I can sense some of you walking out of the room at this point, which is fine, because others aren't for everyone – I get it.) When the club is turned into a walking one, the pleasures of reading and the pleasures of being with others are combined with the pleasures of walking – walking in nature, I should add, on Hampstead Heath, which is where the club sets off, on the last Sunday of every month, under the leadership of Emily Rhodes, who is about as literary and erudite as one is allowed to be these days.

The book under discussion this morning is *Childhood* by Tove Ditlevsen, a late Danish author who had a hard time of it growing up. The book is autobiographical, at least somewhat, and it tells the story of Tove's childhood, which the author likens to a long and narrow coffin that can never be escaped – charming. But however bleak the wording, the point is a persuasive one: that we are wedded to how we were brought up, and must live with the consequences of that wedding; that we are the answer to the questions of our youth, regardless of whether that youth was harsh or felicitous or bruising or benign.

Emily rounds us up, sets a topic of discussion, and then leads us into the woods. People instinctively split into pairs or small groups, wherein they begin discussing whether Tove's mother was a psychopath. I fall in with Kasia.

'I'm Kasia.'

'Ben.'

'Nice to meet you. The opening paragraph made me glad I don't have children. You?'

Kasia and I discuss the book for some minutes, then have a quick chat about Poland, and her childhood in the eastern city of Lublin. Just as we're getting into our stride (in both senses), Emily insists that we pause beneath a tree for some general discussion. I can't help fearing that one or two members of the group might not be able to resist offering expansive thought-splurges during said general discussion, but in the event contributions (on the matter of memory and socialism and Copenhagen) are concise and interesting. When I venture to ask a question along the lines of, 'Is it surprising that Tove would rather risk oblivion than embarrassment?', I am reminded of being a tosspot in seminars at university. Nonetheless, I'm enjoying myself, am enjoying this. I've not discussed a book with a group of people for *years*. It's nostalgic. Or rather – it's nice to be reminded of something I love doing, *through the act of doing it*.

Discussion persists. There's agreement that being a woman in 1920s Copenhagen wasn't a piece of cake ('You could argue that the most violent act performed on Tove is not physical but societal', says Alan from Bradford originally); and there's disagreement about whether the author-narrator is arrogant or not. There's also disagreement about whether cyclists should be tolerated on the heath, after one nearly dismembers Emily.

We switch partners, walk and talk for another twenty minutes, then pause in a meadow, where Emily hands out shortbread biscuits and asks us to think about the relationship between Tove and her father. When it becomes clear that Nick from New Hampshire is no longer listening to what I have to say about Tove and her father, I lean back on the grass and watch the seldom clouds slip shyly across the sky, and then Emily standing smartly in front of a scrum of trees, whose ample green liveries are dancing and shimmering in the breeze. (Forgive me. I'm getting carried away. This is what happens when a book casts a spell – you start to think and talk in the manner of the book, and before you know it you literally *are* a melancholic eight-year-old Danish shoplifter. For better or worse, reading is impressive in this way. It flirts with us. It coaxes our sense of self. It leads us astray, and sets us apart, and begs us to follow.)

We get back on our feet and pick up the pace – back towards the beginning. The group is fluid now. People drop back to share a thought. Others catch up to make a joke. The mood, as far as I can tell, is good and bright and fair. The gentle exercise helps: it stimulates the brain and wakens the heart. What's more, the enveloping nature quietly encourages ideas and honesty; while the act of walking side by side seems to promote discussion in a way that static, face-to-face talking doesn't.

We linger at the end, reluctant to disband. I join a small group to continue swilling the idea of childhood as a coffin. I recite those lines of Larkin, about your parents fucking you up but not meaning to, and a pair of Marys nod appreciatively despite the bad language. Before we call it a day, a few book tips are swapped. Kasia recommends *Scoop* by Evelyn Waugh, while one of the Marys reckons the latest by Robert Galbraith. (Not exactly woke, this pair.) I suggest a coffee, and perhaps a continuation of the talk, but there's general agreement that getting poked in the eye would be preferable to paying what they charge for a coffee around here.

6 August

Walking home from the library, I go a new way – just for a nose, to be honest. I pass a house bearing a blue plaque, which always get my attention. Turns out the painter Mondrian lived at the address. This information by itself isn't much fun, but the memory it prompts certainly is. I was in an art gallery in St Ives, being given a tour of some of the marquee artworks. Our guide asked us to consider a work by Mondrian (who, it's fair to say, didn't really go in for realism). The guide then asked the group for its thoughts. Everybody was silent until a girl of ten or eleven volunteered that she did something similar in art once and got an F. I laughed then and I laugh now – the latter a trace of the former somehow, an echo. Nice, in any case, that such moments can have a sort of afterlife – or after*lives*, in fact – owing to the simple act of remembrance.

9 August

Call me easily pleased but I've always been satisfied without wheels on my feet. There's something so obviously and deeply counter-intuitive about their addition. But at the same time – and here's a case of the brain wanting to have its cake and eat it too – I've always been totally seduced by images of streamlined Americans blading on a Californian promenade, looking like life's ultimate and sexiest victors. While on top of this seduction is the fact that I'm scheduled to attend a roller disco the weekend after next, and feel that I really ought to learn how to move on wheels before I attempt to dance on them.

'I'm a bit scared,' says Meg, standing outside the London Skate Centre, where we've come to hire some skates.

'That's fair enough.'

'The first time I went ice skating was the only time I went ice skating. My granddad took me. I was really good. A natural. He even used the word exceptional. But then I fell on my face and it turned purple, and I never went back.'

'This is different, Meg.'

'But is it though?'

'Yeah.'

'Really?'

'No, not really, but we're here now. So let's get our skates on, shall we?'

We enter the shop. It contains: a lot of hazardous footwear and loads of photos of the manager in his heyday, when he was a professional figure skater. He kits us out – blades, knee pads, wrist pads. It's quite a bit of gear, which is always a warning sign. Lawn bowls didn't require any of this getup, and nor did bingo.

'Any advice?' I ask the manager.

'Knees bent and don't look down.'

'Which is also true for life.'

'If you say so, sir.'

We carry our blades towards Hyde Park, one of London's largest. We mean to cut our teeth on one of the park's slick walkways. Opposite the park, I notice a blue plaque affixed to a townhouse informing that J. M. Barrie, inventor of Peter Pan, used to live in the building – when he wasn't in the park bending his knees and not looking down, presumably.

For those not in the swim, Peter Pan is the most famous big kid in the world. I like the guy. I'm supportive of his desire to stay youthful and vibrant and full of beans and so on. Protecting one's inner child is important, even if you were objectively unbearable until the age of fourteen.

However, Peter Pan went too far, I fancy. I mean, he needn't have been *that* worried about getting on a bit. It's almost offensive to old age. Someone needs to grab him by the shoulders and explain to him that you can have a right laugh right up until the age of 75 (after which point it becomes physically impossible).

When it comes to fictional characters with age-related issues, I prefer Benjamin Button. To get to the end of your life looking like Brad Pitt at eighteen, but with the wisdom of a centurion? What's not to like about that?

Anyway, into the park. Our first job is getting into the gear. I get a spot of cramp in my midriff trying to yank the boots on – just as I did when I went wakeboarding that time. What is it with the pursuit of fun and cramp? Why do the two tend to come as a pair? Maybe it's my body protesting the change; maybe it's my body expressing its ardent desire to remain loyal to the repertoire of movements it's grown accustomed to. Maybe cramp is a sign to back down, to give up. Or maybe it's the price of admission to a meaningful life.

In any case, it's fair to say I don't fly out of the blocks. Indeed, it's fair to say I struggle to remain upright. For the first five minutes, I don't attempt to go anywhere. Instead, I just try to get used to bending my knees and not looking down. But the thing is, you *want* to look down. It's instinctive. That's where all the trouble lies. That's where you need to iron a few things out. I don't trust my wheels to behave themselves – I need to monitor their movements. And bending your knees doesn't feel right either. It's not a position I associate with motion. I don't walk with my knees bent.

'Are you just going to stand there?' asks Megan sweetly.

'I'm trying not to fall over.'

'They're knee pads, by the way. Not elbow pads. You've put them on wrong.'

'Look, leave me to me, okay? Besides, you can hardly talk. You're still sat on your arse.'

'I want to see how you get on first.'

Not very well is how I get on. Trouble is, I want my rollerblades to behave like shoes, but they won't, because it's not in their nature. It's quickly apparent that if I'm going to get anywhere, I'll need to change my mindset. I need to stop trying to walk, and start trying to roll.

Despite this emotive pep talk, for the next ten minutes I continue to look like a drunkard trying to catch a grasshopper. Such is my performance, I'm not only getting looks from the public but explicit discouragement. One guy pats me on the back (unhelpful) and says 'Give up, mate. You're shit' (also unhelpful).

I'm shit because I'm nervous. And I'm nervous because rollerblading is hard and so is the ground. I need to stop fearing collapse. I need to stop guarding against falling over. I need to *embrace* the risk. I need to do this by suppressing my fear of broken bones, and allowing the wheels on my feet to do what they're destined to, which is to roll. Rollerblading is like plenty of things that are new and weird: the harder you resist, the harder it becomes.

'Ben.'

'What?'

'Being scared just makes disaster more likely.'

'I fucking know that, alright?'

'Well get going then.'

'I'm just having a think, okay?'

When I finally bite the bullet and let the wheels roll, they roll me straight towards, and then into, a silver lime tree (gifted to Hyde Park by Berlin in 1988). Needless to say – and for those who appreciate things in high definition – while moving towards the tree my arms were flailing about all over the place. The sudden burst of movement causes my heart rate to rise to at least 190, a potentially fatal level if sustained. This is clearly a disproportionate response on the part of my heart – I mean, I literally rolled about two metres at 0.8 mph.

Clutching the tree, I notice I'm beneath – albeit some distance from – one of the bedrooms of Kensington Palace, home of the Duke and Duchess of Cambridge. Just my sodding luck that the only time in my life I'm within range of Kate Middleton, I chance to be on wheels clutching a lime tree.

By now, Megan's on her feet. I know because she keeps telling me. She's shuffling happily along like an old woman in slippers. Or a penguin in jean shorts. She's looking down, and her knees aren't bent, and she's emitting a single distended cry of 'whoooooaaaaaahhhhhhhh' in roughly F sharp, but is nevertheless making progress.

In fact, she's definitely making progress. She's picking up speed. She zooms past me unapologetically, buzzing more than anyone's buzzed before, her face lit from behind by pure serotonin. Then, approaching a speed bump, her brio falters and she begins to moan in panic. The speed bump does its job – it reduces Megan's speed. It also causes her to roll backwards, lose her balance, and tip onto her arse. She lands on her coccyx but is claiming to have a head injury.

It's a case of history repeating itself, I'm afraid. The incident on the ice-rink when she was seven and started happy but ended up blue has reared its ugly head, and that ugly head is saying, 'I did warn you, Megan.'

It's sad to behold. Until her fall from grace, she'd been doing wonderfully. For a full minute-and-a-half she was punching above her weight. She was a 'natural'. But then she stacked it and now she's terrified to get back in the saddle, lest the same thing happens again. Life was fun, and then it hurt, and now she wants to go home. Could it be that the best bit of our lives is that blissful window between the removal of stabilisers and our first almighty crash? Could it be that the best bit of our lives is the fleeting bridge that connects innocence and experience? Could it be that the best bit of our lives is roughly five minutes long?

Because I'm yet to fall, I up the ante: I quicken my pace, attempt to change direction, have a go at using the brake. The latter, I quickly discover, is more of a trap than an asset. The last thing you want to do when rollerblading is allow your weight to shift onto your heels. If you do that, the wheels will go one way and you'll go the other. It's what happened to Meg. But the thing with the brake is – to operate it, you have to shift your weight onto your heels. I mean, what kind of a sick joke is that? Your means of slowing down is also your means of *going* down. By seeking salvation, you are also courting disaster.

Nonetheless, I'm having fun. My growing competence, the extra thrill that comes with speed, even the sound of the wheels on the path – it's all a source of pleasure. Make no mistake, the anomaly of having eight wheels underfoot is growing on me. If Kate spotted me now, she wouldn't look twice. She'd be utterly unmoved and indifferent. Which is just how it should be.

I look more than twice at Meg, that's for sure. She makes quite the picture. Her confidence knocked, she looks like Bambi on ice. She keeps getting frustrated and trying to sit down, but can't even manage that. Then she gives up trying to sit down and just stands there, frozen, refusing to continue.

'What's up?'

'I want to take them off but when I try and sit down it feels like I'm going to fall over.'

'I see.'

'And I don't like that people are watching me.'

'Shall we call it a day?'

'I liked it at the beginning. I was happy then.'

'I know, darling.'

'But I don't know how to stop.'

'Would you allow me to demonstrate?'

'Okay.'

I fail to demonstrate. Instead, I skate as well as I can, as fast as I can, for as long as I can, my arms thrusting superbly in sync with my legs like pistons. I reach the end of the path, turn, come back towards Meg, absolutely (or relatively) flying.

She's filming me. She looks proud. This might be the first physical thing I've ever done that's made her happy. I glide nonchalantly towards her, wave to the camera, stand up straight, take in the sun, the moment, the resplendent complexity of life – and then successfully demonstrate the art of hubris by attempting to brake and somehow finding myself briefly horizontal and in mid-air before ending up less briefly on my backside, having landed heavily and without nonchalance on my hip.

Megan's a good 30 metres away, but I can nonetheless hear the distinct sound of her pissing herself. Looking at her, you'd be forgiven for thinking that when it comes to acute merriment, very few things top watching a loved one fall over.

17

I almost pull a neck muscle trying to seem happy

Wherein the author gets out his binoculars, jumps off a cliff, plays his part in a farcical reworking of Cinderella and considers the complexity of fun.

13 August

Over the past months, I've got no closer to defining fun, but I do feel better placed to discuss its complexity. On top of being wildly subjective, fun is also fickle. While today it's one thing to you and another to me, tomorrow there's a fair chance the whole thing will turn around and it will be to you what it was to me, and to me what it was to you. The upshot? Fun is hard to prescribe and hard to plan, because it can't be trusted to turn up. You can put it in the diary, for next Thursday or whenever, but to do so would be a bit like scheduling HAPPINESS or JOY or PRIDE for 17 September 2026. I'm not saying that planned things can't be fun, because they can, and I'm not saying putting Scrabble or parkour or judo in the diary is a bad idea, because it's not. Being intentional and forward-thinking can definitely do wonders for your fun life. I'm just saying don't bank on fun showing up, because it's flaky as hell.

If we accept that fun is hard to pin down and hard to rely on – then what? Where do we go from there? Do we just accept that there's nothing that can be done and hope for the best? No. We don't. And the reason we don't is because although fun is prone to arriving unannounced via the back door, *you can be better at having a back door.* As far as self-development mantras go, this has to be one of the worst ever to be articulated or committed to print. So let me put it another way: it is in your gift to develop your *sense of fun* – that is, your openness to it, your propensity for it, your awareness of it. And by developing your sense of fun, you will necessarily improve your chances of hearing fun knocking gently on your back door. (Forgive all the back-door imagery if, like me, you don't have a back door. The back door is basically a symbol for the portal through which the unexpected and spontaneous arrives. But you knew that.)

So how do we get better at having a back door? How do we sharpen our sense of fun? In truth, I'm not sure, but I do have a hunch. My hunch is that developing one's sense of fun might involve ditching a few things, and taking up some others; that it might involve a certain amount of overhaul. You might want to tweak some relationships, for a start. You might want to address some dependencies. You might want to think again about spending four hours on your phone every day, or six evenings a week half-cut. You might want to get less distracted and more attentive, less robotic and more spontaneous, less self-regarding and more forward-facing. You might want, once a week perhaps, and just for a few hours, to be deliberately kind. You might want to start talking to people more. You might want to sit down and have a think about all the things you used to love, and all the people you used to love, and ask yourself which are likely to have you back. You might want to join a softball team. You might want to renovate a canal boat. You might want to start writing poetry again. You might want to walk nowhere in particular for half an hour every evening. You might want to make a list of all of the things that make you sad, and just sit with it awhile. You might want to bake some muffins. You might want to escape. You might want to start wearing odd socks, or a bandanna, or a novelty tie. You might want to stop wearing a tie. You might want to stop wearing anything at all.

And you might want to take everything I say with a huge pinch of salt because I'm in no way an authority, on anything, at all. Like Sophocles, the only thing I know is that I haven't got a clue.[41] You might also want to object to all of the above on the grounds that life is too serious for fun. You might want to object

---

[41] Socrates. Not Sophocles. FFS.

on the grounds that life is tough and the idea of giving up even ten minutes to something as spurious and saccharine as *developing a sense of fun* is laughable and indulgent. You might want to object on the grounds that you've got bigger things to worry about. To such objections I might say: a keener sense of fun might actually increase your ability to cope with what's on your plate, rather than hinder it, by making you, if only fractionally, more resilient and judicious and philosophical and hopeful. To such objections I might say that a keen sense of fun should be an element of everyone's arsenal, in their everyday battle with the slings and arrows of life. I might say that no matter how bombarding and stressful life can be, we can help ourselves in small ways. We can make small alterations to how we think and perceive and react. We can tinker with our software. We can reclaim our calm. We can retrieve our zest. We can be better at having a back door – where levity and lightness and jollity and joy might randomly call. And we can also tell people who don't know what they're talking about to mind their own business. We can also do that.

I've come to believe that fun is ultimately a way of seeing things. (In the first instance, anyhow. You will eventually have to get into the kayak or conversation, or onto the pogo stick or dancefloor – you can't just look at the damn things your whole life.) I've come to believe that fun comes down to perspective, that it boils down to attitude, that it is, at the end of the day, about where your head's at. If you suspect your perspective is off, and your attitude isn't what it could be, and your head's nowhere to be seen – then join the club. I am not holier than thou. Not by a long chalk. What I am is at least partly persuaded that we've got some agency over our mindsets, some control over our heads. So maybe schedule a conversation with yours. It might not turn up, but hey, at least you tried. End of rant.

17 August

Improv is short for improvisation, or improvisational theatre. It is a form of drama that is unscripted and usually (though not always) comedic. Formerly a way of training actors, improv is now a recognised artform in its own right. It was massive in Chicago in the 1950s and 60s, and has been spreading its tentacles in a spontaneous fashion ever since.

I have some experience of improv, but only in a domestic setting. Once or twice a year something will come over me – often when washing up – and I'll feel compelled to ad lib nonsensically in a New York accent. It happens to Megan as well sometimes, though she'll always be from Yorkshire. It happened to both of us at the same time once, and it made for an unusual half an hour.

I head down to Leicester Square on the tube, whence it's a short hop to the Arts Theatre, where City Academy run their improv classes. I find the 'golden door' mentioned in the invite, and then hesitate. Because I'm nervous. Because I feel like I felt when I went ecstatic dancing that time. Because my comfort zone is down here, on the street, alone, perving on the urban environment. It's not up there, among strangers with dramatic instincts, straining to improvise.

There are ten of us in the class. Our teacher, Justin (though he could be making that up), invites us to create a circle. Abrupt flashbacks to drama units at university, when, in my first year, I was invited to make a circle about twice a week for what felt like a lifetime (but was actually two terms), after which point – having nailed circle making – I was able to avoid practical modules by focusing on Shakespeare.

When Justin says he's going to lead a meditation, I've got a mindful to leave, but to his credit he keeps it mercifully short.

After warming up our minds, Justin tells us one or two things we might not know. He says that improv got big in the UK following the success of the television show *Whose Line Is It Anyway?* – wherein a bunch of Americans mucked about sans agenda for half an hour – and that the principles of improv are very useful in the workplace, with the likes of Google and Apple employing its techniques to boost morale and foster cohesion. I enjoy trying to imagine the unplanned development of technology in a Scouse accent.

Then we introduce ourselves and explain our motives for coming. I'm Justin and I'm being paid to be here. I'm Nick and I want to be quick on my feet in the workplace. I'm David from Colombia and I want to make friends. I'm Caroline from Eastbourne and I want to be an actor. I'm Danny from Seattle and I gotta let off steam somehow. It's hard to say why exactly, but I absolutely dread this sort of thing. If I had to read out a poem, or a recipe, or improvise a sentence, I'd be fine, I'd feel okay, I wouldn't go to bits. But when the task is to introduce myself, a portion of my brain shuts down, and another portion of it freaks out. Don't know why it just—

'Hello my name is Ben' – Christ, I'm barely audible – 'and I'm here because I want to try new things, and leave my comfort zone, and become quick on my feet in the workplace.' No I don't. No I don't at all. I don't even *have* a workplace. For the love of God, why is it so hard to say who I am?

We start with a game of Simon Says, which (Justin says) is an exercise in *really* listening rather than only *half* listening. I find the game alarming on two fronts: how quick I am to submit to authority (I just shoved a finger up my nose), and how often I get caught out and do things that Simon didn't say.

Next is an exercise designed to loosen our faces, and shake off some inhibition: when Justin says 'ding', we all have to stop bouncing on the spot and pull the biggest, cheesiest, happiest faces of our lives. Then we have to go around the circle showing our big, cheesy, happy faces to everyone else in the group. Outcome: I almost pull a neck muscle trying to seem happy. So it goes.

Then it's a game called Zip, Zap, Boing, or something equally unpalatable. We're in a circle (what is it with circles?) and the idea is to send energy around the circle, and across the circle, and back the other way around the circle, by zipping and zapping and so on. I'm crap at the game. I lose my two lives before anyone else. I trip the circuit each chance I get. The best part of the game is when I'm out of it and only have to stand there and let the energy pass through me. At the end of the game, for the benefit of the group, Justin gives me a pep talk. He says that mistakes are inevitable, both in improv and in life, and that, in this room at least, they should be made with joy rather than shame. He says that trying to be perfect is the perfect way to kill joy and make ourselves feel rubbish. To have fun, he says, you must be prepared to look stupid. The word amateur, he says, has its roots in the Latin for love. You must learn to love your mistakes, he says (before dropping his mic to a round of applause).

Finally, Justin splits the group into three and allocates a fairy tale to each. My group is asked to improvise a version of *Cinderella*. I'm cast as one of the ugly sisters, and don't do a bad turn if I'm honest. I probably give Cinderella a bit too much grief when I'm getting ready for the ball, and I probably come on a bit strong to Prince Charming when I get there, but all things considered it's not a bad effort. There's a nice moment when Prince Charming, very shy and retiring up to this point, gets fed up with my advances and snaps, 'Ugly Sister Number One. You are doing yourself no favours and need to back down at once.' I pretend to be offended, sashay away, and make a meal of calling myself an Uber.

After the class, a group of us repair to the Porcupine across the street, which turns out to be far more comfortable than its name would suggest. We have a laugh remembering our initial awkwardness, and all the joyful mistakes, and our pathetic attempts to resemble office furniture. People tell their stories, or tiny parts of them anyway: where they grew up, how they came to London, what they think of the city. We find it easier to tell these stories, I feel, because of what we've just done, because of the vulnerability we've already shown. People speak freely and without fear of judgment. (Which isn't to say that people aren't judging; I mean, there's absolutely no way I'm not going to judge Danny from Seattle for putting cream in his tea.) Not once does anyone mention work. Which is interesting when you consider the extent to which work dominates our lives.

20 August

I nip over to the Isle of Wight to see my Auntie Pat and decide – on a whim, because I'm that kind of guy these days, which is to say still without dependents or a proper job – to stick around for a couple of nights to see if I can't sniff out some of the old f-stuff. To this end, I first cycle from Ryde to Cowes, before proceeding south-westward through scorched countryside bordered with busy and buzzing hedgerows to my digs for the night – a hammock in the woods, not far from Yarmouth.

But what a hammock! (State of the art, well-hung.) And what woods! (Ancient, semi-natural.) The helmsman of Camp Wight, an erudite and encyclopaedic eco-warrior called Thomas, is hospitable indeed. First he gets a fire going for me in a recycled washing-machine drum, and then he takes me to the edge of a wheat field to point out certain constellations and tell me roughly 150 things about the natural world. About a dozen of these things pertain to glow worms. At Thomas' insistence, we go on the hunt for a vibrant example. Our hunt takes us all around the campsite, with Thomas leading the way in the dark. After a fruitless lap, and with Thomas growing increasingly piqued that the worms should have the temerity not to appear in public, we finally spot one, exactly where we started, just beside my hammock. So it goes.

21 August

After a tipoff from Thomas, I'm back on the bike and heading south to Freshwater Bay, where I'm due for a session of coasteering, which essentially involves navigating a stretch of coastline come hell or highwater and in a wetsuit.

Our instructors are Izzy, Basil and Louis. Izzy is the most senior of the three, and is the right balance of stern and affable; Louis is the least senior of the three, and is principally a DJ at a bar up the road called The Hut; and Basil is in the middle and has a crush on Benedict Cumberbatch, having taught the actor how to surf earlier in the summer.

After equipping us with buoyancy aids and unmissable helmets, Izzy assembles the group on the beach. We number about a dozen, ranging in age from twelve to 58. After a safety briefing (i.e. pay attention and follow the leader), we enter the water and proceed, by hook or by crook, along the shoreline. Doing so, we clamber over rocks, are washed through natural tunnels, explore prehistoric caves, and swim around ancient headlands. Along the way, we learn about the geological personality of the landmass, about the limpets and anemones, and about the various algae that pattern the cliff face. Coasteering is adventure and education, adrenaline and information, nature and exertion – which, in terms of fun, are sound pairings indeed. I doff my helmet.

After more wading and scrambling and swimming, we come to the final challenge: to climb the cliff face and then jump from a natural platform about 30 feet above sea level. I'm not much of a climber. I've got about as much upper-body strength as an ironing board. But buoyed by adrenaline and the encouragement of Basil, I manage to ascend to the jumping platform (albeit very slowly and without grace).

At the summit, crouched in a small alcove not designed for the purpose, I prepare for my plummet – which essentially involves briefly paying attention to the majestic views of the English Channel and then panicking. Realising that there's only one way out, I leap – somehow managing to tilt on my way down and land square on my arse.

Among other things, I feel a rush of pride and a pang of happiness upon entering the water, the likes of which you're unlikely to get at home with your feet up. I'm no expert, but I'd say that the kind of emotional cocktail I'm enjoying right now is one you have to earn – by deed, by discomfort, by ordeal.

I bob around in the sea on my back, careless of my cuts, mindless of my scrapes. I close my eyes and listen to the distant sound of gulls and children shrieking (in pleasure, one assumes, rather than terror). For five minutes, it's a kind of heaven.[42]

* * *

---

[42] Said bobbing would result in a sunburnt nose. So bear that in mind the next time you think you're in heaven.

I jump back on the saddle, and shoot off once more in pursuit of diversion. I find it in spades at Newtown National nature reserve, which is managed by the National Trust and is about twenty minutes along the coast. I've paid a Geordie called Dave Fairlamb a modest amount of money to show me around for a couple of hours. A compound of Ant, Dec, and one of the hairy bikers, Dave's knowledge and enthusiasm are immediately infectious. As we make our way through the former rotten borough of Newtown (which once had about nineteen MPs for its seven residents), Dave tells me that for a big chunk of his life he was in a heavy metal band, and about as into birds as your average worm. He transitioned from metal to ornithology in his mid-twenties, when head-banging started to suffer from the law of diminishing returns. After holding several posts for the RSPB, Dave moved to the Isle of Wight about three years ago when his partner got a job on the island. He quickly set up Natural Links, whose prevailing concern is to nurture and celebrate our links to the natural world.

Dave is all link by the look of it. As we pass through a meadow, he can't walk a metre before pointing something out: a Glanville fritillary butterfly, the sound of grasshoppers, the spectre of a buzzard, a dashing red squirrel. The Isle of Wight has a ton of the latter, says Dave. I ask if this has anything to do with the greys not being able to afford the ferry crossing, which is famously prohibitive, but Dave's attention has been caught by a curious moth – which is probably for the better.

We reach the salt marshlands. It is a beautiful setting, and one that's made better by the kind of brilliant blue sky I associate with other places, with elsewhere. Dave tells me that only those types of flora that can put up with being under seawater twice a day can flourish here, like sea lavender and samphire. Then he tells me that if I turn my binoculars around, I'll stand a better chance of admiring the Canada Geese. I ask Dave what his favourite bird is.

'I've got two. The fulmar, because it is just utterly beautiful to behold.'

'Fair enough. And the other?'

'The peregrine. Because it shoots down on pigeons at speeds of up to 200 miles per hour and knocks them out cold.'

'Also fair enough. And your least favourite?'

'I don't have one. They're all just doing their thing. But I get a lot of people moaning about sparrowhawks. They say, "Dave, can you do something about the sparrowhawks? They're eating all my blue tits." And I say, "If they didn't eat the blue tits, Carol, before long there'd be blue tits working in the Co-op and driving the buses."'

It's not just the likes of me Dave takes for a walk. It's not just tourists on the lookout for amusement. He also does bird-song sessions with the blind and partially sighted, as well as with local teenagers who are down in the dumps or down on their luck. 'They really take to it,' he says. 'It's unleashing. Nature takes them to a better place. Ah, would you look at that grey mullet!' When I start scanning the sky with my binoculars, I reckon Dave is ready to give up on me.[43]

When we pause for a sandwich, Dave shares with me a few of the things that blow his mind about birds. Not the least of them is when a cuckoo drops its egg in the nest of a reed warbler (which is just something they do apparently) and the cuckoo chick, when it hatches, instinctively mimics the sound of a group of reed warbler chicks, so that the mother reed warbler will fall for the mother cuckoo's scam. 'It's beyond our ken,' says Dave.

---

[43] For the 1 per cent who – like me – were unaware, a grey mullet is a fish.

'And do you know what? I'm glad it is. Because mystery is more pleasing than knowledge. Although that being said, I'm glad I know how to make a good shepherd's pie.'

Although Dave's passion is infectious, his knowledge is not so easily caught, it being the fruit of decades of paying attention. But by rubbing shoulders with others – like Dave for example – bits of their ken stand to fall off and land on you. And you never know, such bits might take root and flower, might grow into something larger and lifelong. I'm not a card-carrying twitcher just yet, but I reckon I've got the makings of one.

'What's that one, Dave?' I say, gesturing to an excitable pied specimen wagging its tail like there's no tomorrow.

'That's a dog, Ben. Shall we call it a day?' [44]

---

[44] Twitcher is not a synonym for birdwatcher, as I thought. Twitchers are an altogether different specimen. In short, they're more bonkers. They get wind of a rare bird having been sighted somewhere, start twitching compulsively with excitement, and then set off to wheresoever the rare bird has been spotted. I was delighted to learn that twitchers have developed their own little language. For example, a twitcher who sets off to see a rare bird but arrives too late, is said to have *dipped out*. As a result of their near miss, the twitcher might rightly feel utterly *gripped off*. My stepdad's mate is a proper twitcher. He once travelled to Egypt during the Arab Spring against the advice of the British Foreign Office to avoid dipping out. He had a few rounds fired over his head when he knowingly trespassed on the grounds of a local magnate on the outskirts of Cairo. When I asked him to sum up the appeal of twitching in a nutshell, he refused to do so, lest it encouraged a flurry of new twitchers, which could result in more traffic en route to Haversham in the event of a willow tit sighting, for example. Hardcore.

18

The sort of person who embraces a sudden downpour

Wherein the author visits his grandmother, invents a Belgian philosopher, promotes the virtues of planning and sits on a bench again.

23 August

I visit my nan. Before I'm even through the door, she's offered me a brace of toasted sandwiches and begun filling me in on the gossip: Grandad's got a man bag; so-and-so's leg is practically falling off; the postman got a puncture; the council don't know their ears from their elbows. That sort of thing.

My auntie drops in while I'm here, which is nice. She says she saw a programme on the telly recently and is now seriously considering selling her house to buy a motorhome and travel the country. Well, you should see the look on my nan's face as my auntie outlines her dream. You'd think Auntie Jo was describing how she planned to marmelise her children and sell the resultant jars on eBay.

'What is it, Mum?' says Jo.

'Oh, nothing.'

'No, come on – what is it?'

'I just don't think it's a very good idea, that's all. Just swanning off like that. Just disappearing in a truck like that.'

'It wouldn't be for a while yet, Mum. Not for five years at least. You probably won't even be ...'

'Probably won't even be alive? Is that it? Well, you're probably right. Which is all the more reason for you to abandon the idea at once. You'd have nobody to contact in an emergency.'

As one can put oneself in harm's way, so can one put oneself in fun's way. How? Well, by visiting your nan for a start. And if you don't have one, consider borrowing someone else's. And I mean that seriously. You can volunteer to drop in on older members of your community for a cup of tea and a natter. I started doing it when I lived in Wimbledon, after my housemate Winnie had moved into a care home. I used to visit a bloke called Rod once a fortnight or so. Rod was a good laugh, despite being a complete misanthrope. According to Rod, the best things about the 21st century so far have been the interview Prince Andrew gave to the BBC about his links to Jeffrey Epstein, and the fact that reproduction rates are going down. For fun, Rod liked to watch old episodes of *Mastermind* and reward himself with a thimble of Grand Marnier every time he got a question right. It wasn't always a laugh visiting Rod, though. He could be quite mercurial. He once blew my head off and told me to leave when I suggested that self-driving vehicles sounded a bit dangerous. Oh, well. You've got to take the rough with the smooth, I suppose.

24 August

Improv. I turn up feeling as stiff and self-conscious as last week, suggesting that such things as inhibition aren't easily got rid of. We start with the most perfunctory meditation I've ever taken part in. We're asked to close our eyes and breathe in. That's it. That's the extent of it. We're not even invited to breathe out. I'm delighted.

For the benefit of Hyacinth, a social worker from Peckham, who missed the first session, Justin quickly recaps what we learned last week. Namely: that structure facilitates spontaneity; that being present is productive; and that failure is joyful (in this context, anyway: I once failed a drugs test at the Slovenian border and can confirm it wasn't joyful).

We skip the 'Happy Face' exercise, and move on to the Zip, Zap game we're all so fond of. It's meant to test our reflexes and attentiveness, but mostly it just tests my patience. It doesn't help that I mess up immediately; doesn't help when the girl to the right of me, to kick things off, zips the energy in my direction and I just look at it and say nothing, as if she were offering me a platter of liver and onions. I'm quick to own my mistake, however.

'I'm sorry, everyone! I'm sorry, I'm sorry. Jeez, what am I like? God, I'm useless. I pre-meditated. That's what I did. I had a zap ready to go and in the event it wasn't called for. And so I froze. Ah, yikes. I've literally messed up immediately. But it's cool, I feel loved, I feel joyful. Shall we go again?'

'If we could, Ben, that would be grand,' says Justin.

After Zip, Zap, there's a game called Bippity, Boppity, Boo. In short, one person enters the middle of a circle, selects someone in the ring of the circle, goes up to that person, then attempts to say 'bippity, boppity, boo' before the other person can say 'boo'. Neat, huh? The person in the middle has some tricks up their sleeve, however – to catch the other person out. They can say a few things other than 'bippity, boppity, boo', with each thing requiring a different response from the person they're confronting. The person in the middle can just say 'boo', in which case the other person mustn't say anything. The person in the middle can start counting elephants, as in 'elephant 1, elephant 2, elephant 3', in which case the other person has to turn into an elephant by pinching their nose and crossing their arms in a way suggestive of a trunk. If they don't achieve this elephantine transformation before the person in the middle has counted to three elephants, they joyfully lose. And the final thing the person in the middle can say is 'James Bond, secret agent, 007, licence to kill', in which case the other person has to pose in a way suggestive of James Bond holding a gun. The highlight of the game – and indeed of my entire experience of improv so far – is when Hyacinth panics and gives James Bond a trunk.

My personal lowlight comes during the next game, when I have a small altercation with Justin. It's a story game, with each

HERE COMES THE FUN

person in the circle contributing one word of the story. Boris. Went. To. The. Asylum. Etc. Basically what happens is I get stitched up by the person before me, and it seems to me that the only way to rescue the sentence in a grammatically and syntactically correct way is to introduce a new person, Jeremy, whose sudden arrival on a moon made of mashed up carrot puts Justin's nose out of joint no end. He stops the game.

'What are you doing, Ben?'

'Hm?'

'Jeremy?'

'Yeah.'

'That's called throwing a bomb.'

'Is it?'

'Improv requires humility. You need to be a team player.'

'I just felt that—'

'We can't have Jeremys turning up out of nowhere. It's not fair.'

'I just felt that the only way to rescue the sentence in terms of its grammar and so on was to interpret the "so" that came before Jeremy as a conjunction rather than an intensifier.'

Justin shakes his head. He can't believe what he's hearing. 'Erm. I need to choose my words carefully, here. Which is ironic, erm. Look, Ben, just don't – just try not to overthink it, okay?'[45]

---

[45] On reflection, I think Justin had a point. I should have just said a word – melon, for example – and not given the slightest toss about such things as sense and meaning and elegance. I'm not delighted to say so, but I do have a habit of overthinking things, and that habit of overthinking things does have a habit of getting in the way of things like merriment. It is curious and tantalising to consider that the 'good life' – pondered for millennia by the greatest minds – might turn out be the one containing as little thought as possible.

We finish the session with a game that I do a bit better in. Two people are given a topic or scenario – they're fishing, for example. One kicks things off by asking a question, and the other has to reply with a question of their own, one that is roughly on topic, rather than a total non-sequitur. For example, 'Have you caught anything? / Do you like popcorn?' would be the end of the road for whoever asked about popcorn. The goal is to stay on stage for as long as possible. The best stretch of dialogue, for my money, is between deadpan Hyacinth and quick-on-his-feet Nick. The scenario is 'traffic jam', and it's fair to say that it's not always obvious how the questions are related. Hyacinth almost cocks up about five times in the space of seven seconds. See if you can spot where.

'It's a nice day,' says Hyacinth. 'Isn't it?'

'Doesn't the traffic bother you?' says Nick.

'Nah. Not really. What traffic?'

'Have you ever seen it this bad?'

'Don't know what you're talking about. What are you talking about?'

'Can't you see the traffic?'

'Do I need to?' (This gets a cheer.)

'Do you need glasses?'

'Are you talking to me?' (Ditto.)

'Are you getting hostile?'

'Maybe the traffic's driving me mad?'

'What traffic?'

'What?'

'Didn't you say there was no traffic?'

'Did I?'

'I'm pretty sure you did, yeah.'

'Was that a question?'

'Oh fuck.'

At which point the pair buckle, everyone starts laughing, Hyacinth is crowned champion, and we all go on our way – with me wondering how I might make Nick and Hyacinth pretending to be in a traffic jam a recurring feature of my lifestyle.

When I get home, I tell Meg how the class went and so on. I'm just running through the details, really, more in a spirit of despair than in an effort to amuse, and yet she's absolutely creasing up. When I do an impression of Hyacinth nearly cocking up five times in seven seconds, she's almost wetting herself, which of course sets me off, and before you know it the pair of us are inexplicably in tears, me at the sight of Megan laughing so much, and Megan at the thought of Hyacinth saying, 'It's a nice day. Isn't it?'

Could it be that improv is Type 2 fun? Could it be that I'm going down to Leicester Square every Wednesday for a couple of hours in order to return with the means of making Megan laugh?

28 August

Bench. A woman sits down next to me. She listens to a voicemail. It's in Polish. When the message is done, I turn and say hello in that tongue. She's Ukrainian, in fact, but understands Polish and has a lot of Polish friends. She works in the fancy off-licence, Bottle Apostle, and is proud to do so. She tells me they hold a free tasting session each Friday, when they open two bottles of something interesting, and have a drink and a chat with whoever pops in. I admit to not really knowing much about wine, which is the lady's cue to set about dismantling my ignorance. The next ten minutes turn out to be the richest and most rewarding of my day. Not just social, not just uplifting, not just a small infusion of optimism into the tyres of my mindset – not only these things, but also informative, also educational. She might be making it all up of course. She might be improvising out of her backside. But I'll give her the benefit of the doubt. And I'll be turning up for the tasting, thank you very much.

It starts to rain. Ordinarily – or previously – I would get up and take shelter somewhere, but not today. Today I just sit and let it rain on me, quietly and stupidly proud of myself for having become the sort of person that embraces a sudden downpour.

No sooner has this self-satisfied train of thought come to an end, than I'm on my feet and dashing to the charity shop, thinking, 'Actually, sod that for a laugh.'

29 August

These days, I write for a living rather than a laugh. Contrary to appearances, my writing isn't – or is rarely – pointless. To inject a bit of whimsy into my craft, therefore, and somewhat inspired by the improv, I've started writing a limerick a day. I chose the limerick form because it's probably the poetic form least likely to test your will to live. I'm on a 42-day stretch. There are days when I give the poem half an hour, and try to make it half-decent, or fractionally meaningful, or satirical or whatever. Example:

> *A philosopher thinking in Ghent*
> *Gave up the bad habit for Lent.*
> *When asked to explain*
> *Their thoughtless refrain*
> *They said, 'I couldn't possibly comment.'*

It's still naff and doesn't scan, and is wanting for many things, but you can see that some effort went in. Which isn't the case on those days when I give the limerick less than a minute and as much thought as I give the former triple jumper Jonathan Edwards, which is to say, not a lot. The latter type of poem is an imperfect example of automatic writing, and therefore an awkward window unto my soul. Example:

> *A toddler residing in Mayo*
> *Used to play the piano*
> *He gave up the damn thing*
> *When his mum became King*
> *And could no longer drive him to lessons.*

If the above is anything to go by (which it probably isn't), my automatic self is prone to giving up; from the west coast of Ireland; and in possession of a parental complex of some kind.

Despite being less than wonderful at it, the practice of writing a limerick each day has nevertheless been fun. It's hard to say with certainty why this is so, but I'd say the combination of absorption, silliness and word-based creativity works a treat somehow. Also satisfying at some level, I fancy, is being reminded of the simple and enduring magic of something coming from nothing; of words arriving from nowhere; of the quietly miraculous appearance of a Belgian philosopher.

I posted a couple of my limericks on Twitter once, foolishly thinking to measure their quality this way, and maybe get a lucrative book deal, but the response was so modest as to be statistically insignificant (i.e. there was no response). Not one of my 184 followers was compelled to press a button indicating approval. Alas – I persist without an audience, which is for the better really. Things done for nothing have a knack of offering most.

By the way, here's today's effort:

> *For some the quintessence of fun*
> *Is parading themselves in the sun*
> *But for others instead*
> *It's the marital bed*
> *And for others still it's breaking the rules unnecessarily*

31 August

Improv. I wasn't in the mood for it, to be frank – but then it changed my mood. Which makes me think that oftentimes you don't have to be in the mood for fun because it will be in the mood for you. Although fun is largely a way of seeing the world, it is also sometimes utterly inconsiderate of your senses, of your predispositions, of your leanings. Sometimes fun ignores your attitude. Sometimes it overrules you and your mood. Sometimes it is just too good to resist. All this is to say that when I turn up to improv this evening I'm feeling fully impervious to gaiety and joy and merriment (even scornful of such things), and yet within five minutes of pretending to be an unbearably vain and self-important celebrity at a press junket, another part of me has been summoned from beneath a pile of pressing concerns and abiding considerations, and I'm feeling, if not on top of the world, then a lot higher up than I was.

Fun does a job on me, but I had to turn up for it to do so. And the reason I turned up was because I had committed myself. On this occasion, that the event had been scheduled was key. Had it not been in the diary, I would have left the library two hours ago and followed my low mood home, where I would have moped around feeling somewhat bothered and bored for a while, before consuming half a bottle of vinegary wine and some television. (Now that I spell it out, I think I might have made the wrong decision coming to improv ...)

Yes, fun is sensibility. Yes, fun is attitudinal. Yes, fun is unreliable and prone to absenteeism. Yes, it's those things, but it's not a law unto itself. It is not so ethereal as to be unmanageable, ungraspable. It's important to recognise that there are some practical steps you can take to get a handle on the stuff. It's important to recognise that, when it comes to fun, you do have agency. It's important to recognise that you can – by design, and through commitment – put yourself in certain places where fun has been known to hang out. And it's important to recognise that you can put yourself in those places – like this rehearsal studio above a bar in Leicester Square, for example – habitually and routinely and repeatedly. Fun might not be reliable, but that's not to say you can't be.

By signing up to something in advance, we are hedging ourselves against future bad moods. At a guess, we might only be in the mood for something like improv about 25 minutes a week. The rest of the time, given the option, and for whatever combination of reasons, we'd likely turn it down. We'd most likely demur and fall back on our go-to uses of disposable time, be those what they may. In those short spells of willingness – in those 25-minute windows – we need to make decisions that will do us good when we're feeling low and sluggish. In those short spells, we need to make single decisions – signing up for an improv course, say – that are actually seven decisions: one for every Wednesday evening going forward.

I'm not saying that *planning* is foolproof. I'm not saying there won't be times when your Swedish lesson backfires, or the idea of your sushi-making class is so intensely off-putting that you opt to take yourself off to Nando's for two-and-a-half hours instead. I'm not saying by making something regular, its effect will be similarly regulated. Not at all. What I am saying is that an informal commitment to something novel and social and light-hearted will prove rewarding and enjoyable far more often than it won't. By gently obligating ourselves to regular instalments of something we've identified as potentially fun, we arm ourselves against the more pedestrian features of our personality.

Anyway. Back to the action. Back to today's session. More than anything else, I enjoy watching a scene between David from Colombia and Caroline from Eastbourne. They've been given a setting (Disneyland), and told to basically freestyle from there. Of the thousands of ways he could have taken it, upon Justin's cry of 'action!' David starts jumping up and down in faux distress and shouting 'Mummy! Mummy! Mummy!', with his fists clenched and his eyes shut tight. What's interesting – or more interesting – is that David's not playing for laughs. He's being totally earnest. When it comes to kicking off scenes in ways that suggest unresolved issues stemming from childhood, David certainly has form, but this performance is his magnum opus. All Caroline can do in the face of David's livid infant is put her hand to her mouth in amused disbelief. All Justin can do, meanwhile, is shout 'cut!', before gently reminding David not to make Caroline's life harder than it needs to be.

David isn't the only one to be brought up short, mind you. I too get nipped in the bud during a scene with Hyacinth, the social worker from Peckham who's about as deadpan as it's possible to be. We're at a tennis match, spectating, and things are going quite well, in that we've established that we're married and are behaving like a team. We're even getting a couple of laughs, for example when Hyacinth remarks how lovely it is to be sitting in the front row about a second after I've pulled out some binoculars. And we get another little laugh when I ask Hyacinth who it is that Venus is playing and she says, 'I can't be sure, but I think it could be Pluto.' Despite our good work, Justin abruptly terminates the scene when I introduce, out of nowhere, a ridiculous reason for being at the tennis – i.e. I've sold the marital home and have put all the money on Pluto winning because I need the windfall to pay for life-saving brain surgery. According to Justin, it was at this point in the scene that he stopped caring, which might tell us more about Justin (i.e. that he's lacking in empathy) than it does about the suitability of my fabrication.

19

It might be helpful to consider life as a pie

Wherein the author goes on the hunt for conclusions, puts fun in its place, wonders if improv should be understood as an awkward branch of psychotherapy and puts a pie in the oven.

4 September

Library. Because they have similar stickers, I accidentally shelve a book about parenting in the paranormal section. Easily done, I imagine, similar stickers or not.

Towards the end of my shift, I go around the shelves reading last lines at random. My favourite is from *The Handmaid's Tale*. 'Any questions?'

My shift finishes at 1 but I stay on until nearly 2, just for the hell of it. Not a bad yardstick of enjoyment, that – how long you stick around after your shift's done. When I worked at Burton Menswear, I was out of the door before my shift had even started, if that's not too confusing an exaggeration.

7 September

I said last week that some of the stuff David from Colombia instinctively comes out with might reveal certain things about who he is, and how he became to be so. Well, I'd say the same is probably true for all of us. One person in the class keeps mentioning frogs, for instance, while another person cannot disguise their contempt and discomfort whenever the idea of romantic love comes up. Over the past weeks, I've become convinced that improv should be understood as a bizarre strand of psychotherapy. Here's something you can do at home with a loved one who you suspect might have deep-seated psycho-logical complications: tell them they're a butcher and you're a customer on the hunt for something a bit different, and then say 'action!' It might precipitate the end of the relationship, it might bring you closer together: in any case, you will learn something. What have I learnt about myself through improv? What has been revealed to me? In what ways has the tip of my tongue been telling? Well, to be honest, based on what I've seen, it would appear that my authentic self is a forgetful bisexual who wants to be famous.

12 September

Bench. I'm about to leave when a friend enters the scene, which is a nice thing to happen. He's across the road, arm in arm with his housemate, Jane. They hooked up through Share and Care, the organisation that matched me with my old landlady Winnie. My mate clocked that I didn't mind the set-up with Winnie, and has given it a go. Good on him.

Jane's a nice enough lady. We've met a few times. Reads a lot, I'm told. A book a day almost. Read one of mine and didn't think much of it. I tried to talk her round, but the lady wasn't for turning. Said she knew a waste of time when she read one. I follow the pair of them up the road and pinch Adam's bum outside the post office. Not exactly PC, but worth it for his reaction – which is to laugh first and turn around second.

Ah, the bench. It will always give you something. It will always bear a fruit. And if it doesn't, if it gives you nothing, if it gives you zilch, if it gives you no audio or aesthetic souvenir – then you can still count yourself fortunate, because it is a rare and precious thing to pass an hour untroubled.

If I had to pick one thing, of all the fun things I've sampled, to take on a desert island, I think it would be sitting on the bench. You might think such a selection absurd, or even dishonest. You might say to me: 'So you'd be content sitting on a bench all your life, would you?'

Of course not. Exclusive and unending bench-sitting would be an unmitigated disaster. Each fun thing has its ideal ration.

For rollerblading, it's once in a blue moon. For ecstatic dancing, it's even less than that. For football, it's roughly once a fortnight. For conversation, it's once or twice a day. And for the bench, for just sitting and taking in the world, or one tiny corner of it, it's three times a week for roughly an hour.

But those hours punch above their weight. Believe it or not, sitting on a bench has many strings to its bow. It is reminiscence. It is novelty. It is conversation. It is curiosity. It is learning. It is beauty. It is familiar. It is strange. It is chance. It is fate. It is the natural world. It is the built environment. It is personal. It is social. It is minor. It is major. It is common. It is rare. It is ongoing. It is frail. It is calm. It is chaos. It is all of the world, and so little at once. It is a cross-section of occurrence. It is those lines of Blake:

> *To see a World in a Grain of Sand*
> *And a Heaven in a Wild Flower*
> *Hold Infinity in the palm of your hand*
> *And Eternity in an hour*

And if nothing else, it is flipping cheap.

14 September

One of the central virtues of improv is that it allows – nay, demands – a direct and comprehensive relegation of the self, and all the manifold concerns and burdens that are inextricable from it. Whereas other pastimes achieve a degree of unselfing almost by accident – fishing, say, or bingo – improv is deliberate in its ambition to get rid of you. It might sound odd, and it might be erroneous to say so, but at its best improv can feel like it's got nothing to do with you, which only makes the sport more attractive and rewarding on a personal level.

A highlight of the final session is when David from Colombia, having learned his lesson about being a furious toddler, casts himself on more than one occasion as a frail pensioner. Another highlight is when we play a game which involves two people improvising around a given scenario – nothing new there – but with the added element of Justin shouting 'new choice!' whenever he wants one of the pair to provide an alternative to their previous answer. When it's my turn, I'm put in a nightclub with deadpan Hyacinth.

'Do you come here often?' I ask.

'What's that you say? Do I come here often? I'm afraid to say that I do.'

'So what's your name?'

'Sally.'

'New choice!'

'Betty.'

'New choice!'

'Nigella.'

'Would you like to dance, Nigella?' I ask.

'Yes, alright then.'

'New choice!'

'No thanks.'

'New choice!'

'I would but I have to go to the toilet.'

'Why's that?'

'To powder my nose.'

'New choice!'

'To urinate.'

'New choice!'

'To cry.'

'Why, what's up?'

'I'm feeling upset.'

'New choice!'

'I lost my job today.'

'New choice!'

'I've got pancreatic cancer.'

'I'd love to be your doctor.'

'Really?'

'New choice!'

'I've got private health insurance, thank you.'

'New choice!'

'I was only kidding when I said I have cancer.'

'That's good.'

'New choice!'

'That's weird.'

'New choice!'

'That's very honest of you.'

'That's interesting because my friends always say that I'm honest. What's your name again?'

'Steve.'

'New choice!'

'Brad.'

'New choice!'

'Ambrose.'

'Would you like to have some fun, Ambrose?'

'Yes.'

'New choice!'

'No.'

'New choice!'

'Fuck it, why not?'

'And cut!'

The above is inarguably jam-packed with utter, nonsensical tosh. And therein lies its value, as far as I'm concerned. It's so alarmingly pointless and goalless and aimless and useless, that it is an excellent corrective to our everyday orientations, which tend to be anything but. By being beside the point, improv gains its significance – as a tonic, a leaven, an elixir. As with fun, improv's apparent lack of purpose belies its important ability to make us feel good, to make us feel alive. I will definitely be coming back. If I remember to sign up before my mood swings.

19 September

In the 1950s, psychologists James Olds and Peter Milner, in a series of ground-breaking experiments involving rats and pleasure, found that some rats would self-stimulate as often as 2,000 times per hour, at the expense of all else, including food and sex. Given the chance, they'd allow pleasure to take over their world. Given the choice, they'd let pleasure ruin them.

Fun can only be but a piece of the puzzle. Its role will only ever be supportive, rather than starring. If you gave fun the main part it would falter before the interval. It would forget its lines. It would draw a blank. It would cause any critics in the front row to stand up and leave. *It wouldn't be able to cope.*

But that much is obvious. It will surprise nobody that trampolining is subject to the law of diminishing returns. That too many cherries might compromise the cake. That you can be on wheels, on holiday, on drugs – and still be utterly miserable. It will surprise nobody that fun is mercurial. That fun is flimsy. That fun is incapable of filling a life, not even if you keep pouring it in. It will surprise nobody that, on top of fun, a life needs certain amounts of love, seriousness, sacrifice, sadness, competition, challenge, achievement, loss, purpose, idleness, vocation, suffering, duty and boredom.

If we accept that a good life has a goodly number of parts, the question becomes a matter of organising the variety, of getting the balance right. To this end, it might be helpful to consider life as a pie. A Life of Pie, if you will. All elements of life – suffering, surprise, responsibility – will have their representative wedge. No two wedges will be exactly the same size, and no two pies will be alike. No recipe is gospel, and no ratio is supreme. Some pies will have larger slices of this, others slimmer slices of that. Yours might have a giant tranche of challenge, a modest slice of love, and just a wee sliver of fun – and that might be fine by you.

But if that's not fine by you, then here's the good news: you can reorganise your pie. You can tinker with its portions. You can play with its fillings. You can fatten certain constituents – a sense of purpose, say – and you can flatten certain others – passive escapism, for example. You can don a figurative apron, pull up some figurative sleeves, delve into that figurative pudding and rearrange the innards. You can make the fun slice bigger. You can make the stress slice smaller. You can bulk up the love portion. You can diminish time in the bath. You can add meaning, or you can take it away. You can season the whole thing with kindness, or you can pimp up the crust with a herb of your choice. If you'll indulge me for a second: *There is an I in the middle of pie.* So get baking, people.

There are a million things you can do to your pie – to get it back on track, to get it ready for the oven, to transform it beyond recognition – and just the one thing you can't: and that's nothing at all. You can't do nothing at all. Because a pie left alone will be thoughtlessly filled with some of life's least appealing elements, like navel-gazing and dread. Because a pie left alone has a mind of its own.

If this book has a message, then it might as well be this: *consider thy pie – or your pie will consider you.* (No, hang on, that second bit doesn't work, does it? When would a pie ever be in a position to consider something? Look, give me five minutes, I need to think about this ...)[46]

---

[46] I thought about this and was unable to come up with anything better. Meaning the book's message remains: consider thy pie, or your pie will consider you. Which I'm sure you'll agree is a really awful message.

20

Toward the foothills of euphoria

Wherein the author goes to a summer camp, enjoys cheerleading, gets hit in the face, marvels at a doctor, learns to sign a Lady Gaga song, produces a worm and goes home early.

23 September

A 'summer camp' is an American institution. As far as I understand, it's primarily for kids and adolescents whose parents don't want them hanging around during the school holiday. The youngsters get shipped off somewhere for a couple of months, Dakota say, or Maine, where they play volleyball more or less continuously until they've grown by five per cent, either physically or spiritually.

Camp Wildfire is a British version of this American institution, albeit with two major differences: it's exclusively for adults and only goes on for a weekend. I don't mind saying that the idea of playing volleyball for 48 hours with a thousand unfamiliar adults in an ancient woodland in Kent, with prices starting at £250 (if you pitch your own tent), almost made me retch. Which is why I booked a ticket.

For the four months after I booked my ticket, I forgot all about summer camp. It wasn't until yesterday (the day before camp started) that I took a look at the website, to see if anything was required of me in advance. It was. I had to do two things: pledge allegiance to one of four patrols (badgers, hawks, squirrels or slugs) and enrol in whichever of the scheduled activities took my fancy. Only I couldn't, because all the activities that took my fancy – like quad biking and paddle boarding and mountain biking and Japanese sword fighting – were already full, meaning I had to spend my credits on whatever was left. Which is why I'm booked up for cheerleading and pottery, among other things.

Of all the activities on offer, one in particular gave me the creeps. Just the thought of it. Just the prospect of how stratospherically terrible I'd be at it. Don't get me wrong, the pursuit of fun necessitates trying things you wouldn't ordinarily be up for. So much is admitted. But the pursuit of fun – in my book anyway – also necessitates the avoidance of things that are guaranteed to make you angry and acutely miserable, things that are bound by their nature to trigger feelings of acute self-loathing. Things like raft building. My dad was a shipwright in the dock-yard and could build a raft in his sleep. I, on the other hand, couldn't build one in my dreams. Not without going crazy and getting a life-changing splinter. I'd have more fun conducting electricity than building a raft, I really would.

Another activity I was happy to miss out on – while we're on the topic – was nipple-tassel making. I mean, I've got a curious nature, but it's not that flipping curious. I'm more than up for engaging fully with things that are pointless, because I under-stand that fun and pointlessness are kind of related. But there is always a line. And nipple-tassel making, I'm not afraid to say, is on the wrong side of it.

I'm on the train to Borough Green and Wrotham – from where there'll be a shuttle bus to the camp – and as things stand, I have zero appetite for what lies in store. This isn't a reflection on what lies in store, rather a reflection of my state of mind. I'm elsewhere – at work, under the thumb, preoccupied with my occupation. Even after months of thinking and reading and learning about the importance of switching off and tuning in, I'm on my way to what is essentially a fun camp listening almost exclusively to the Shit FM playing in my head. When we reach Borough Green, and it's time to alight, I leave my travel pillow on the overhead shelf. An ill omen if ever there was one.[47]

There's a queue for the shuttle bus. I join the back and by my reckoning ought to get a place on the next one, due in ten minutes. I ask the guy behind me – Alex – what he does for fun,

---

[47] The concept of Shit FM – the negative DJ in our minds – is Helen Russell's if I'm not mistaken. Russell is the author of *The Year of Living Danishly* and *How to be Sad*, among other titles.

and he says he walks around the park listening to podcasts. I ask him again, and this time make it absolutely clear that I'm asking how he has fun and not how he stops himself having a break-down. His answer is the same, though he does add that there was a conference in Mexico last year that he nearly went on. Crikey.

* * *

The bus deposits us in a field on the edge of acres of towering pines and limes. Entering the campsite, I give several things a wide berth straight off the bat. Right by the main entrance, an 'initiation' ceremony is in full swing. Each 'patrol' – that is, your random animal alias – is being whipped up into a partisan frenzy by the patrol leaders, in a fashion suggestive of an ideological youth camp (I imagine). Everyone's wearing patrol uniform – kerchiefs and hats – and some have even been branded with their animal of choice. The four tribes have now entered an arena, where the 'games' will take place. The spectacle is gladiatorial. The Badgers look ready to draw blood. The Slugs are champing at the bit (which is a surreal image). For me, there is something dystopian about it all. How quickly – and based on next to noth-ing – will people take sides and go nuts! I read too much Tajfel during my Psychology A level to happily embrace any of this nonsense.[48] Instead of joining in with the harmless tribalism, I get a coffee and have a nice little chat with the barista, who tells

---

[48] Henri Tajfel was a psychologist of prejudice and intergroup rela-tions. He spent time in a prisoner of war camp, an experience that prompted and informed his later work, which sought to demonstrate how 'ordinary' prejudice is (or can be); how quickly a person will favour a randomly assigned 'in group' and punish a randomly assigned 'out group'.

me that in Australia there's a new type of coffee called 'a magic', which is between a flat white and a cortado. Now that's the sort of thing that gets me going.

What doesn't get me going is tent erection. It's not easy to find a patch, for a start. I've pitched up late and there's barely room for a small one. According to the instructions, the tent takes seven minutes to establish, which is interesting because it takes me over an hour. Once I've got it up, I say hello to my neighbours: it takes me most of the evening. I notice a pattern: the younger the camper the harder they find casual social interaction. A group of lads in their early twenties can barely look at me. Though maybe that's got less to do with their maladaptation (on account of society being shifted online) and more to do with the fact that I'm wearing pink socks with green shorts.

I go up to the main festival site, via the 'intrepid woodland' – those ancient pines and limes I mentioned. There are no activities planned for tonight, just live music, a couple of lectures and a bit of comedy, so I get myself a ginger beer at the bar (I'm going dry this weekend), and enter the auditorium (which is essentially a big tent) for a talk on nudity and naturism. The two speakers are in the buff, and are less interested in promoting naturism and more interested in discussing body positivity, which is fair enough. In short, they're saying that as a society we're majorly trending towards body negativity. They share research carried out at a venerable institution (whose identity I forget) that showed that six per cent of those surveyed had had suicidal thoughts in relation to their body. That's shocking. It's one thing weighing up your belly and grimacing somewhat, but it's another thing entirely to be so disappointed with your body that you'd consider killing yourself. At risk of extrapolating too readily and wildly, the six per cent figure (which we must accept comes with a siz-able margin of error) says that something's majorly up with our messaging, with our society's comms. There will always be people with body dysmorphia. And there will always be people who beat themselves up because of how they look, or how they think they look. But six per cent suggests a systemic error, a cultural fault. It suggests that the models are bogus, that the pressure is too intense, that the ideals and standards of beauty are phony and irrational. *It doesn't matter what you look like.* That should be the message. Not everyone will hear the message. Fine. Not everyone will pay heed to the message. Granted. But that should be the message. One way to kick start your journey to body positivity, argues the man hanging out on stage, is to throw caution to the wind and cycle to work in the buff. 'Unless you live in Stoke,' he adds, intriguingly.

Following the naturists on stage is a comedian called Rosie Jones, who you might have seen on the telly. It's a cracking set. Rosie is smart and engaging and daft and irreverent and, yeah, right up my cup of tea. She's also self-aware. Rosie explains her rise to fame thus: 'I'm disabled. I'm gay. And I'm a prick. The BBC love me.' At one point she drops the mic accidentally and it completely conks out. She laments: 'Ah. Now the mic's disabled, too. It'll probably get a fucking award.' A particular highlight is an extended anecdote about Jones being voted the 96th most powerful lesbian in the UK, which I find oddly uplifting. The mechanics of satisfaction will never fail to baf-fle me.

Buoyed by the brilliance of Jones, I've got enough juice in the tank for a bit of dancing. I've missed the live bands, and have to make do with a DJ, who's clearly into music that lacks a storytelling element. Ordinarily, I would run for the hills in this type of situation, but on this occasion I stick around on the edge of the dancefloor and close my eyes and just sort of shift my weight from side to side, at one point getting caught up in a bit of hessian sack. When my low-level anxiety drops to almost immeasurable levels, I move into the centre of the dancefloor, where, paradoxically, I feel much less intimidated and self-conscious. This idea of the edge being scarier than the centre makes me think of rollerblading and grief and all the other things that become less threatening the more you open yourself up to them. Thinking about this makes me think that perhaps I should stop thinking and just focus on the music.

Which is what I do. I focus on the music. And I dance. And I don't just dance, I *enjoy* dancing. I can't say I'm utterly unaware or totally oblivious, because I'm not. I'm still somewhat conscious of those around me (which is useful for health and safety reasons) and am still somewhat under the illusion that people are clocking me and silently slagging me off. But still, to be in the middle of a dance floor, dancing to music without words, alone, sober, and to actually be taking some pleasure from the experience, represents something approximate to progress or growth, which isn't to be sniffed at. When someone in a fox costume spills a pint of lager on me and isn't even aware that they've done so, I decide the disco is slipping *infra dignitatem* and head for the tents.

24 September

Camping is also *infra dignitatem*. Yes I left the travel pillow on the train, and yes I didn't think to bring along a blindfold or some earplugs, but on reflection the light and noise pollution were actually secondary afflictions next to the simple travail of having to sleep in a bag on the ground. It was Type 4 fun without a shadow of doubt, which is to say, you didn't think it would be, and it definitely fucking wasn't. When a guy tried to get into my tent just after dawn, asking for shelter because he had precisely no idea where his tent was, I just pushed the crown of his head backwards whence it came and zipped up the portal.

My alarm goes off at 8.30 a.m. because I've got dodgeball at 9. I thought it would be good to start with something active, but now I'm not so sure. The prospect was good, and now it's bad – more evidence of the instability of all things. The queue for the showers is already the stuff of legend, and the queue for coffee isn't far behind. I enjoy the sight of a hundred random individuals brushing their teeth as I head back to the intrepid forest, where a dodgeball court has been established. I've never played the game, nor seen it played. I haven't even seen the film with Vince Vaughn and Ben Stiller that did well at the box office.[49] We're split into two teams of seven, and positioned on either side of a dividing line constructed from logs, resting upon which are several pink balls the size of huge oranges or tiny pumpkins. On the whistle, you charge for the balls. If you get one, you throw it at an opponent. If you hit them, they're out. If they catch the ball, you're out – and vice versa. The team containing the last person standing is the winner.

It's a pretty simple game. And it's a pretty manic one, too. All things considered, it's not a bad way to start the day. It's certainly preferable to how I normally start the day, which is by drinking two instant coffees and procrastinating for an hour.

---

[49] I've now seen the film and am struggling to understand how it did well at the box office.

The game takes a step back in my estimation, however, when I get hit flush on the side of the face while stooping to pick up a ball. Just a millisecond before being hit, my mindset was trending in the right direction. Just a millisecond after, it wasn't. How quickly things can change! How fragile is felicity! I'm left with an imprint of the ball's logo on the side of my face, and a ringing sound in my ears.

There's this to be said for dodgeball: it offers an insight into the fundamental distribution of global personality types. That is, within any dodgeball game, there'll be a healthy range of psychopathologies on display. There'll be the lunatic player, and the passive-aggressive player, and the largely indifferent player, and the terrified player, and the Machiavellian player, and the accident-prone player and so on. In case you're interested, I'm the type of player who's desperate to win but too scared to attack; the type of player who will hide behind a tree until everyone else is pretty much dead, and then dash confidently and zestfully towards a loose ball, only to get hit flush in the face at the key moment. We move on.

10.30 a.m. I head to the arena for cheerleading. The instructor (Lois) doesn't waste any time: she issues the pompoms and then immediately launches into the routine we'll be performing at the end of the session (in front of an audience that is healthy now and getting healthier by the minute). Not long into the class, Lois tells me in no uncertain terms that I need to give it more sass, which is not something I thought I'd ever be asked to provide any amount of, let alone more of. To her credit, Lois is not making any allowance for the fact that I'm clearly someone that is only here because quad biking was fully booked. She treats me as she's treating everyone else – which is to say, on the basis that

I've done this sort of thing before. When she shouts for more vim, I give her what I can. When she pleads for more bounce, I deliver what I'm able. When she calls for more hips, I think, 'Not them again ...' When she begs for more *glee* – I lose a bit of respect for her if I'm honest. But I do what I can. I give Lois as much glee as my physiology and personality will allow, and it seems to be enough.

At the end of the routine, Lois wants us to finish with a personal flourish, with a bit of freestyling. One girl does a high kick. One girl does the splits. One girl does a backflip. What I do is bring the pompoms together, lower them to shin height, and then sort of run around randomly in that position for a while, as if chasing away a chicken. After we've rehearsed the whole routine a few times, we're split into teams for a dance battle. We're asked to come up with a team name and chant, and to quickly choreograph a way of entering the arena enthusiastically from all sides. It's fair to say that I don't contribute much to the brainstorming session.

When it comes to our performance, I don't embarrass myself. I manage to get through the routine, albeit with certain steps missing and certain others inexplicably introduced. When it comes to the audience vote, my team – 'The Glee Girls' – comes last, though I'm sure we'll bounce back. Just when we're all thinking that cheerleading is over and it's time to move on with our lives, Lois looks at her watch and says, 'You know what? We've still got five minutes. Do you want to do it one more time all together?' I don't mind saying that I'm the first to say yes.[50]

---

[50] The final performance was filmed and shared with all participants. When Megan saw the video it took her a long time to come to terms with what she'd seen. I just posted it on Twitter if you fancy a butcher's.

2.00 p.m. Life drawing. My attendance is a small triumph of hope over experience. Which is to say I don't fancy my chances, and already feel apologetic towards the model. Nonetheless, it proves an enjoyable hour. While the model shifts from pose to pose, the instructor (Rod), in an effort to unlock our potential for the sport, encourages us to take a different approach with each drawing. He suggests we draw lefthanded, that we draw without looking at the paper, that we draw without looking at the model. Rod's efforts are largely in vain, alas. The reason being that whenever I put pencil to paper, the result communicates with unbearable clarity that I have no talent for drawing whatsoever. After each dodgy attempt, Rod is kind enough to suggest that all is not lost; to suggest that each attempt is free from what came before – but I'm not buying it, and nor is Rod if he's honest.

It's not that I don't *try* to get on board with what Rod is saying, and treat each sketch as a clean break, untainted by my earlier efforts, but it's just very hard to do so when the out-come on every occasion is almost sub-human. Unfortunately, there's just no amount of mental gymnastics that can alter the fact that when it comes to draughtsmanship I've got three left feet and a lazy eye. It's no surprise that my best effort is the one where I wasn't allowed to look at the paper: I was spared the sight of my progress (or lack thereof), and therefore kept in a state of innocence until it was revealed that instead of drawing a woman on a chair I'd drafted some kind of weather forecast.

Sometimes I overegg my incompetence a touch, because generally speaking it's easier to write superlatively than accu-rately. But on this occasion, there's no overegging: my efforts are objectively off-the-chart awful. I'm tempted to put this down to a lack of practice. But I would be kidding myself. Because even when I was at primary school and used to draw regularly, I was wretched. I was crap compared to my peers. I was awful relative to people that stank. My work was never hung on the fridge. Instead, it went straight in the freezer.[51]

And yet – notwithstanding my outstanding inability, and my hyperawareness of being graphically challenged – the session is a pleasure. On top of drawing's becalming properties, some of Rod's encouragements and inducements are fun to be on the receiving end of, 'Don't use your brain!' not the least of them. I hardly need to point out that not using one's noggin so much is threatening to become this book's only identifiable theme.

At the end of the session, with my drawings fanned out before me, I'm caught in two minds whether to keep them or not. Rod decides for me: while absentmindedly tidying up after the session, he gobbles up my oeuvre in a fist and shoves the lot in a bin, as if the disposal was a fait accompli.

After the class, I find a shady spot under a tree and sit and read for a while. There are umpteen 'drop in' activities about to start elsewhere in the forest – juggling, hula hooping, trampolining – but sometimes you have to know when to apply the brakes to learning, when to call time on novelty, when to give new sensations a breather. So I sit and read the beginning of a book called *Beginners*, which says that when babies are learning to walk they can fall over up to 70 times an hour, which is inspiring in a weird way.

8.30 p.m. I attend the pub quiz in the auditorium. And I'm not the only one: it's rammed in here. Trivia definitely has a wide

---

[51] If this book sometimes reads like an account of my general incompetence, then that's fine, since one of the many keys to one of the many mysteries of fun is the ability to be good at being crap.

(and almost inexplicable) appeal. I recall the daily quizzes on the cruise ship, which were always well attended, with many people preferring the chance to answer questions about 60s pop music to the various temptations of Helsinki.

I join up with a bunch of other people (most of them Cambridge graduates) and over the next hour or so do my impression of a spare part, which I've got down to a tee. On the plus side, I do learn a thing or two – what Richard III looked like, for example – though it must be said that this modest benefit is dwarfed by the significant cost of being reminded that I have about as much general knowledge as a cheese sandwich. I provide one correct answer – eleven. The question was: 'Leicester City striker Jamie Vardy holds the record for scoring in the highest number of consecutive games. How many?' If we are what we pay attention to, then I'm in big trouble. And so is the person who knew the name of Kim Kardashian's cat.

After the quiz there's an informal lecture by Dr Helen Czerski, a physicist and oceanographer, who's here to rant about a few things from the world of science, including cement, champagne, the idea that science is a series of miraculous breakthroughs made by individual geniuses (when it's really about a lot of people trying and failing), and an ocean-dwelling worm called *Syllis ramosa* that, at a certain point in its life, will grow a pair of eyes on its backside, the better to forage for plankton. Dr Czerski is a brilliant speaker. She is clear and fluent and passionate. I marvel at her. I marvel at what she says, what she shows, what she explains, what she argues, what she illumines. As far as I'm concerned, marvelling is up there, in a phenomenological sense, with any other positive verb in the continuous tense, including laughing and smiling and delighting, and so on. It's marvellous. End of.

At the end of her talk, Dr Czerski is asked a question about her champagne research. She's asked whether she was still able to enjoy champagne despite having thought about it so much. In response, Dr Czerski says: 'It's that classic question of Richard Feynman: is a flower more or less pretty for being understood? But to answer your question, I'm more than able to enjoy champagne.'[52]

On that note, Dr Czerski calls it a day. And on that note, I set off towards the dance tent, where a gypsy swing band are in full stride. I venture into the pack and let my body answer the questions of the music, let myself go a bit, let myself trespass toward the foothills of euphoria. The unbroken run of momentary emotional upticks that I've experienced over the last 24 hours, unsullied by the flotsam of ordinary life, has somehow built up a head of steam, has somehow cleared a path in the thicket and led me here, to this small patch of careless surrender.

I feel happy. And serene. And exhausted. And unburdened. And unblemished. And as good as I can remember ever feeling. But I also feel oddly and distinctly on the brink of despair, on the brink of tears. And perhaps that's right. Perhaps that's not odd. Perhaps despair is a close neighbour of pure happiness. And

---

[52] A friend is studying music in Manchester. She will sit all day dissecting pieces by Mozart and Sibelius. When I last spoke to her, she said: 'I was in the office, poring over some sheet music, listening again and again to "Eine Kleine Nachtmusik", and it was boring me to tears. It felt like I was killing it. Killing its beauty. Then, going home on the bus, admittedly after a few drinks, I was listening to Bowie's "Moonage Daydream", and looking out the window at the Oxford Road, and the people, and the lights in the rain, and I could have cried for joy. Now my question is: what am I to do? Stop studying and just ride the bus all the time?'

perhaps that's why we subconsciously shy away from the latter, why we daren't get too close to it, why we're curiously satisfied with a satisfactory life, with the likes of bliss and despair safely at bay. Perhaps the appeal of satisfactory lies in its distance from pain.

I can guess what you're thinking. *Just dance man.* There I was, happily bopping to a seven-piece band, not a care in the world, feeling unthinkably good, and then I go and spoil it all by saying something stupid like: 'But what's curious is that I also feel oddly and distinctly on the brink of despair ...' Then I go and spoil it all by thinking about the flowers, and about what makes them wonderful, and about how long they'll last, rather than delighting in the damn things and leaving it at that.[53]

25 September

9.00 a.m. First up, Zorbing. What a way to start the day: climbing into a massive inflatable (or inflated, rather) orb and then going at it like a hamster on a treadmill. During the safety briefing, it's obvious to the others that I'm not desperate to get started.

'He's hungover,' says a lady called Kerry. 'Look at him. He's hungover. I've never seen anyone look so hungover.'

'I'm feeling fine actually, Kerry, but thanks for the feedback.'

'Look at him. He's fucking hungover.'

'I'm not, Kerry.'

---

[53] If you're interested, see *The Pleasures of Finding Things Out*, a 1981 BBC documentary about Richard Feynman. I think Feynman, had he been at Camp Wildfire, and alongside me on the dance floor that night, would have said: 'Your emotional state is richer and more beautiful for being complex, my friend. Now move those damn hips and cry if you have to!'

'Yes you fucking are. I'll tell you what – I'm going first before he gets in there and throws up all over the place.'

If you want to know what it feels like to be in a tumble dryer (when it's on), have a go at Zorbing. If you don't, then don't. If you want to injure your shoulder and then moan about it for the rest of the day, have a go at Zorbing. If you don't, then don't. After the initial – and welcome – double shot of adrenaline, the appeal of Zorbing wanes pretty quickly. I'm not going to invest in one. Let's put it that way. One thing in its favour: it certainly wakes you up. Which makes me wonder if starting the day with fun might not be the maximal approach to the stuff. I mean to say: if you've only got time or appetite for one small bit of fun a day, have it first thing, have it straight off the bat, let it get the ball rolling, let it set the tone, let it slap your soul around the chops, let it put a spring in your step before you bore yourself to tears in front of spreadsheets. Want some advice? Get out of bed and into your Zorb. It's not impractical at all.

10.30 a.m. I'm sitting on a bale of hay, beneath a canopy of leafy trees, bathed in dappled sunlight, cradling a ukulele, and all but under the nose of Eric, our instructor. A swift anatomy lesson – 'Here's the saddle, here's the bridge, here's the nub, here's the neck' – is followed by an introduction to chords F, C and A minor, which are easier to master than you might imagine. Next Eric and his helpers distribute a selection of songs, and we get cracking on 'Dance the Night Away' by The Mavericks, the first lines of which – 'Here comes my happiness again / Right back to where it should have been' – speak to me personally. Indeed, I briefly imagine the song being used when this book is made into a film (which will somehow manage to star Olivia Colman). But then the rest of the song happens and all thoughts of including it on the soundtrack disappear, because it's basically about a bloke going out on the lash and chasing 'senoritas' after being dumped by his girlfriend, probably for being an absolute dipstick.

Next we play an Elvis number, and after that it's 'Three Birds' by Bob Marley, and finally it's 'Riptide' by Vance Joy. Once more, the opening lines chime with the thrust and gist of my ongoing experiment. 'I was scared of dentists and the dark / I was scared of pretty girls and starting conversations.' At this point, I stop paying attention to the lyrics, in case the song turns out to be gently misogynistic and promotive of debauchery in a way I can't in all conscience support. Instead, I just hum. And it's nice, just humming and strumming – really nice, in fact. I'm sat on my bale, bathed in my dappled sunlight, beneath the pastoral gaze of my gentle Eric, living my best life. (Or my life at least.) It's a special few minutes, playing that last number, with the couple behind me singing along sweetly, and the worst of the ukulele players having the grace to be bad quietly. There's something fraternal and rejuvenating about the experience, something tender and resonant, that elevates it to the sweetest of spots, and makes the ukulele workshop my number one bit of fun so far.

12.30 p.m. After lunch, it's back in the forest for pottery. It's 'primitive' pottery according to the menu, which basically means there's no chance of us ending up in a similar position to the one Demi Moore and Patrick Swayze found themselves in at the beginning of *Ghost*, and every chance of us being handed a lump of clay and told to just get on with it. First we're asked to squeeze and squash and massage the clay until it's lost all of its wrinkles and fissures. Notwithstanding the moment when I get a spot of cramp in my thumb, it's quite a nice task: just squeezing and handling the clay, without objective or assignment, and in total silence. (Curiously, nobody in the group is talking. Perhaps people are tiring of being social, or perhaps it's an effect of handling the clay.) The spell is broken when our instructor calls time on our trance and poses a challenge: to turn our clay into a shallow dish, first by flattening our ball, and then by crimping and pinching its edges until we have a basin of sorts. When we've all done that, we're given a choice: to either continue working on what we've got – adding detail, embellishing, refining – or to squash the clay back into a ball and then let our imaginations go wild. I instinctively squash the clay back into a ball – see, I'm learning; I didn't give it a second's thought – before staring at it gormlessly for five minutes, not knowing how to proceed, as blank as the canvas before me.

Eventually, I start rolling the ball into a sausage. Then I flatten the sausage until it resembles a tongue – a long, rectangular tongue. At this point, I'm tempted to join the ends together and make a ring, but fancy that would be too neat, too simple, and so reject the option of completion, and create a rough horseshoe instead. When I allow one bar of the shoe to rest against the inside of the other, I end up with a weird, slightly tilted number 6. The structure is now self-supporting, with each end of the tongue supported by the other. More than anything else, it resembles a worm in thought, with the worm's chin sort of resting on its fist (were worms to have chins and fists). A bit like the Rodin sculpture *The Thinker*. When the instructor comes over to have a look, he nods knowingly, as if seeing deep into my soul, and says: 'Cook it at a low heat initially, and then crank it up as high as it will go. If you shove it in at maximum, it'll probably explode.'

I take my wriggly philosopher over to the display table, which bears all the items produced so far this weekend. It is a tableau in both senses – at once a piece of handy furniture, and a document of the human imagination. A glance at the output gives no clear indication whether we're doomed as a species or destined for ever greater things. There's a tiny pair of clay clogs, a castle, a flower, a dagger, a phallus, two figures embracing, and about a dozen ash trays.

4.00 p.m. I chance on a British Sign Language workshop, and am invited to join. (At first, because the invitation is signed, I think that I'm being told by the instructor to mind my own business.) It's a diverting half-hour, and the fact that the skill I'm being introduced to is potentially useful, and connective and social, makes the session better still – qualitatively speaking. I learn how to sign a Lady Gaga song, and I learn how to sign my name, and I learn that the sign for Liverpool is also the sign for lesbian, which will doubtless prove a useful economy whenever I find myself in that city.

5.00 p.m. I head back to the tent, meaning to have a quick nap before returning to the fold. But when I get to the tent, instead of getting in the thing and having a snooze, I start to take it down. A part of me has clearly decided that enough is enough, that I'm done for the weekend. The plan was to stay for the duration: to have a blowout tonight and then head home tomorrow. But if there's anything I know about fun (which there isn't), it's that you've got to know when to stop. When I call at the information tent to enquire about the shuttle to the station, the lady says, almost sympathetically, that I'm the first to do so.

6.30 p.m. The journey back to London gives me a chance to reflect on the weekend, and how it was, in a way, a summation of the journey I've been on this past year; how it was, in a way, a chance to apply some of the tools I've picked up during that time; how it was, in a way, an opportunity to put certain things into practice, like letting go, and switching off, and saying yes, and opening up, and not having a clue but being okay about the fact. The journey back to London gives me a chance to reflect on *my relationship with fun*. (Which is a useful thing to be able to do at this stage of the book.)

But I don't take it. I don't take the chance to reflect on those things. Instead, I whip out my laptop and connect to the internet and spend the next hour flitting between news and work, between comparison and worry. Last night I was gazing at the stars, now I'm gazing at my navel (which is neither in nor out, as it happens). This afternoon I was in the zone moulding a worm, now I'm simultaneously checking football scores and researching gastroenteritis.

We are not works in progress. That formulation is too teleological, too mechanical, too goal-driven. Instead, we are a thousand shades of human – always were, always will be. We are stupid and sublime, prosaic and profound, open and closed, happy and sad – and everything in between. We can – by effort, by design, by hook or by crook – tinker with the ratios; but we'll never be anything absolutely, so long as we live.

Self-development is hard to measure. We haven't got the best view, for a start, and because we're with ourselves all the time, it's difficult to spot or sense the incremental changes. It's true with our appearance, for example. I can't see how I've changed since last summer, because the alteration has been too gradual, but my friend, Tony, who hadn't seen me for a year, told me last week: 'You've got old, man. And you look permanently confused. How did that happen?'

I mention the above (how tricky tracking change can be), because when I get back home to the flat and put the kettle on, and a load of washing in, and a few things on the shared calendar, and a favourite album on, and a few questions to Meg about her weekend, all within about five minutes, she says, 'What the fuck is up with you? You're acting … *happy*.'

When she says this, I'm genuinely taken aback. I'm taken aback because I didn't see the question coming. And I didn't see the question coming because I didn't see a difference, didn't *feel* a difference. I shrug my shoulders and tell her I must be buzzing, that this must be the effect of pottery and sleep-deprivation, and that she'd better get used to it. 'I'm going out for a walk,' she says. 'Give you a chance to calm down.'

I make a cup of tea and drink it on the front steps looking out onto the street and the trees. (What the fuck *is* wrong with me?) And there, at the top of those steps, I admit to myself that I'm feeling – as well as exhausted and alive, etc. – a tiny bit proud. (If you want to go and be sick, by all means do.) I admit to myself that I'm feeling a wee bit pleased with myself. With how the weekend went, I mean. Not just what I did – the dancing, the chatting, the learning, the failing – but also what I didn't do (which is to say a bunch of things I've been doing routinely for recreational purposes for most of my adult life, which ultimately do me no good whatsoever).

Some things added, some things taken away. You'd expect such an equation – if my understanding of mathematics is sound – to more or less take you back to where you started. You'd expect the result to be roughly the same. But not all additions are equal, and not all subtractions are alike. I added cheerleading and took away the internet. I added dodgeball and took away

38 units of alcohol and a pair of hangovers. I added a tendency to talk and dance, and took away an inclination to hide. I added a measure of quiet self-appreciation, and took away a slice of noisy self-loathing. And the sum was positive. The outcome was good.

I'm not going to wax lyrical about it, because tomorrow's another day, and we're all fundamentally messed up and flaky, and emotional states are by their nature ephemeral and fleeting, but I have to say that the fun camp served me well, that it did me some good, with the caveat that I will never again in my life sleep in a bag or attempt to draw anything.

Apart from conclusions, maybe. I might draw a few of those now and again, when needs must. Like now, for example. I'll draw a conclusion now if you don't mind. And here it is: I seem to get cramp a lot. And here's another one: there's an apparent relationship between contentment and minor injuries. And here's another: any year that results in an invitation to the engagement party of a man called Derek who you met on a cruise is an indisputably good one. And here's another: one conclusion will never be sufficient. And here's another: when I get back on the Boditrax machine, nearly a year after weighing in 23 years heavier than I am, it transpires that I've somehow managed to put on another eighteen months. You've got to laugh.

Acknowledgements

When it comes to books, there are no immaculate conceptions, only messy ones that involve lots of people doing lots of things so that a book might find its feet, might put on weight, might rise to a certain height and set sail. These people include the lad who taught me how to wakeboard (after a fashion), down at Hove Lagoon. They include Andy Dalton, who picked me for central midfield and then took me out on a bike. They include Jim Brook, who invited me to a dodgy café so that he might show me his cryptic prowess. They include a squad of veritable diamonds at Primrose Hill Community Library (which ought to be visited and thoroughly patronised at once).They include Natasha and Anna at Shelter. Emily Rhodes, whose walking book club must be the finest of its kind on the planet. The good people at Ambassador cruise line (not least those doing the rowing). My better three-quarters, Megan Menzies, who suffered through my daily bouts of book-based moaning. Liz Baker and her colleagues at Wilkin & Sons. The Irish quartet and Mormon duo who made my Camino so memorable. Everyone at Icon Books, though especially Ellen Conlon, Sophie Lazar and Emily Cary-Elwes, who constitute a publishing triangle so colossal as to be visible from space. My agent, Ed Wilson, and everyone at Johnson & Alcock, who I'm reliably informed are on the look-out for emotive cookbooks set in Sicily featuring Gareth Southgate. My friends and family, who provide an irresistible and ongoing cause for climbing out of bed each morning. Booksellers of the world! Margaret from Liverpool, who got me up on the dancefloor. Dr Helen Czerski, who made me marvel in a tent. Rosie Jones, who made me laugh in same. My improv teacher at City Academy, who did a fine job of making it up as he went along. My ukulele instructor. My pottery chief. My life-drawing guru. Everyone on the Isle of Wight, though mostly Dave Fairlamb, Simon Clark, Mark at Call It What You Want (a top-notch eatery in Cowes where you don't get to choose), and the coasteering team down at Freshwater Bay. Richard at the Avenue Cookery School in Wandsworth. The esteemed life coach Andy Hix, who got me chatting about vaccines. The esteemed bridge maestro Rollo, who gave me a tantalising glimpse of a better world. The team of sales reps at the Independent Alliance. Yourself for picking up this tome. Jemma, Philip and Nigel for getting me up and down in one piece. My cheerleading coach. The vascular surgeon from County Clare who told me her idea of fun was eating toast in the bath. The good people at Ruskin Park community garden. Whoever invented Microsoft Word. The pigs of Kentish Town City Farm. And Keira Knightley.